THE SUSTAINING HAND

STUDIES IN
GOVERNMENT AND PUBLIC POLICY

THE
SUSTAINING
HAND

COMMUNITY LEADERSHIP
AND CORPORATE POWER

Second Edition, Revised

BRYAN D. JONES
and
LYNN W. BACHELOR

UNIVERSITY PRESS OF KANSAS

Published by the University Press of Kansas (Lawrence, Kansas 66049),
which was organized by the Kansas Board of Regents and is operated
and funded by Emporia State University, Fort Hays State University,
Kansas State University, Pittsburg State University,
the University of Kansas, and Wichita State University

Library of Congress Cataloging in Publication Data

Jones, Bryan D.
The sustaining hand : community leadership and corporate power /
Bryan D. Jones and Lynn W. Bachelor − 2nd ed., rev.
p.   cm. − (Studies in government and public policy)
Includes index.
1. Automobile industry and trade−Michigan−
Case studies. 2. Michigan−Industries−Location−
Case studies. 3. Business and politics−Michigan−
Case studies. 4. General Motors Corporation.
I. Bachelor, Lynn W., 1947-   . II. Title. III. Series.
HD9710.U53M433 1993 338.4'76292'09774 93-12434
ISBN 0-7006-0598-3
ISBN 0-7006-0599-1 (pbk.)

Printed in the United States of America

10 9 8 7 6 5 4 3 2 1

The paper used in this publication meets the
minimum requirements of the American
National Standard of Paper for Printed
Library Materials Z39.48-1984.

TO OUR FAMILIES, WHO SUSTAIN US

Behind the frenzy of official activity was the unmistakable guiding and sustaining, indeed controlling hand of the General Motors Corporation.

—Michigan Supreme Court Justice James A. Ryan, 1981

There is nothing wrong with Detroit that three or four factories can't solve.

—Detroit Mayor Coleman A. Young

Contents

List of Figures and Tables   ix
Preface to the Second Edition   xi
Preface to the First Edition   xiii

Part 1
Detroit, Public Policy, and the Automobile

1 Private Power and Public Policy   3
2 The Automotive Public Economy   21
3 Detroit: Industrial Democracy or Capitalist Oligarchy?   40
4 The American Automobile Industry under Pressure   55

Part 2
The Decision at Milwaukee Junction

5 General Motors Searches for Sites   73
6 The Bureaucracy in Action: Meeting General Motors'
    Timetable   90
7 The Trappings of Democracy   109
8 The Democratic Steam Roller: Poletown in Court   123
9 The Politics of Tax Loss   134
10 Street Theater: Organized Opposition to the
    Poletown Redevelopment Project   143

Part 3
Plants in the Hinterland

11 Pontiac: The Company Town and the Exurbs   165
12 Flint: Political Maneuvering and Buick City   185

Part 4
Urban Regimes and Solution-Sets

13 Automobile Politics: A View from the 1990s   205
14 The Chrysler Jefferson Project: Poletown Revisited?   217
15 Urban Power, Political Decision Making, and the
   Automobile Industry   233

Notes   255
Index   275

List of Figures and Tables

FIGURES

2.1 Employment in state and local governments and in automobile production in Michigan   24

2.2 Scatterplot of employment in state and local governments and in automobile production in Michigan, lagged by one year   26

2.3 Revenues derived from selected taxes by the state of Michigan   27

2.4 Expenditures for selected functions by the state of Michigan   29

2.5 Number of motor vehicles produced in Detroit, Flint, and Pontiac   31

2.6 Total revenues, adjusted for inflation, raised by Detroit, Flint, and Pontiac   34

2.7 Total outstanding debt, adjusted for inflation, in Detroit, Flint, and Pontiac   35

4.1 Sales of passenger cars by domestic manufacturers   60

4.2 Penetration of the American automotive market by imports   61

4.3 Profits of the automotive manufacturing industry after taxes   64

4.4 Capital expenditures by American automobile manufacturers, in constant dollars   68

5.1 Proposed alternative sites for General Motors' Detroit Assembly Plant   81

5.2 Layout of the Central Industrial Park project   88

10.1 Black population in the Central Industrial Park area   146

10.2 Polish-American population in the Central Industrial
     Park area   146

12.1 Politics and economics in Flint   187

13.1 Motor vehicle sales in the United States   209

TABLES

6.1 Projected Costs and Sources of Revenue, Central
    Industrial Park Project, October 1980   96

6.2 Financial Arrangements, Central Industrial Park Project,
    Spring 1981   97

6.3 Sources of Revenue from the Public Sector and Project Costs
    of the Detroit General Motors Assembly Plant, April 1982   98

9.1 Estimate of Retained and Captured Taxes, Central
    Industrial Park Project, Selected Years   140

10.1 Distribution of Income by Race, Central Industrial
     Park Project Area   145

13.1 Repayment Schedule for Loans from the Federal
     Government for the Central Industrial Park Project   214

Preface to the
Second Edition

In his textbook on state and local government, John Harrigan cites the earlier edition of this work as exemplifying a pluralist counterattack on the political economy movement.[1] We hesitate to characterize our approach as pluralist, at least as that term is commonly used, but we did intend the first edition of this book to serve as a foil to the genre of works that see politicians as having the same interests as business executives. We thought then, and continue to think, that politicians and business executives in cities have fundamentally different interests that can be directly traced to the incentives facing them. These incentives are as simple as the electoral motive for politicians and the profit motive for business executives. Furthermore, within very broad limits, neither is subservient to the other. Rather, they are interdependent in complex ways, so that different interactions between the business and political communities generate different urban regimes in different cities (or the same city at different points in time). Today this is an important theme in urban political economy, although it certainly was not when we drafted the first edition.[2]

We have taken the opportunity in preparing this second edition to refine and extend our argument. First, we have provided updates to all of the plant location decisions that we reported in the first edition in chapter 13. Second, we have added in chapter 14 another case study of an automotive plant location decision—the Jefferson Avenue Chrysler assembly plant in Detroit. We use this material to show how urban regimes develop characteristic solution-sets to economic development problems, which then are applied almost routinely to superficially similar situations. What once were adaptive and creative policy initiatives become routine, and may not work as intended. We see this variant of institutionalization as an important constraint on the interaction between the urban economic and political systems. Hence our use of the term *set* in both senses: as a collection of elements and as a readiness to respond.

Finally, we have rewritten both the introductory and the concluding chapters to reflect these extensions of our argument. We argue that urban regimes are defined as much by their solution-sets as by the nature of the participants in their governing coalitions. That is, ideas are as important in distinguishing regimes as are participants, although of course the two are intertwined. The rest of the chapters, which detail the auto-city responses to the vast restructuring of the automobile industry during the early 1980s, are unchanged from the first edition.

Our approach to urban political economy leaves much room for the operation of chance factors, institutional drag, and political leadership. We argue that urban regimes are often established through the actions of political leaders, and that they are reliant on a pattern of interactions among politicians, business executives, labor unions, and other private groups. These interactions generate a characteristic solution-set for the regime, by which we mean a "package" of problem-definitions and preferred solutions. That is, an urban regime tends to see its problems and its policy solutions together. It is very rare for a regime to "discover" a problem and then engage in a systematic search for a policy solution. Solution-sets may be incrementally modified through negotiations among participants, thus allowing adjustment to changing circumstances. But they can also become glaringly dysfunctional, attracting new participants to the policy process, participants who question the basic premises of the existing urban regime. At such times a major episodic regime alteration can occur.

One can always envision a different pattern of interactions leading to different solution-sets, and thereby different policy actions. So long as this can happen, a somewhat different urban political world is possible, and there remains a real and important role for public leadership. Constraints, of course, exist and are powerful in channeling urban regimes. Indeed, this book faces squarely the actions of urban regimes under severe constraints. That we find such room for political interplay reinforces our thesis that political leaders are independently powerful in the city.

We appreciate the careful and critical reviews given this edition by Denny Judd and Clarence Stone. The intensity of their comments is testimony to the vigorous and open debate that characterizes urban political economy today. Mike Briggs of the University Press of Kansas provided the expert guidance for the project that we have come to know as the routine standard of excellence at the press.

Preface to the
First Edition

Once in a great while one gets a chance to observe firsthand an event that is not only important itself but also symbolizes the interplay of social forces in a particularly graphic manner. For us, that event was the destruction of an urban neighborhood in Detroit so that an automotive assembly plant could be built in its place. This is the highest order of modern urban drama: the human suffering that goes with the replacement of the obsolete with the productive; the struggle of the city to save its economic base; the awesome power of the Corporation, the City, and the Church acting in consort.

It was this urban drama, in its early stages, that stimulated the research that has produced this book. Yet the case itself, along with decisions about assembly plants in other Michigan communities, served primarily as a vehicle for the examination of the role of the multinational industrial corporation in decision making in the local community. We find that the giant corporation, in the words of Michigan Supreme Court Justice James Ryan, both guides and sustains the policy process in the modern industrial city. It performs this dual role by providing a large proportion of the livelihoods for the citizens of the community. By sustaining, it guides political choices. Its business decisions have more impact on the policies of the community than do its attempts at political influence. In the words of Charles Lindblom, the market is surely a prison.

In a narrower sense, the cases that serve as the principal foci of the book caused us to look seriously, for the first time, at the effect of automobile production on the city. Much has been written on the consequences of automobile consumption for the modern city: the politics of highways, the decline of mass transit, the decentralization of the metropolis, the problems of traffic congestion and pollution. Yet urbanists have written little on the effects of automobile production on communities. For those cities that depend on automotive manufacture, directly and indirectly, the consequences of changes in production are even greater than the consequences of changing patterns of consumption.

As in any social-science research project, we have accumulated numerous debts. These include the public and corporate officials who gave generously of their time and expertise as we struggled to understand the complexities of economic development; the office staff of the Department of Political Science at Wayne State University, particularly Marie MacQuarrie and Paula Sanch, who patiently typed our many revisions; Clarence Stone and Paul Schumaker, who reviewed the manuscript for the University Press of Kansas and offered numerous suggestions for improvements; and the press staff, which has ably guided the manuscript through the publication process at the press.

PART 1

DETROIT, PUBLIC POLICY, AND THE AUTOMOBILE

1

Private Power and Public Policy

The determinism of the change of forms is not rigorous . . . the same local conditions can give birth to apparently different outcomes under the influence of unknown or unknowable factors.

— René Thom

The year was 1905, and William Crapo Durant had a problem. Durant, of Flint, Michigan, had made millions for himself and his fellow Flint investors in the Durant-Dort Carriage Company, and now he controlled the nascent and undercapitalized Buick Motor Company. His transmission and engine operations in Flint were unable to keep pace with his assembly operations in Jackson, Michigan, ninety miles away. And the small building in Jackson was capable of producing only five to eight automobiles a day, less than a fifth of orders.

Durant, an industrial dreamer second to none, was up to the challenge. He purchased a large tract of farmland to the northwest of the city of Flint; by 1907 the largest industrial building in the world would stand on the site, producing 8,487 automobiles in 1908.[1]

Durant's immediate problem, however, was to raise the necessary capital. He publicly asked the banks of Jackson to invest $100,000 in Buick, with the guarantee that all Buick operations would be consolidated in that city. Durant offered a similar package to the citizens of Bay City. A group of Flint investors rose to the challenge and agreed to buy $80,000 of Buick stock. Durant agreed to "the understanding that the Buick Motor Company will discontinue its Jackson plant and locate its entire business at Flint, commencing construction work upon its new buildings as soon as plans can be prepared and the weather will permit."[2]

3

In the fertile entrepreneurial mind of Billy Durant, the founder of General Motors, was born a strategy that would be used again and again by automobile companies. Taking advantage of their special roles in the creation of wealth in capitalist society,[3] the directors of automotive and other industrial concerns have attempted to extract benefits from city officials who wish to preserve or increase the vitality of their local economies. The leverage of industrialists comes from the simple fact of the mobility of capital; the constraints on public officials come from the geographic confines of the modern statutory city.

INDIVIDUAL DECISIONS
AND THE POLITICAL ECONOMY

Just over seventy-six years after Billy Durant agreed to build an assembly plant in Flint, Thomas A. Murphy, chairman of the board of General Motors, wrote to Mayor Coleman A. Young of Detroit that General Motors would "cause an automotive assembly plant to be built on the Detroit-Hamtramck site if the site criteria requirements detailed on the attachment to this letter are accomplished."[4] Murphy went on to detail the site requirements in six single-spaced pages. The requirements ranged from changes in zoning specifications to a demand for tax abatement.

Both Durant and Murphy succeeded in gaining concessions from city fathers. It would seem, on first examination, that the relationship between the automobile companies and the cities that are dependent on automotive manufacture is simple: the companies are in a position to extract maximum concessions, and the cities are in no position to deny anything. Yet surface appearances can be misleading. The relationship between cities and companies is far more complex, and city officials are not without resources themselves in their dealings with industry.

There is a more fundamental issue here: How do human actions relate to the broader public economy? In the view of some observers, human decisions are at best reflections of more fundamental social trends. Moreover, it seems clear to some analysts that capitalists always prevail over politicians: "Because of its control over resources, the capitalist class is usually able to manipulate governments to its own ends."[5] Other social scientists see complexity and flux rather than structure and determinism. Raymond Boudon writes that "the strategic and innovative dimension of human action makes all empirical lawlike statements on social change mere conjectures."[6]

We are convinced that neither of these perspectives is particularly useful in understanding urban politics. The issue is not whether there is an innovative and strategic dimension to politics; clearly, in our minds, there is.

Nor is there any question that the economy influences politics. The question that will occupy us in this book is whether that strategic and innovative dimension can affect the public economy, or whether the actions of politicians are so constrained by the actions of capitalists that they lack any meaningful autonomy.

Thomas Anton has noted the tendency of political scientists to assume that the sociopolitical world is "essentially stable; we think that the boundaries of political (and thus policy) action are largely predetermined by environmental conditions; and we view politicians as reactive beings, seldom if ever capable of effective forethought in human affairs."[7] Yet, political actors hold values, develop intentions, and formulate strategies to achieve relationships they desire. In the process, they often enough bring about major, as well as minor, changes in the world they inhabit."[8]

We are dealing with a very serious level of analysis problem here. On the one hand, we are interested in the extent of autonomy and strategic innovation that individual decision makers possess. On the other hand, we are also interested in the manner in which economies and political systems interact. It is all too common for analysts who are studying individual decision making to infer that the strategic and innovative choices that are at least occasionally made have great consequences for public policy and for society in general. "Great leader" theories have reemerged, in a somewhat less objectionable form, through the concept of "policy entrepreneur."[9]

The search for certainty in the explanation of social affairs is perhaps a more common "disease" among social scientists. Operating at the broader level of analysis, students of the interaction between the economy and the polity frequently deduce that individual decision makers are severely constrained by the socioeconomic structure. Economic forces so greatly influence the policy actions of political leaders that such actions may be satisfactorily predicted from economic relations.

On the one hand, individual political leaders make decisions, interacting with economic elites, political activists, and mass publics. On the other hand, the political system interacts with the economy. The linkages between the two levels of analysis are generally forged by fiat: either great leaders and policy entrepreneurs obviously affect the political economy, or the economic structure is so set as to make meaningless any individual effort at change. This implicit refusal to devote any energy toward the study of the linkages between the two levels has left us with a social science that is characterized by bouncing back and forth from one level to another, with the crosswalking process being poorly understood.

This state of affairs is not limited to social science. The evolutionary biologist Stephen J. Gould has similarly criticized evolutionary biology, writing: "Rudyard Kipling asked how the leopard got its spots, the rhino its wrinkled skin. He called his answers 'just so' stories. When evolutionists try to explain form and behavior, they also tell 'just so' stories – and the agent is natural selection."[10] The "just so" stories of social science involve more agents: structuralism, policy entrepreneurship, political and economic competition. But the movement between theory and data is oftentimes just as facile.

This state of affairs has led one of us to propose that the levels of analysis be viewed as causally related. That is, while it is the case that individual decisions and group actions are constrained by the existing political economy, it is also the case that the interactions among individuals and groups affect the direction, scope, and velocity of social change at the *broader level of the public economy. Political ecology*, the interactions of groups and the decisions of individuals, can alter the structure of the political economy, but individual decisions are not made in a social vacuum. They are constrained, and are often heavily constrained, by the broader *public economy.* The result is a complex and reciprocal causal interaction between the two levels of analysis.[11] This means that changes in the political ecology can alter the political economy, which, in turn, changes the incentive structure that political and economic actors face.

The assertion that the decisions of individuals and groups, the political ecology of public policy, and the broader public economy of a society are causally related is, of course, no more than a perspective guiding further inquiry. The causal linkages between the two levels of analysis are so complex as to defy analysis at present. Nevertheless, it is a perspective that will allow us to place the actions of individual decision makers in context and will force us to analyze the actual constraints on their actions, as well as the potential effects of their activities on the public economy.[12]

CITIES, PLANTS, AND AUTOMOBILES

One way to examine the connection between the actions of political decision makers and the public economy within which they operate is to study extreme cases, that is, cases in which the autonomy of political actors is likely to be either very low or very high. If reasonable observers conclude that actors whose autonomy is severely constrained by the operation of the political economy do exhibit "strategic and innovative" decision making, then we have very real evidence that the political economy does not completely determine the policy actions of leaders. By studying the conditions under which they act or don't act, we can more fully understand the constraints on and the opportunities for urban leadership. (Demonstrating that this innovation affects the broader public economy is a more difficult, but not impossible, undertaking.)

The self-conscious study of decision making under extreme conditions of structural constraint is the approach that we take in this book. We examine the responses of public officials in three Michigan cities – Detroit, Flint, and Pontiac – to decisions made by the General Motors Corporation in regard to the location of plants. In each case, General Motors, itself under increasing competition from Japanese automobile manufacturers, chose in the midst of a major recession to replace aging assembly operations with new facilities. In each case, the local economy was heavily dependent on automotive manufacture; in Flint and Pontiac, the dependency was exclusively on General Motors. In the cases of Flint and Pontiac, the corporation simply made a public announcement that new facilities would be built in suburban areas. In the case of Detroit, the company offered the city the opportunity to have the plant, providing the city could secure a suitable site, clear it, and transfer it to the company in a timely fashion. In each case, internal city politics complicated the process. In each case the political executive had the room to maneuver, although it was not always used. To complete the picture, we study a final assembly plant location decision – the construction of Chrysler's new Detroit Jefferson Avenue assembly plant. This time there was no recession, yet a similar pattern of negotiations between city and company occurred.

A contemporary automobile assembly plant is a work of modern industrial art. Capable of producing as many as 500,000 automobiles per year, it can directly employ as many as six thousand workers. It contains its own power plant, railway system, and water and sewer system. The cost of building it may exceed $600 million, and retooling costs can run as much as $200 million for changeovers of models. It may occupy a square mile of territory, and it is capable of generating large economic spillover effects, including economic activity concerned with supplying parts and materials, transportation, and services for the facility. Yet some of these figures look pale in comparison to the labor-intensive assembly plant of old: the Dodge Main assembly plant of Chrysler, which was abandoned and then destroyed to make way for Detroit's new General Motors assembly plant, employed eighteen thousand workers by 1920 and forty thousand during World War II.

Today the economic importance of an automotive assembly operation makes it a far more attractive acquisition than was the risky operation that Jackson's city fathers refused in 1905. In terms of economic effect on a community, there is probably not a more important single manufacturing facility today than an automobile assembly plant. Some appreciation of the magnitude of the undertaking may be gauged by a comparison with the five-year $750-million public-private economic development plan announced in the fall of 1983 by the governor of Rhode Island, which would have not quite financed one assembly plant of the type built by General Motors in Detroit, where totals for private-sector expenditure ran over $550 million, and public costs ran almost $300 million.

COMMUNITY DECISION MAKING

Simply put, Detroit, Flint, and Pontiac were dealing with a severe threat to their "export industries." Paul Peterson writes that "it is only a modest simplification to equate the interests of cities with their export industries" and goes on to argue that public officials act rationally to maximize that goal, within environmental constraints.[13] For a city, export industries are those businesses that manufacture goods or deliver services that are sold in other regions of the country or in other nations. Export industries create jobs and wealth at the expense of consumers residing in other regions. Hence they transfer wealth to the city from elsewhere. The potential loss of such major manufacturing capacity would be a severe blow to the wealth-creating capacity of the industrial city, whereas the acquisition of one can yield substantial "spillover" benefits to the local economy in the form of employment, construction, and retail sales.

Because there is a tendency for all participants in a city to recognize this, Peterson predicts that, on economic development issues, at least, policy making should occur in a quiescent environment in which rational analysis is the primary decisional mode. There is considerable evidence that more conflict occurs over economic development policies than Peterson suggests, partly because some groups view expenditures that promote future economic growth as detracting from quality-of-life improvements in the present.[14] Moreover, Peterson's assumption that a city has a "unitary interest," which decision makers discover and act upon, has been vigorously criticized as defining away the critical value conflicts in urban society.[15] Nevertheless, his approach has provided a radical departure from prevailing analyses of urban politics. His assumption that local political leaders and economic elites share a common interest and act accordingly contrasts sharply with analyses that first assume that citizens and elites have different interests and then examine the behaviors of political leaders in light of this difference. Earlier elitists viewed, often implicitly, the interests of the economic elite and those of the mass public as being divergent. Peterson sees cooperation, at least on some issues, as flowing from a common interest.

If Peterson is correct, then local policy making on economic-development issues becomes deterministic, barring an occasional mistake on the part of decision makers. They will simply produce policies that maximize the successes of their export industries. Herbert Simon has forcefully criticized this aspect of the assumption of decision-making rationality:

> The classical theory of omniscient rationality is strikingly simple and beautiful. Moreover, it allows us to predict (correctly or not) human behavior without stirring out of our armchairs to observe what such behavior is like. All the predictive power comes from characterizing the shape of the

environment within which the behavior takes place. The environment, combined with the assumptions of rationality, fully determines the behavior.[16]

Two Issues

As the above discussion implies, there are at least two major issues in the study of community decision making. These are, first, the extent of convergence of interests between politicians, citizens, and economic elites and, second, the extent to which the rational decision-making model applies regardless of the configuration of interests. Whereas Paul Peterson has described the interests of all three decision-making elements as unitary, Robert Dahl's earlier analysis depicted them as plural. In Dahl's formulation, mass preferences are diffuse and ill formed and give leaders considerable leeway. Leaders will not share a unitary interest because, at least in industrial society, a plurality of interests exists. An activist stratum is poised to give definition to diffuse social interests and to promote them in the political process.

In the view of the pluralists, elections are real and meaningful mechanisms for bending the actions of political leaders toward the preferences of the organized groups that spring up in an open society. These groups, rooted in a social order made complex by the Industrial Revolution, have real power because of the variety of power resources that a complex society provides. Elections force political leaders to consider the preferences of these groups, or at least the preferences of the leaders of these groups.[17]

So-called elitists, though they generally accept the notion of plural social interests, have not accepted the argument that these interests are reflected in the policy process. At least three elitist positions have been developed. The first argues that economic and political elites are essentially from the same upper levels of the social strata and that they regularly interact in a variety of situations. This regularity of interaction through schooling, clubs, and business associations forms, through the socialization process, a common class consciousness. This class holds disproportionate social, economic, and political power, so disproportionate that it forms a ruling elite. Political and economic power may be conceptually separate, but both domains are controlled by the same individuals.[18]

The evidence concerning the existence of a culturally defined upper class in the United States is strong.[19] The problem lies in demonstrating a connection between the wishes of this class and the outcomes of public policy. Here the evidence is weak and is difficult to evaluate because it is subject to varying interpretations. If, for example, elites tend to lose on highly visible issues where their interests are pitted against a popular cause but are able to take considerable advantage when the issue is implemented, is this to be counted in favor of the proposition?

A second approach recognizes that the backgrounds of political leaders and economic elites are distinct but treats the offices that political leaders hold as being secondary to those that are held by economic elites. Hence, economic elites are able to control the behavior of political leaders in Congress, in executive agencies, and in positions at the state and local level. This approach, which is most closely associated with the name of sociologist C. Wright Mills, has emphasized the control that the upper class exercises over the institutional "command posts" in society. It is through these command posts that the economic elite is able to control the behavior of the politicians who hold the less important governmental positions. As a consequence of the association of power with the command positions in business and government, this approach has been termed *institutional elitism.*

Elitists offer two different sets of reasons for political leaders doing the bidding of business elites. Some analysts see this control as deliberate. For example, Michael Parenti writes that culture is an instrument of control that elites use consciously. These elites "consciously try to keep tight control over the command positions of social institutions and over the flow of symbols, values, information, rules, and choices which are the stuff of culture."[20] Others have seen this control as a natural consequence of the structure of capitalist society. Political leaders work to support the existing order and, in particular, to support the capital accumulation that they assume to be necessary to promote the common good. In the process, they aid the capitalist class to the detriment of the proletariat.[21] The similarities between this approach and Peterson's are worth noting.

A third approach is the *systemic power* argument of Clarence Stone. Stone recognizes the divergence of interests between economic elites and political leaders, but he has rejected the argument that leaders generally act on behalf of their constituents, even their organized ones. Elected officials are cross-pressured by the demands of constituents, on the one hand, and the necessity of cooperating with members of the upper strata, on the other. Cooperation is made necessary because of the disproportionate resources that upper-class individuals possess. They and their enterprises are mobile; they can leave town. They occupy advantageous positions in the status hierarchy; because prestige is a resource that is perceived to lead to policy success, politicians, who are usually from working-class backgrounds, are attracted to the elites. Finally, social elites possess disproportionate private power, occupying positions in local business corporations and nonprofit organizations, and they can mobilize the necessary resources for accomplishing civic projects.[22]

The second issue concerns the mode of decision making that community actors employ. If economic and political leaders share a common interest, at least on issues of capital accumulation, then the major issue in the study of community policy making concerns the decisional mode. Community values are set, at least on many issues facing the community, and the only matter of concern is how to implement these values. Whether these values are put into practice through informed, rational decision making is an empirical question. It is very likely that the course of public policy can be affected by any limits on organizational rationality. Strong restraints on organizational rationality will exist as long as we have indeterminism in the social world, institutional limitations on the abilities of individuals within an organizational setting to receive and process information, and human tendencies toward exercising selective attention, information distortion, and miscalculation when making decisions. Hence there is always the possibility that the course of policy will be different in a nonrational world from what it would be in a strictly rational one.

The situation is far more complex when common community values do not drive the decision-making process. If different actors on economic-development issues pursue different interests, then the limits on rationality can interact in complex ways with the process of bargaining and negotiation among leaders who represent social interests in the community. The effects on the course of policy will be correspondingly complex. One possibility, however, is that the decision-making discretion of some actors will be more circumscribed by the power configuration than will that of others, placing a premium on the decision-making skills of the former individuals. If business executives are more powerful, then politicians will need to be more skillful.

THE INTERESTS OF POLITICIANS AND BUSINESSMEN

It is possible that the unitary interest is born of common values among governing elites but diverges significantly from the interests of citizens. This view is forcefully argued by sociologists John Logan and Harvey Molotch. They write that "for those who count, the city is a growth machine, one that can increase aggregate rents and trap related wealth for those in the right position to benefit."[23] In this formulation of the process of city politics, economic and political elites are unified by their interest in increasing the value of land and other fixed assets.

Consensus on the unitary interest in increasing the price of land is maintained through manipulation: "Elites use their growth consensus to eliminate any alternative vision of the purpose of local government or the meaning of community."[24] Stephen Elkin echoes this approach, writing that government officials and businessmen holding fixed assets in the city agree on efforts to "enhance the value of their fixed assets by attracting mobile capital to the city."[25]

The motive to cooperate certainly characterizes many local business concerns, especially utilities, banks, retailers, real estate developers, and the local media. These businesses are greatly influenced by the economic vitality of the locality. There exists, however, a group of businessmen who have scant interest in city policies that enhance the value of capital assets. These are the captains of the region's export industries, the very group of individuals most responsible for wealth creation in the city. To the extent that their manufacturing facilities increase in value, perhaps because of the general desirability of their location, these export-oriented businesses will be subject to higher taxes. Yet the facilities themselves are unlikely to be sold unless they are obsolete. It is possible that these businesses will have diversified by investing in downtown redevelopment schemes that tie them more closely into the alleged interest in land inflation of the local "growth machine." It is just as likely that they will have diversified by buying other manufacturing firms, or by using their cash to decrease their common stock in circulation.

It is clear that the classic captains of industry have no corporate interest in joining forces with the "growth machine." They may do so for extrinsic reasons—they feel a sense of civic responsibility, or they are induced to do so because of incentives granted by city government. Hence we must look for a more sophisticated model of government-business relations than that offered by the proponents of a "unitary interest" in cities. The "growth machine" model fails to take into consideration a fundamental divergence of interests between the corporations responsible for the region's export industries, which are not affected by the economic condition of the immediate locale, and those businesses which rely on the region's economic vitality for sustenance. Peterson's notion of interests stemming from support for export industries is also problematic, because elites in many communities have determined that they do not want the pollution and congestion that often come with manufacturing facilities. Indeed, the location of manufacturing plants in a community may actually detract from the value of land, because certain other uses of adjacent property will be precluded.

Moreover, the interests of political leaders often differ radically from those of any subset of economic elites. Economic elites really do derive their power from the positions they occupy in the private economy, as the institutional elitists claim. But the economic elites generally act out of the interest, as they perceive it, of the corporations they run, not in the interest of their class. Their future well-being is connected through a system of structured incentives with the corporations they lead, not to some diffuse class interest. These elites are interested in the profitability of their firms, which can be almost completely disconnected from the economic viability of the local community or from the well-being of their fellow capitalists. In specific situations, of course, the interest of the corporation is not always clear, and ample room exists for both miscalculation and the pursuit of individual interests. Businessmen continue to be involved in all sorts of civic projects in most cities today. But corporate executives are judged by their impact on the balance sheets of their companies, and they generally act accordingly.

Just as the leaders of corporations put the welfare of their enterprises before the general interest of the general community or even the interest of the business community, political leaders are primarily concerned with the enhancement of the political entities they head. As John Mollenkopf notes, "Government intervention follows its own logic."[26] Success in enhancing the political entity is a more complex concept than is success in enhancing the position of a corporation. Certainly it includes economic enhancement, but it also includes enhancing the general well-being of citizens within the entity. Elections provide a powerful reminder of that obligation and are fundamental in forging a political interest distinct from the business community. However, the existence of elections does not mean that elected leaders simply adopt the perspectives of their constituents. On the other hand, simply because political leaders pursue economic-development policies rather than neighborhood-investment strategies does not necessarily mean that they are capitulating to the dictates of the business community. The interests of political leaders can be (and often are) different from either. Political leaders, because of their unique positions in society, represent interests that do not conform to any other set of interests, although of course any particular leader may be heavily influenced by (or even be captive to) such interests.

Because the interests of politicians and businessmen differ, city officials often want things from the business community that are not in the interest of that community to produce. In many policy arenas, but especially in the arena of economic-development policy, the wishes of city officials are very often different from the interests of any segment of the business community. Indeed, the whole conception of economic-development policies is to encourage businessmen to do things that they would not do on their own. Moreover, both location-based and export-based businesses have incentives to try to negotiate as large a public sector package as possible for their projects. Even if these policies are perversely abused to the self-serving interests of the business community, their very existence suggests a fundamental difference between the interests of public officials and those of business leaders. Development policies also divide the business community, but in a curious way. Location-based elites have incentives to support packages for export-oriented firms, but the reverse is not true. Because executives of export industries have little interest in increasing the values of their fixed assets, they tend to be indifferent about development schemes that are not directly related to their own businesses.

Because of this fundamental difference, the interaction between business leaders and public officials is generally not a rational discussion of the alternative strategies of economic improvement. Businessmen, seeking the improvement of the profitability of their firms, have a strong motive for seeking the maximum benefit from governments. Governmental leaders, however, have a motive not to comply, but they find themselves at a disadvantage. Business leaders, particularly those based in export, can threaten to move their enterprises, and it is in the nature of the bargaining process that they will ask for more than they need. Political leaders, however, do not know just how much they must provide to make their community the most attractive location. This asymmetry of information leads to the extraction of more benefits from the public sector than are absolutely necessary to influence the corporate decision in regard to location, an amount that we have referred to elsewhere as "the corporate surplus."[27]

Increased mobility for firms has changed the extent to which business has influenced local politics. Roger Friedland and William T. Bielby write:

> Increasingly the dominant economic units are more locationally independent firms which can move between cities, if not countries. Because of their superior economic power, such dominant economic units are less dependent on [traditional] political participation to secure necessary public policies. . . . Control over key economic processes allows dominant businesses to shape and limit the parameters within which political conflicts will take place.[28]

There is, nevertheless, considerable room for political maneuvering. Mollenkopf writes that the "progrowth coalitions" that are established and nurtured (in his view) by politicians "are not a transmission belt by which outside interests manipulate or directly control government. The reverse is rather more true: programmatic initiatives launched by such coalitions have tended to reshape the contours of private sector interests."[29] Mollenkopf is correct that businessmen are continually responding to initiatives of politicians, but he probably underemphasizes the extent to which the economic development policies of politicians are a response to actions taken by elements of the business community. Moreover, as we noted above, land-based local elites have strong motive to initiate redevelopment schemes. In the case of industrial urban renewal, however, politicians must initiate because they need the cooperation of industrialists, and that cooperation will not normally be offered. Because politicians command considerable resources, and because they, as initiators, have the first opportunity to delineate the nature of the issue that underpins the interaction, politicians are many times the primary definers of urban regimes. Moreover, the success of politicians is contingent on visible public actions, such as redevelopment projects, giving them further motivation to initiate. That they operate in a capitalist political economy and a federal structure that dictates that local governments are responsible, in large part, for raising revenue does not change this fundamental fact of urban politics, although clearly these facets of the urban political economy channel the activities of urban politicians.

We shall argue that a pattern of interaction between governmental officials and the business community emerges on economic-development policies and that this pattern certainly constrains political leaders but still leaves them room to maneuver. Because of what might be called loose coupling between business leaders and politicians and, more broadly, between the private economy and the public sector, different leaders, with differing abilities, will exploit the situation differently, and different outcomes will be produced.

Ironically, then, superficially similar circumstances can produce radically different public-policy outcomes. It is difficult to know beforehand just how a political leader will react to a set of circumstances. Hence, knowing the circumstances will usually suffice to predict outcomes, but not always. Moreover, because exceptional, nonroutine actions on the part of leaders can affect the general circumstances, the course of events can be changed by acts of leadership. Political leaders, however, are at a decided disadvantage on issues of economic development, and it is critical that the constraints of capital mobility be factored into any discussion of political entrepreneurship.

URBAN REGIMES AND SOLUTION-SETS

An urban regime may be defined as a pattern of interactions among governmental officials and business elites that is forged in order to "make and carry out governing decisions."[30] Clarence Stone argues that informal relations between business and political elites are necessary to solve problems in cities, because government alone cannot command the resources to do so. Similarly, Elkin claims that "there can be no study of city politics without the study of city economy."[31] These interactions among and between the two major classes of elites in cities, according to Stone and Elkin, result in characteristic patterns or ways of doing things in cities. These patterns are different from city to city, but are all reflections of the dependence of the city polity on the city economy.

Stone's approach to urban regimes emphasizes the manner in which co-operation among urban actors is induced and sustained. "A regime takes its character from the composition of its governing coalition and the way the members are related to one another."[32] What a regime is and what it can accomplish are both related to patterns of interactions among members. According to Stone, these interactions often derive from patterns established among upper-status citizens occupying important positions in the business community and the nonprofit sector. While we agree with Stone that previous interactions among important private and nonprofit actors are important, we would stress the independent importance of politicians. Moreover, we note the possibility of radical regime change based on new ideas that activate new participants (and to which old participants in the governing coalition must adjust).

While these interactions often have their genesis in the history of business-government relations in the city, they can be dramatically altered in a very brief period of time. This can occur through the actions of an activist mayor either seeking the cooperation of other civic actors or determined to construct a new governing coalition. If, however, city politics are as dependent on the city's economic vitality as many students of the city have suggested, then the mayor must approach the business community in order to achieve public goals. Businesses must react to initiatives coming from the political sector, if only because they have less reason to pursue collective city ends. Furthermore, a substantial segment of the business community, that involved in export industries, has little need for the public powers of city government. While it is true that developers desiring particular locations for their projects are dependent on city government, corporations whose facilities are not dependent on specific locations, including many manufacturing and service organizations, have little need to influence city politicians.

Even banks and large retailers, once the mainstays of central business districts, are less wedded to specific locations than was the case in the past. Electronic communications have made banks less reliant on central geographic locations, and the dispersal of population in metropolitan areas and the mobility of that population has given retailers a plethora of locational choices. Hence even those business concerns tied most closely to economic vitality may have fewer ties to politicians than in the past. Established firms, of course, may vigorously engage in city politics to defend their investments. Increases in capital mobility have nevertheless allowed businesses to be less dependent on city politicians than before.

This suggests that politicians, and in particular mayors, are often more responsible for regime formation than are businessmen. There exists great variability in the way in which regimes emerge, but the role of the political leader is generally crucial. This is especially true in cities where the business community is organized primarily through export industries or other mobile corporations. In a modern urban economy, this organizational form is increasingly prevalent. Consequently, urban regimes are probably forged at the initiative of politicians more frequently than by business executives, ironically, because politicians need business more than business executives need the city.

What is more important than the issue of initiation, however, is the question of participation. New regimes emerge when new participants are attracted to the policy arena. New participants are attracted through new ideas, fresh policy proposals that appeal to them. Hence there exists a fundamental interaction between regime composition and the ideas it espouses through its policy proposals and symbolic announcements.

Once established, urban regimes get codified in general practices that become characteristic of the regime. These include both informal interactions among politicians and businessmen, and formal procedures established by city agencies. For example, many cities have established economic development departments as part of city government to plan and conduct programs that attract industry, and various quasi-public agencies such as economic development corporations and downtown development corporations have been established to foster cooperation between the private and public sectors. All such arrangements reflect the general characteristics of the regime and vary considerably from place to place.

One may think of these organizational arrangements, and the economic development and other policies supported by these arrangements, as the *solution-set* of the regime. An urban regime can be faced with many opportunities and problems, including issues of social order, equity, and economic vitality. How a regime chooses to emphasize these broad goals helps to define the regime but so does the particular policy mix it chooses within these broad categories. Such policies and priorities emerge out of the interactions among regime participants.[33]

Even within a regime emphasizing economic development, there are various ways in which cities may pursue economic growth. These include downtown commercial development, residential enhancement, and attracting industry through a variety of means. Industry might be wooed through tax abatements and land write-downs, through infrastructure development, or even through the nurturing of human capital. Each approach involves a different understanding of the causal connections between public policies and industrial location. It is even not inconceivable that a city would concentrate on life-style enhancements for its current residents, paying little attention to economic growth initiatives. Hence the accumulation of policies in a priority area are important in defining a regime's solution-set.

Most city governments are characterized by multiple policy arenas, and each arena can have considerable independence from the mayor and city council. Moreover, the city's governing coalition often has little interest in many urban policy arenas, even though those affected by policies formulated in that arena are very concerned. At times, these areas may intrude on the macropolitics of the city, but normally they remain in the background. Each of these arenas may be typified by a solution-set that may or may not be consistent with the general priorities of the governing coalition. The lack of policy integration in cities preoccupied an earlier generation of urban scholars.[34] Hence it is possible that a single urban regime will be characterized by multiple solution-sets, each defined by a policy subsystem. We are mostly concerned with solution-sets that are emphasized by political leaders, however, because they are most important in attaching a policy definition to the regime.

Whatever the specific policies, solution-sets are characteristic patterns of solutions to problems and opportunities facing the city. As we shall see, these solution-sets often emerge from an interaction between past solution-sets and the current activities of city politicians and other urban actors. They reflect the understandings of governing elites about the causal connections between a city's problems (or opportunities) and potential policy solutions. Once in place, solution-sets tend to dominate city problem solving. This happens for several reasons, including the tendency of leaders to engage in limited search most of the time, and the fact that solutions are often codified in city agencies, which then dominate the search process with their known and preferred policy options. Because of these tendencies, *policy stasis* is a dominant characteristic of urban regimes.

Changes in urban regimes often occur when new actors devise new solution-sets for the problems facing the city. It is not unusual to find that solution-sets are generated (or, more likely, modified from past policy activities) in periods of extreme stress or when new political leaders emerge. New participants enter politics (or old participants become more active, not infrequently in defense of the status quo) because elements of the solution-set are valued in different ways by different urban actors. It is also typical to find that these solution-sets are applied to problems in a more routine fashion afterward – even when they are no longer appropriate. This process of incremental changes in policy understandings and outputs interspersed with bursts of creativity in policy activities that are associated with new understandings of policy issues has been described by Baumgartner and Jones as a *punctuated equilibrium* model.[35] In this book, we will illustrate both the development of a creative set of economic-development policies by mayors in Detroit and Flint in a crisis atmosphere and the less successful application of the same approach in later seemingly similar situations.

The agenda theories of John Kingdon emphasize the connection between "streams" of problems and "streams" of solution proposals that unify in more or less random fashion.[36] We agree with much of Kingdon's formulation, because it separates problems from solutions, sees both as subject to politics, and suggests that the purveyors of solutions have motive to try to gain acceptance of a problem definition that is compatible with their solution.[37]

Cities, however, are forced to deal with recurring problems, and economic development is one of the most important of these. It is clear, moreover, that the solution-set must be workable – in the sense of being capable of mobilizing support. The perceived probability of success is one aspect of a solution-set that can help attract support and can even limit consideration of less easily achievable, but better (in a long-run cost/benefit sense), solution-sets. Indeed, a regime's viability is limited by its capacity to "mobilize resources commensurate with the requirements of its main policy agenda."[38]

We argue that urban regimes codify solutions and problem definitions into a solution-set that tends to dominate policymaking for a period of time. It would be a mistake to view an urban regime solely in terms of its participants.

Rather, solution-sets and participants are related interactively. At times, participants and solution-sets coexist in stasis; at others, new participants mobilized by political leaders put forth new ideas. This implies that no urban regime may be understood apart from the historical context of both the past solutions used by the regime in dealing with its recurring problems such as economic stagnation and the historical context of the way in which urban elites have understood the problem. Only through such an approach can one begin to understand the development of what might be called the Detroit model of urban industrial renewal: projects on a vast scale with massive public intervention and direction in partnership with multinational manufacturing corporations.

In our view, the solution-set developed by a regime is an important defining characteristic – as important as the participants involved in the regime's governing coalition. Clearly the two are connected – participants carry favored solutions into politics, and certain solutions attract certain kinds of participants. But two different cities with the same kinds of participants can develop different solution-sets, at least within limits. Most important, a focus on solution-sets highlights the strong role of policy as both an independent and a dependent variable – not only a passive result of the actions of participants, but also an active force attracting new actors into the fray. The specific connection between participants and characteristic solution-sets becomes an empirical issue – one tailor-made for the strong tradition of the case approach in urban studies.

CONCLUSIONS

We shall argue, then, that politicians and business leaders bring different interests and motivations to their interchanges concerning community economic development. We recognize the "privileged position" that business leaders occupy in communities, and we realize that this position yields them special advantage in the policy process. As Friedland has noted, these resources, in order to be effective, do not have to be employed in what we normally think of as politics.[39] The simple understanding of the possibility of capital mobility colors the entire bargaining process between political leaders and leaders of corporations. However, we find problematic the stifling determinism that characterizes the views of the so-called elitists, the theories of modern Marxists, and the rational decision-making approach of the public-choice theorists that defines away value conflicts. By ignoring the "strategic and innovative" dimension of politics, such approaches banish from consideration what may well be a major source of social change: creative, albeit constrained, leadership. By ignoring the role of politicians in forging governing coalitions, they overlook a major source of innovation in urban politics. Finally, by failing to understand the limits that regime structures place on innovation, they miss the real source of conservativism in urban regimes, thinking instead that it involves the power of businessmen over politicians or a commonality of interests between the two. We make the case for the independent influence of policy solutions codified into both the formal (bureaucratic) and informal patterns of interaction among regime actors. The cases of plant location in Michigan's auto cities that we examine in this book focuses on these facets of urban governance.

2

The Automotive Public Economy

Detroit, Flint, and Pontiac are all auto cities. While each had an existence prior to the emergence of the automobile on the American scene, each experienced its greatest growth because of the automobile. In the late 1970s and early 1980s each experienced its most rapid decline because of the automobile—or more precisely, because of the lackluster performance of the American automobile-manufacturing industry during that period.

The connections between the economic health of Michigan cities and automotive manufacture are clear and direct. Because the links between economic well-being in Michigan and the success of the three major automobile-manufacturing companies are so obvious, it has been easy for some observers to conclude that politics and public policy in Michigan cities are just as dominated by the concerns of automotive manufacture. This observation has occasionally been made with pride, occasionally with disdain. Carl Crow, in the former vein, commented in 1945: "Buick is Flint and Flint Buick. It is not far-fetched to say that the relationship between the city and the industry has been like that of a self-sacrificing father and a successful son."[1]

In a more unfavorable and more analytical vein, Richard Child Hill has written:

> As massive social investment subsidies flow to downtown developers and transnational auto corporations, the city administration [of Detroit] has sharply reduced social consumption services to Detroit residents. . . . Mobilizing public incentives to leverage private resources, city officials now call themselves "entrepreneurs in the public interest." But . . . this version of the public interest boils down to the needs of private investors.[2]

There are two distinct components to the question of the relationships between automotive manufacture and public policies. One has to do with the broad connections between economy and government, the other with the specific interactions between public and private decision makers. Through the public powers to tax and to incur debt, governments use the productive capacity of the private economy to generate the resources necessary to produce public services. They are also open to influence from a variety of sources, not the least of which is the business community. These two separate components of the linkages between private enterprise and public policies are not related in a simple manner. We begin our examination of these connections by exploring the dependence of the public sector in Michigan and in our three auto cities on the health of the automobile-manufacturing industry. While the connection between economic health and automotive manufacture is clear, the links between the size of the public sector and automotive manufacture are not at all evident.

This exploration, of course, can be recognized as a central concern of political science: the issue of why government grows in modern society. Much has been written on this issue, and the various explanations of governmental growth have been subjected to empirical test.[3] Our task is both more simple and more complex. We seek to examine the relationship between a particular "export industry" of a political system and the public policies produced by that system.[4] Government may grow because that export industry is successful, but it may grow for other reasons as well. It may contract as a consequence of decline in key industries, but the contraction may not be in proportion to the industrial decline. Raising taxes or increasing levels of debt is always possible. Moreover, contraction can bring about an alteration in public-spending priorities, with increases in welfare and decreases in more positive governmental services.

MICHIGAN AND THE AUTOMOBILE

The economies of Detroit, Flint, and Pontiac are part and parcel of a regional economy that encompasses all of southeast Michigan and much of the state. The state's economy, of course, is heavily dependent on automotive manufacture, but just how dependent is often overlooked. During 1978 there were around 750,000 automotive-related manufacturing jobs in Michigan, about 19 percent of the state's total employment. This figure did not include nonmanufacturing jobs that were dependent on the auto industry—such as jobs in banking, advertising, trucking, railroads, and insurance.[5] In a study of supplier firms in southeast Michigan, David I. Verway found that 82 percent were directly linked to the automotive industry.[6] In 1978, 64 percent of all manufacturing jobs in Michigan were in automotive or automotive-linked firms; in 1980 the percentage still stood at over 61 percent.[7] In 1982, 36 percent of all passenger cars and 30 percent of all trucks produced in the United States were produced in Michigan, and over 42 percent of all jobs in the motor-vehicle industry nationally were in Michigan.[8]

Michigan's preeminent position in automotive manufacture came partly from the location of early automotive entrepreneurs and partly because of the willingness of Detroit bankers to finance the fledgling industry.[9] Flint and Pontiac were also centers of a vigorous carriage-manufacturing industry, and many of the early automotive entrepreneurs had had experience in that industry—including Billy Durant, the founder of General Motors. The carriage industry was so vigorous in Flint that the city fathers had nicknamed the city "Vehicle City" several years before the advent of the automobile.[10]

Whatever the particular circumstances leading to the development of the automobile industry in southeastern Michigan, that development was an established fact by 1920. The construction of GM's world headquarters in Detroit in 1919 made Detroit the corporate center for the company; Ford's headquarters were already established in the "surrounded" suburb of Highland Park. In 1920 a civic directory claimed that 94 percent of all automotive-manufacturing facilities in the United States were located within a 100-mile radius of Detroit.[11] While this was probably a considerable exaggeration—industry figures indicate that about 35 percent of all passenger cars produced in the United States were produced in Michigan—the statement indicates the depth of the commitment that Detroit's civic boosters had made to the automotive industry.

MICHIGAN'S PUBLIC ECONOMY

While the Michigan economy's dependence on the automobile is clear, the public economy's dependence on the automobile is not so clear. The level of public expenditures by Michigan's state and local governments is driven by the health of the statewide economy, but it is also driven by such factors as need because of increased population and citizens' demand for services. Moreover, funds spent in Michigan by Michigan governments are not necessarily raised by Michigan governments. Michigan, like all states, is part of a complex intergovernmental fiscal system. In 1978 the federal government provided 23.2 percent of all public monies spent by Michigan governments, a figure that had declined to 21.7 percent by 1981.[12] Thus the level of expenditures by Michigan governments is a function of local economic conditions and local political demands, as well as national political circumstances.

The state itself is also characterized by a complex fiscal intergovernmental system. Through a system of tax sharing and intergovernmental
grants the state provides 37.2 percent of the total funds spent by Michigan's
local governments.[13] The effect of this intergovernmental complexity is to
insulate, to a certain extent, local expenditures from the vagaries of the local
economy.

Conditions in the automotive industry do constrain, but do not
determine, expenditures in the public sector in Michigan. The absence of
tight linkages between the size of the public sector and the performance of
the private sector may be seen by examining figure 2.1, which charts the
number of automobiles produced in Michigan and the level of state and local
public employment there. The number of automobiles produced in the state
directly affects the state's automotive-based payroll and, therefore, the
impact of the automotive industry on the state's overall level of economic
activity. The number of automobiles produced is related to overall consumer
demand for automobiles, as well as to the relative demand for various types
of cars, since Michigan plants are not entirely representative of all plants. In
the past, for example, Michigan plants tended to produced a higher
proportion of larger-sized models and were thus affected by ups and downs

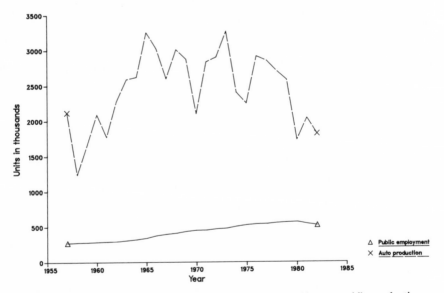

Figure 2.1. Employment in state and local governments and in automobile production
in Michigan. Automotive production is far more volatile than the production of public
services. Source: David I. Verway, ed., *Michigan Statistical Abstract, Eighteenth
Edition* (Detroit: Bureau of Business Research, Wayne State University, 1984),
tables X-1 and XVI-2.

in consumer demand for larger models. But public employment in the state is not related simply to automotive production. The cyclical nature of automotive production is not reflected in the size of the public-sector work force.

Governmental budget cycles do not correspond to economic cycles. In order to simulate the delayed effect that economic conditions have on governmental budgets, we have introduced a one-year lag on the data for automotive production. The correlation between these two series (corrected for trend) is 0.46, which is moderate by social-science standards. The reason for the rather modest correlation is that Michigan automotive production experienced several peaks and troughs during the period 1956–82, but government employment never fell until 1981. There is, however, evidence of attenuated public-sector growth in years after there were declines in automotive production. More importantly, during the severe recession in the automotive industry that began in 1979, governmental employment in Michigan fell substantially, from almost 570,000 in 1980 to 522,000 in 1982. This suggests that the size of Michigan's public sector is not determined by the success of the automotive industry but that it is constrained by it. With a severe-enough downturn in the automotive economy, such as that from 1979 to 1982, the size of the public sector will shrink. However, as we shall see below, the relative shrinkage is far less than that experienced by the automotive-related private economy and, indeed, by the private economy as a whole.

Public employment, at least until 1979, grew steadily, while production was highly variable. Employment in the automotive industry is keyed to production, with layoffs occurring when production declines and with call backs occurring when production increases. Thus, employment in the public sector is not related simply either to employment in the automotive sector or to production in that sector. This in itself may not be particularly earthshaking. The very nature of the private sector allows it to adjust more rapidly to changing economic circumstances than the public sector can. What is perhaps more surprising is that the size of the public sector is not related simply to longer-run trends in the automotive industry. This is illustrated in figure 2.2, which shows the scattergram between automotive production, with a lag of one year, and public employment in Michigan. This chart can be divided into three basic regions, generally (but not exactly) associated with time periods. The first region, at the lower left, corresponds to the late 1950s and the early 1960s. This was an era of solid growth in the automotive economy but of very low growth in the public sector. The second region, approximately corresponding to the period of the middle 1960s to the late 1970s, indicates modest growth in the automotive sector but explosive growth in government. The third region, at the upper part of the chart, corresponds basically to the late 1970s and the

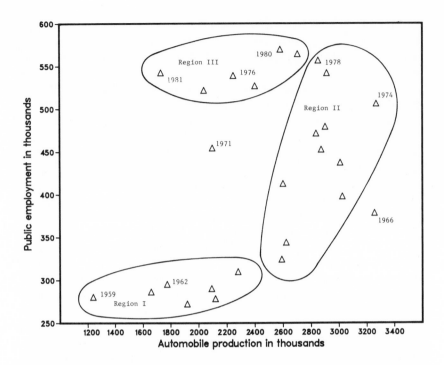

Figure 2.2. Scatterplot of employment in state and local governments and in automobile production in Michigan, lagged by one year. Employment in the public sector does not depend in a simple manner on the state of the automotive economy. Source: David I. Verway, ed., *Michigan Statistical Abstract, Eighteenth Edition* (Detroit: Bureau of Business Research, Wayne State University, 1984), tables X-1 and XVI-2.

early 1980s—an era of rapid decline in automotive productivity but only slight decline in the size of the public sector. Indeed, the period of 1977 through 1980 was a period of substantial and sustained decline in automotive production but of continued growth in government.

The years between 1954 and 1978 were characterized nationally by sustained growth in the public sector and by the emergence of a complex system of fiscal federalism. It is not surprising that Michigan was affected by this trend. What is surprising are the resulting complex relationships between the state's economy and its public sector—relationships illustrated by figures 2.1 and 2.2.

Another way of looking at the resiliency of the public sector in the face of a decline in the private sector is through the estimates of personal income prepared by the Bureau of Economic Analysis. Between the first quarter of 1981 and the last quarter of 1982, personal income in Michigan that was derived from private nonfarm activities declined by 14.2 percent, adjusted for inflation. Income from the manufacture of durable goods, which in Michigan is almost entirely related to the production of automobiles and trucks, declined by 24.5 percent. But income whose source was state or local government declined only 2.3 percent during that period.[14] While the recession was ravaging Michigan's private sector, it was doing less visible damage to the state's public sector. Spending levels were buoyed by increases in local taxes, by questionable accounting procedures at the state level, and by increased borrowing at both levels. (State-income-tax rates were not raised until 1983.)

Governmental resources were not uniformly affected by the recession, nor were governmental functions. Decline in the private sector was not uniform; the durable-goods sector, particularly the automotive economy, contracted much more severely than did other sectors. Consequently, state

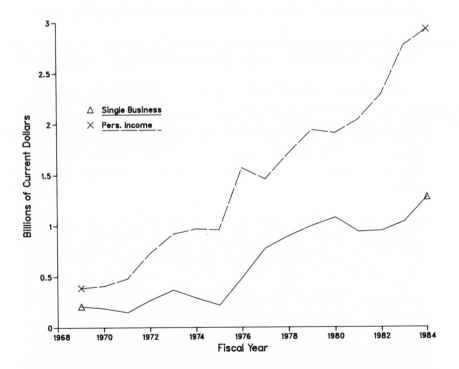

Figure 2.3. Revenues derived from selected taxes by the state of Michigan. Business taxes have been a less reliable source of public-sector income than have personal income taxes, because they are more affected by business cycles. Source: Department of Management and Budget, State of Michigan, *State of Michigan Comprehensive Annual Financial Report,* various years.

revenues from the corporate sector, particularly the manufacturing component of the corporate sector, dropped more rapidly than did other sources of revenue. Figure 2.3 compares state revenues from the personal income tax with those from the single business tax. The single business tax is a levy on the costs and profits of doing business. It replaced eight other business taxes, including the corporate income tax, in 1976; figure 2.3 presents corporate-income-tax figures prior to that year. The single business tax, which approximates a value-added tax by requiring corporations to pay taxes on the total of employee compensation costs, profits, interest, and depreciation, falls most heavily on the state's larger corporations.[15]

The graph shows that the collapse in state revenues in 1981 was due in good measure to the decline in tax revenues from the single business tax. Receipts from the personal income tax were more stable, declining substantially relative to inflation between 1979 and 1981 but resuming growth thereafter.

Similarly, governmental priorities were altered during the severe recession, as is indicated by figure 2.4. Long-term growth in expenditures for health and welfare in Michigan have been greater than for education, but the recession that began in 1979 caused a radical reversal in levels of expenditure for these two functions. Welfare and health expenditures continued to grow at the prerecession rate, but service levels suffered in the face of continued inflation and steeply increased demand. Education, however, fared far worse: spending for education dropped dramatically, even in current dollars, as the state called upon localities to increase their contributions to elementary and secondary education. The collapse of the automobile industry had caused the state to reorient its spending priorities radically.

The complex relationships between the public and private sectors in Michigan are not unique. Nationally, expenditures by local governments fluctuate less than does private sector productivity. For example, Terry Clark and Lorna Ferguson note: "Growth curves of city revenues are smooth, varying little with business cycles. By contrast, several private sector indicators show sharp cyclical patterns."[16] These authors also present data indicating only modest correlations between measures of private-sector resources and various fiscal-policy indicators among a sampling of American cities.[17]

DETROIT, FLINT, PONTIAC, AND THE AUTOMOBILE

In 1940, popular historian Arthur Pound wrote that Detroit was primarily the "social underpinning for motor car construction. It has other

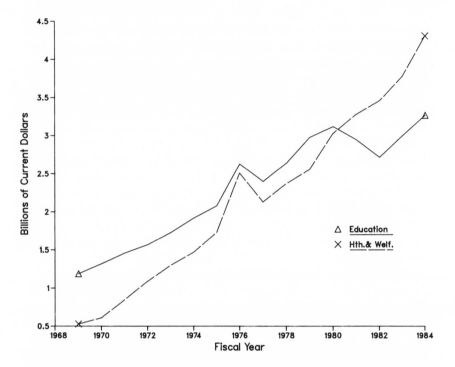

Figure 2.4. Expenditures for selected functions by the state of Michigan. The recession caused a dramatic shift in state spending priorities. Source: Department of Management and Budget, State of Michigan, *State of Michigan Comprehensive Annual Financial Report*, various years.

uses and graces; but fundamentally modern Detroit exists to build and sell motor cars, and once it quits doing that it will lose its chief reason for existence.''[18] What was true in 1940 is still true today, and it is even more true for Flint and Pontiac. While Detroit is home to the headquarters of General Motors and to Chrysler and GM assembly plants, along with various suppliers, it also contains commercial and industrial concerns that are not directly connected to automotive manufacture, such as Stroh Brewery (closed in 1985) and the headquarters of the Burroughs Corporation. Flint and Pontiac, however, come very close to being General Motors company towns. The Flint area contains no fewer than fourteen General Motors facilities, including Buick headquarters and assembly operations, AC Sparkplug headquarters and manufacturing operations, two Fisher Body plants, and a Chevrolet Division truck assembly plant and engine factory. Pontiac lost its Pontiac Division assembly plant in 1983, but it is still home to Pontiac corporate headquarters, GMC headquarters, and a GMC assembly plant.

General Motors' activities peaked in Flint in 1978, with 76,933 people employed and an annual payroll (excluding fringe benefits) of $1,865,837,000. GM activities reached their highest point in Pontiac one year later, with 39,200 people employed and a payroll of $650,000,000.[19]

These figures do not include economic activity that is either directly tied to General Motors, such as suppliers, or indirectly, such as banking, insurance, and retail trade. Nevertheless, they are all the more startling when compared to the size of the labor force. In the Flint metropolitan region, estimates by the Michigan Employment Security Commission set the labor force at 216,000 in 1978, of which 17,000 were unemployed and 85,600 were employed in manufacturing. Fully 90 percent of all manufacturing jobs in the Flint region were provided by General Motors, and almost 39 percent of all jobs were provided by General Motors. With the recession in the automobile industry that started in 1979, employment in Flint fell, and jobs with General Motors fell more rapidly. Nevertheless, in 1982 GM provided almost 32 percent of all jobs in the Flint region.[20]

The recession of 1979 to 1983 was devastating to the economies of the Michigan cities that were dependent on the automobile industry. As can be seen in figure 2.5, automobile production in the three cities plummeted after 1977 in Detroit and after 1979 in Flint and Pontiac.[21] The reason for the earlier decline of automobile production in Detroit relates to the problems of Chrysler Motor Company, whose assembly operations are concentrated in Detroit. Production in 1980 in Detroit was around one-quarter of the 1976 peak; by 1982 it was about one-third. Production took a dive in Flint and Pontiac, if somewhat less dramatically.

As production declined, unemployment rates skyrocketed. By 1982, unemployment in the Detroit metropolitan region had reached 15.9 percent, with the city's rate standing at 20.3 percent. Flint's rate reached 20.8 percent that year, the nation's highest.

CENTER CITIES

Although the economies of the Flint and Detroit regions were reasonably healthy until the oil embargo of 1974, the cities of Detroit, Flint, and Pontiac themselves had begun to experience the classic syndrome of urban decline years before. Both Detroit and Flint are older industrial cities, surrounded by surburbs. Pontiac, while technically part of the Detroit metropolis, has all of the symptoms of urban decline and is surrounded by affluent suburbs.

Between 1970 (a bad year economically) and 1977 (a good year), Detroit lost 47,000 jobs, more than 9 percent of its work force. Between

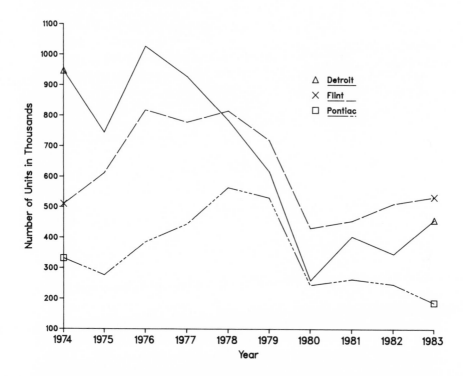

Figure 2.5. Number of motor vehicles produced in Detroit, Flint, and Pontiac. Source: David I. Verway, ed., *Michigan Statistical Abstract, Seventeenth Edition* (Detroit: Bureau of Business Research, Wayne State University, 1982), table XIV-2.

1970 and 1980 the population of the city declined from 1,514,063 to 1,192,222, and changed from 44 percent to 63 percent black. During this same period, property values declined 1.5 percent, while the rest of the metropolis experienced an increase of 116.5 percent. Flint also experienced a decline in population, from a 1970 population of 193,317 to 159,576, as did Pontiac (from 85,279 to 76,270). However, Flint and Pontiac did not experience the decline in property values that Detroit did; Flint's state-equalized property valuation rose by 29.9 percent during that period. This was nevertheless substantially less than the statewide average. Detroit's income tax (levied in 1979 at 1 percent on residents and 0.5 percent on nonresident workers) also yielded less, on a per capita basis, than did similar taxes in Flint and Pontiac. Per capita yield in Detroit was $70; in Flint, $127; in Pontiac, $142. These last two figures are highest in the state among cities that levy an income tax; the large number of nonresident workers at General Motors facilities inflates tax collections in these two cities.[22]

The Detroit region, center of automotive production, has been affected as much or more than any other metropolis in the world by automobile *consumption.* The region is supplied with a superb network of freeways. With Henry Ford's five-dollar day and his dream of the mass-produced automobile for the workingman, geographic mobility became truly possible for the semiskilled worker on the automobile assembly line. In Detroit, as in Flint, suburban sprawl definitely included the working-class family. The classic concentric city of the Chicago school of urban studies emerged. As one moved further from the urban core, neighborhood well-being improved.[23] Yet the residential mobility that caused this concentric pattern also channeled into distinct sectors those who were fleeing from the center city. Into Oakland County, to the north of Detroit, moved the middle and upper classes; into western and southwestern Wayne County, and into Macomb County to the northeast, moved the factory workers, the clerks, and the lower middle class.[24] "Like the 'big bang' theory of the universe, the sectors are continuously retreating from the core urban area, guided by major transportation corridors."[25]

The "concentric sector" development of the Detroit region has resulted in large geographic variability in such measures of class differences as occupation, income, and housing value. For example, the 1980 housing value of Bloomfield Township (adjacent to Pontiac and home to many automobile executives) averaged 5.98 times that of Detroit. But a typical house in Bloomfield Township cost 4.65 times the average house in Ferndale, in southwest Oakland County, and 5.63 times the average house in the "downriver" (southwest Wayne County) community of River Rouge.[26] Nevertheless, the image of Detroit versus the suburbs does have validity. Between March 1977 and March 1980, the nominal median family income rose 26 percent, to $26,086, in the Detroit SMSA (Standard Metropolitan Statistical Area) but fell 11 percent, to $15,984, in the city.[27] More than 46 percent of Detroiters were housed in buildings that had been constructed before 1940, and many of these had deteriorated; the figure for the SMSA was 24 percent.[28] The city's unemployment is about five percentage points higher than that in the SMSA, but this masks considerable variability within the city. Among blacks, the unemployment rate in 1983 was estimated at 32.7 percent, and among blacks aged 16 to 19 at 66.7 percent.[29]

The static figures above mask a volatile migratory dynamics. Between 1970 and 1980 the city of Detroit lost more than half of its white population. In 1980, 138,000 suburban residents had lived in Detroit only five years earlier. Businesses also migrated, or simply died: between 1963 and 1982 the number of manufacturing jobs in Detroit declined from 200,000 to less than 100,000. Suburban manufacturing jobs grew by 100,000 between 1963 and 1977, but declined thereafter.[30]

COPING WITH DECLINE

Even in good economic times, Detroit, Flint, and Pontiac had suffered. Economic downturns affected these cities even more severely than the state of Michigan as a whole. These economic trends affected the fiscal situation of Michigan's manufacturing cities both in straightforward and in complex ways.

We noted above that economic trends in the private sector and expenditures in the public sector do not move in tandem. The continued increase in demands for public expenditures in the face of a languishing or declining economy has been termed *fiscal stress* and has been subjected to considerable scholarly scrutiny. One of the most striking findings of the fiscal-stress studies is that different cities, as well as different public-sector leaders, have used radically different strategies in coping with decay in the fiscal conditions of their communities.[31]

Between 1973 and 1983 the United States economy experienced two very serious recessions and one substantial boom. Unlike the fairly stable economic times between World War II and the 1973 Arab oil embargo, the period 1973 to 1983 saw the economy become radically cyclical, with accentuated peaks and troughs. Such economic instability wreaks havoc on the budget planning of governments, but it is especially hard on Michigan's automotive cities. There is a great deal of truth in the adage that the automotive sector falls first in an economic downturn; it also falls further and recovers more rapidly than does the national economy.[32]

In Detroit the increasingly cyclical nature of the local economy was reflected in a deteriorating ability on the part of budget officers to estimate revenues. As one might expect, there is a strong tendency for budget officials to overestimate revenue during downturns and to underestimate it during upturns. During the period between 1962, when Detroit's municipal income tax went into effect, and 1982, budget officials underestimated revenue from this source eight times and overestimated revenue twelve times. The most consistent and severe underestimates came after 1978.[33]

THREE STRATEGIES

These severe underestimates came about because of the rapidly deteriorating revenue situation during the late 1970s. All three auto cities were affected by the decline, but they were affected differently, and they responded differently. Figure 2.6 presents data on city revenues from all sources for the period 1975–83, adjusted for the effects of inflation. Collections (and therefore expenditures) increased in all three cities immediately after 1975, primarily because of increases in intergovernmental aid. Gains in Flint and Pontiac also reflected growth in their own sources of

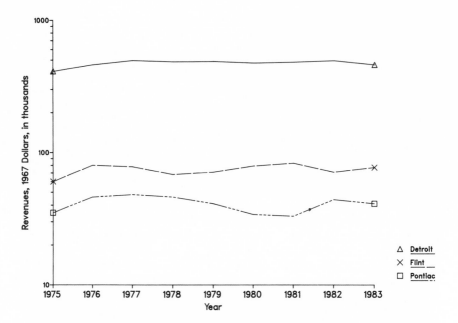

Figure 2.6. Total revenues, adjusted for inflation, raised by Detroit, Flint, and Pontiac. Neither increases in intergovernmental aid nor tax increases (in Detroit) offset the effects of economic decline and inflation on city revenues. Source: *City Government Finances* (Washington, D.C.: Bureau of the Census, various years).

revenue. After 1977, Pontiac experienced a dramatic decline in both intergovernmental aid and its own sources of revenue. Flint experienced little long-term change in either source of revenue, although the curves mask a decline in revenue from the municipal income tax and an increase in property-tax revenues.

Detroit's growth in inflation-adjusted revenue was entirely due to increases in intergovernmental aid, primarily from the federal government. Some idea of the massive infusion of federal funds into Detroit during the Carter presidency is offered by Thomas Anton. He estimates a "replacement ratio"—the extent to which local revenues would have to be increased in order to replace federal grants, holding constant the levels of services—at 38.8 percent for fiscal 1978. Anton reports that federal dollars supported all positions in the departments of Planning, Neighborhood Services, Manpower, and the bulk of positions in the Health Department and supported from 11 to 28 percent of the positions for the five core municipal functions.[34]

A second perspective on the financial status of our auto-city governments is presented in figure 2.7. The total of outstanding debts declined in both Flint and Detroit through 1981, but increased dramatically in Pontiac.

Figure 2.7. Total outstanding debt, adjusted for inflation, in Detroit, Flint, and Pontiac. Debt decreased in Flint as a matter of policy, increased in Pontiac to fund economic-development projects, and declined in Detroit as its bonds fell below investment grade. Source: *City Government Finances* (Washington, D.C.: Bureau of the Census, various years).

Most of the increase in indebtedness in Pontiac was nonguaranteed—that is, not backed by the full faith and credit of the municipality. The majority of these bond issues went for economic-development projects, the largest of which was the Pontiac Silverdome sports stadium.

By 1980, three strategies for coping with fiscal stress had emerged in the three auto cities. Flint had relied on a combination of fiscal conservativism and a growth in indigenous resources to stave off a major decline in services. Though Pontiac had suffered a large decline in revenues, it had responded with an aggressive program of economic development that was heavily reliant on municipal borrowing. Detroit had adroitly exploited intergovernmental aid from the state and federal governments through a combination of political acumen and bureaucratic competence. Mayor Young had forged important political alliances in Lansing and in Washington, and these political connections had paid off in federal aid and in such state-aid packages as the Detroit equity package to offset suburban "exploitation" of city-financed facilities. The city's bureaucracy could be counted on to exploit to the fullest the opportunities for intergovernmental funds in cases where application was necessary. It had become extremely adept at developing project grants during the administration of Mayor Jerome Cavanaugh, and it continued to devote considerable resources to preparing requests for grants.

SECREST AND BEYOND

In the late 1970s, Detroit was struggling with large fiscal problems. Service needs were increasing as the city became poorer as a consequence of the movement of the middle class from the city. Even the black middle class had begun to move to the near suburbs of Southfield and Oak Park. Demands from city unions were intense in the inflationary environment of the period. Yet inflation-adjusted revenues from local sources, after failing to grow for years, had begun to decline in 1978. Mayor Young had crafted a strategy to deal with the problems of high demand and fiscal stagnation. On the one hand, he aggressively pursued aid from both the state and local government. On the other hand, he invested heavily, far too heavily according to his critics, in economic development. More and more of the available federal Community Development Block Grant funds were being invested in economic-development projects, especially projects in the central business district, while less was being earmarked for neighborhood betterment.

The system proved to be a fragile one. Between 1980 and 1981, Detroit experienced a disastrous decline in revenues, which was brought about by the crisis in the automobile industry. Not only did city revenues, especially revenues from the local income tax, decline, but the state of Michigan severely limited its payments to localities as it struggled with its own budgetary nightmare. The city's short-term debt jumped to $130 million, from $50 million the year before. It was evident that the short-term bond market would not be able to absorb such an amount. To compound the crisis, in August of 1980, Moody's Bond Rating Service lowered Detroit's municipal-bond rating from Baa to Ba, which is considered below investment grade.

Mayor Young's response was to appoint a blue-ribbon commission to study the situation and to make recommendations. Headed by Fred Secrest of Ford Motor Company, the Budget Planning and Stabilization Committee included representatives from corporations, banks, and labor unions. The commission first gave Detroit a clean bill of health on financial management; none of the fiscal shenanigans used in New York City during its fiscal crisis were in evidence in Detroit. Then it recommended a "survival package," which consisted of selling deficit-funding bonds, which would convert the short-term debt to longer-term debt; increasing the city income tax; and negotiating wage concessions with municipal unions.[35] The plan was complex; the increase in taxes required both legislative approval and an affirmative vote from citizens. Suburban legislators were hostile toward a tax increase, which would affect commuters. The bond plan would require the approval of state officials, and the city's unions, especially those representing police and fire officers, had been engaged in a protracted struggle with the mayor on a number of issues. The plan carried in the legislature only because of the support of Governor William Milliken. Because he was not able to convince many Republicans to vote for the plan, his lieutenant governor had to cast the deciding vote in the senate. Young skillfully negotiated a wage-concession package with the police officers' association, and all other unions except the building trades agreed to concessions soon thereafter.

While the Secrest survival package alleviated the immediate financial crisis, Detroit has continued to struggle with an extremely unfavorable fiscal situation. Layoffs, reductions in services, and tough bargaining with the city's labor unions have characterized the city's financial policies during the early 1980s. With the cutbacks in federal aid by the Reagan administration, the task was made all the more difficult.

FLINT AND PONTIAC

The cities of Flint and Pontiac also faced desperate fiscal situations. These cities were more dependent on automotive payrolls than was Detroit, but both had stronger property-tax bases. Although Flint was hit hardest by the severe economic decline, its indigenous resources were remarkably robust during the early years of the recession. It faced the least severe fiscal circumstance of the three auto cities. Moreover, Flint's leadership refused to consider a tax increase to fund the wage demands of its strong municipal unions. Mayor James Rutherford, a Democrat and a former police officer, articulated a strongly conservative fiscal philosophy: "Spend, spend, spend is totally unacceptable today. Our pay increases have been minimal. Not this pie-in-the-sky thing Mayor Young did [in the Secrest settlement]."[36]

Pontiac, on the other hand, faced major declines in locally generated resources and in intergovernmental aid. It had embarked upon an economic-development strategy that had not paid high dividends. Its vaunted "Pontiac Plan," an ambitious attempt to revitalize its downtown, had not ever really gotten off the ground. The city had built the Silverdome sports stadium and had attracted professional football and basketball teams to it, but the city had incurred a large debt and increased demand for services. Little in the way of increased economic development had followed. For all its attempts to diversify, the city remained primarily a blue-collar factory town, whose workers increasingly drove in from surrounding Detroit suburbs and whose citizens frequented the numerous shopping centers in the immediate area.

Added to the concentration of service-dependent citizens and a stagnating tax base was a high level of tax resistance. Facing a tax-hostile public, the Pontiac school district had not been able to pass a millage levy for years. School athletics and "enrichment" programs such as music and art were eliminated, and half-day programs were instituted before a millage levy finally succeeded.

Even though it faced a similar fiscal crisis, Pontiac lacked Detroit's political muscle at the state and national levels. It was forced to solve its fiscal problems through cutbacks in services and through layoffs of employees; no Pontiac bailout plan was forthcoming.

CONCLUSIONS

There is little doubt that public policies are affected by decisions made in the private economy. The real issue is just how those effects occur, and with what impact. In Michigan's automotive cities, one would expect clear and direct relations between the automotive economy and public decision making. Yet the explicit connections are by no means clear. Correlations between public-sector activity and automotive production are not large, and public-sector growth occurs even in a stagnating automotive economy. The size and composition of public-sector activity respond to demand as well as supply factors.

Extraordinarily severe economic decline in the manufacturing sector changes the government's revenue base, but it changes demand patterns also. As Michigan's industrial economy virtually collapsed after 1979, demand for social-welfare expenditures rose dramatically. Economic decline forced the state to increase welfare expenditures while cutting overall budget levels. Changes in demand patterns caused increases in some expense categories, while changes in the revenue base forced cuts in others.

Similarly, cities may find it necessary to increase police expenditures, for example, when crime and other indicators of social problems increase, even in the face of declining tax revenues. Indeed, pressures for increases in expenditures for police and other services may proceed completely independently of changes in the crime rate or the revenue situation.[37] Moreover, employee demands in regard to wages and pensions often do not correspond to changes in the revenue situation. Employees of declining cities tend to compare themselves to employees in other governmental jurisdictions, paying scant attention to local financial conditions. Indeed, Michigan's law relating to collective bargaining by public employees requires binding arbitration when there is an impasse, but arbitrators are not allowed to examine the financial condition of the municipality. Ironically, the bill was sponsored by State Senator Coleman A. Young, who has been highly critical of the act since he became mayor.

It would, of course, be a mistake to overemphasize demand factors in the growth of governmental activity. The size of the revenue base does limit public-sector activity, although the complex system of intergovernmental finance can insulate localities to some extent from the vagaries of the local economy. In the long run, however, to sustain a particular level of activity in the face of economic decline means either cutting the cost of services or increasing the proportion of private-sector resources that is taken for public services. After relying heavily on intergovernmental grants during the 1970s, Detroit increased taxes, delayed payment of its deficit, and cut costs at the bottom of the recession of 1979–83.

The connection between the automotive economy and public policies might best be depicted as "slack cables." While clear linkages exist between the economic base provided by automotive manufacture and the size and composition of the public sector, the cables provide considerable slack. From an examination of Michigan's public-expenditure data, one can find no evidence that specific policies and decisions are determined by the automotive economy. In severe downturns, however, the cables are pulled taut, and the manufacturing-dependent polity struggles to meet the social-service needs of its people while it neglects its public infrastructure.

Yet there is at least one area in which private decisions may directly affect public ones: namely, economic-development policy. Cities whose economies are deteriorating have an interest in protecting their bases and, if possible, in attracting new industry. Detroit, Flint, and Pontiac have all pursued aggressive economic-development policies, and each has been accused of tailoring its policies to suit the industry that it was wooing. Only by examining particular decisions can we explore this thesis. Before doing so, however, we will examine the political decision-making structure of the Detroit metropolitan area.

3

Detroit:
Industrial Democracy
or Capitalist Oligarchy?

> There was a time in which the united front was a legitimate political approach to revolution. And that meant working with all elements, including the capitalists and industrialists.
>
> —Detroit's Mayor Coleman A. Young, 1980

"To Detroit, the Constantinople of the West." Thus a well-to-do merchant of Pontiac toasted his guests from Detroit in the 1890s.[1] And indeed, the "city of the straits," located on a narrow body of water connecting Lake Erie with Lake St. Clair and Lake Huron, resembled, geographically, the famous eastern city on the Bosporus. Like the old capital of the Roman Empire, Detroit's lifeblood was commerce. Lumber and copper from the north and foodstuffs from the fertile farms of Michigan's "Thumb" passed through its port. Manufactured goods from the East moved through, serving the farms and communities of Michigan.

Yet even then the analogy was strained. Detroit contained fewer than three hundred thousand people, while Constantinople held more than one million. New York, Philadelphia, and Chicago had decades before become national metropolises, while Detroit was still a provincial capital. More importantly, however, the relatively tranquil Detroit of the 1890s, with its tree-lined boulevards and lingering French flavor, was on the verge of undergoing perhaps the most rapid and complete change in its economic raison d'être that a modern city has ever experienced. Already Detroit had become, like Constantinople, an ethnic polyglot city, as waves of German, Irish, Italian, and, most recently, Polish, immigrants had arrived. The census of 1890 reported that only 20 percent of Detroit's two hundred

40

thousand citizens had been born of native white parents. And industrial development had commenced; the old commercial elite was being joined by the new manufacturers. Iron, steel, tobacco and flour processing, meat packing, carriage manufacture, and machine-tool operations had been established and were growing.

The great transformation, however, was yet to occur. Within twenty short years, Detroit was transformed from a commercial city boasting a moderate manufacturing capacity into an industrial giant, the center of a vast automotive industry employing hundreds of thousands of workers and providing the livelihoods, directly or indirectly, of hundreds of thousands more.

The scope and intensity of the transformation are almost incomprehensible. In 1900, Detroit's population was 300,000; by 1930 it was 1.6 million. Transformed by the same economic forces, Flint, a provincial lumbering and carriage-building town in the Genesee valley, grew from 13,000 in 1900 to 91,600 in 1920 and to 156,500 in 1930. The demand for labor for the automobile factories spawned a vast housing market, and the city grew rapidly outward. Most building during the time was of workers' cottages and two- and three-flat buildings; this gave Detroit its characteristic industrial, sprawling appearance, in sharp contrast to the tenements of East Coast cities.

Industry itself was experiencing a great transformation. In 1905, some twenty-seven hundred factories in Michigan were granted state licenses to produce automobiles.[2] By 1920 only a handful of firms dominated the market, and by 1930 the basis structure of the automotive economy was set, with General Motors and Ford dividing the lion's share of the domestic market. Automobile manufacture had gone from a cottage industry with easy entry (an entrepreneur needed only enough capital to establish an assembly operation, relying on the well-developed supplier system to produce the components) to a tight oligarchy with the entry of new firms being virtually impossible.

MILWAUKEE JUNCTION

Typical of this new industrial order was Milwaukee Junction, where the Michigan Central Railroad joined the Detroit and Milwaukee Railroad not far from General Motors' world headquarters, which was completed in 1921. The rapid industrial expansion after 1900 forced manufacturers to search for space for their factories beyond the city's riverfront and traditional core, which was largely occupied by an earlier generation of industry: shipbuilding, stove manufacture, pharmaceuticals, and tobacco products. The search for space led northeast, to Milwaukee Junction.

During the period of great industrial expansion, the most significant industrial growth in Detroit occurred in three locations: "Outside of Ford's monumental achievements at his Highland Park plant beginning in 1910 and at the River Rouge site after 1917, the most significant industrial growth in Detroit took place in the vicinity of Milwaukee Junction."[3] The area rapidly became home to many of the early entries into the automotive-manufacturing business: Cadillac, Dodge, Studebaker, Detroit Electric, Ford, Packard, and Hupp. In addition, the three major independent producers of automotive bodies—Fisher, Murray, and Wilson—all located at Milwaukee Junction.

All seemed insignificant in comparison to the sprawling Dodge Brothers plant, built there in 1910. Designed by premier industrial architect Albert Kahn, it consisted of thirty-six separate buildings, encompassing more than five million square feet of space. It included its own foundry, powerhouse, and stamping, casting, transmission, and engine operations. The vast assembly building was four stories of bedrock-solid reinforced concrete. Employment there reached seventeen thousand by 1917 and peaked at forty thousand during World War II.

"Dodge Main" was the first major plant organized by the United Automobile Workers in 1936, and in 1937 Dodge Main's Local No. 3 was the largest local union in the country, with a membership of more than twenty-six thousand workers.[4] But if Dodge Main represented the high tide of American industrial might, it also represented the decentralization and decline of urban industrial dominance. Chrysler Corporation bought Dodge in 1928, and the manufacturing components of the operation were gradually phased out. In the 1950s the transmission line was moved to Indiana, and by the 1960s the once-mighty Dodge Main had become Hamtramck Assembly. When it closed in early 1980, Chrysler employed only three thousand workers there.[5]

SOCIAL AND POLITICAL CHANGE

The transformation in economic function brought about radical transformation of the social fabric and the political structure. Historian Oliver Zunz, basing his statement on his painstaking quantitative research of census and land-use data of 1880, 1900, and 1920, describes Detroit in the late nineteenth century, as "a multi-ethnic city, divided into a congeries of ethnic communities which were semi-autonomous." Although the native white elite dominated the commercial and industrial life of the community, the ethnic communities possessed significant cultural and economic autonomy. "Each ethnic group lived in its own section of the city, combined wealthy and less wealthy, rich and poor people, employers and employees . . . and the different communities lived fairly isolated from each other."[6]

Remarkably, by 1920, "that structure of multi-class ethnic communities had completely vanished."[7] Detroit had become the prototypical modern industrial city, with its population separated into two classes, increasingly antagonistic and divided over control of the means of production. The cross-class ethnic communities of the earlier era had disappeared, and Zunz reports that the only significant ethnic clusterings occurred in working-class neighborhoods. Perhaps most importantly, the plural opportunity structure of the nineteenth century, with social mobility possible within ethnic comunities and in the broader community social structure, became "a single opportunity structure in the twentieth century when industry comes to dominate the whole hierarchy of work, to recognize the neighborhood, the culture, and every aspect of life."[8]

With the great industrial and social transformations came a change in the political structure. During the late 1800s and early 1900s, Detroit's government was typical of cities of the day: the mayor-council form, ward elections for the common council (an upper house, elected at large, had been abolished by the state legislature in 1887), and a thoroughly partisan style. The mayor was elected for a two-year term and sat as an ex officio member of the Board of Education, whose members were also elected from wards. The 1880s and 1890s were characterized politically by new German immigrants, who challenged the entrenched Irish in elections to the common council and for control of the local Democratic party. The pattern of alliances changed when Mayor Hazen Pingree was able to pry the German vote from the Democratic party and to build support among Poles for his brand of progressive Republicanism.[9]

The reforms by Pingree, however, failed to curb municipal abuses, which, in the early 1900s, were characterized by recurring scandals as the city government strained to cope with explosive growth and rapid social change. In 1910 the Wabash Railroad had bribed the common council's leader "Honest Tom" Glinnan and virtually every alderman in order to get a street closed for a right of way. In 1912, Henry Leland, founder of Cadillac Motor Company, and thirty-six other members of the city's Protestant elite formed the Good Citizens' League to combat the corruption. The league drew its support from the traditional anti-Catholic wing of the Republican party, but it also was strongly supported by the temperance forces.[10]

In 1918, prodded by the efforts of the Good Citizens' League, the citizens of Detroit adopted a new city charter. The charter abolished the ward system and provided for the election of a nine-member common council, to be elected at large. The Board of Education was also reformed, with seven members to be elected at large. The charter was adopted primarily to suppress ethnic divisions and to increase the power of the white Protestant elite.[11] Ironically, however, it came into effect in an urban world in which ethnic divisions were being transcended by class antagonisms. City government itself became a monolith, similar in organization to the industrial corporation.

The industrialization of Detroit spawned two other massive changes in the social organization, both of which had major political consequences. The first, the unionization of the work force, came just after the Great Depression had devastated the city. The second, the migrations of American blacks and southern whites, reestablished ethnicity as a major organizing force in political and social life. In the eyes of some observers, automotive manufacture had, by the 1960s, created a city of "race and class violence."

The massive social dislocation of the depression in Detroit may be gauged by some figures. In 1929, Ford employed over 128,000 workers in the Detroit region; by 1931 Ford employed only 37,000 workers. Between the spring and fall of 1929, General Motors cut its Pontiac work force from 29,000 to 14,000. In Flint, production dropped to one-seventh of normal.[12]

While the immediate effect of the depression was massive human suffering among industrial workers, the delayed effect was unionization. The great breakthrough for the United Automobile Workers (UAW) occurred during 1936 and 1937, when, following a series of sit-down strikes, General Motors agreed to bargain collectively. Detroit's labor force quickly became the most unionized in the country.

BLACKS IN DETROIT

Detroit had an established Negro community prior to industrialization, in part because of the city's location as a terminal on the underground railroad. But the early industrial period by-passed the black community, and between 1870 and 1910, Detroit's Negro population declined as a percentage of the population. Then, between 1910 and 1920, the black community grew sevenfold, while the while population was doubling.[13] This dramatic increase, brought about by migration from the South, was a result of Henry Ford's policies of promoting employment for blacks in his company, although he concentrated them at his massive Dearborn Rouge Complex. In 1937, 9,825 blacks worked at Rouge, about 12 percent of all workers there. In comparison, General Motors employed only 2,800 Negro workers, mostly in Flint and Pontiac, in 1941.[14]

By the early 1940s, some 100,000 Negroes resided in Detroit, 7.6 percent of the population. Both blacks and organized labor entered municipal politics in Detroit as important factors at about this time. After the race riot of 1943, Mayor Edward Jeffries attacked both blacks and labor, cleverly undermining the "united front" strategy of blacks and the UAW leadership. His overwhelming victory indicated the weakness of the influence that union leaders had on their members' votes when race became an issue. Yet the election "marked the emergence of a close political alliance between black Detroit and the UAW that would remain an important feature of Michigan's political landscape for years."[15]

The labor/black alliance gained a majority interest in the Democratic party during the late 1940s, pushing aside the party's more conservative Irish Catholic wing. But both were relatively uninfluential in municipal politics until the reform administration of Mayor Jerome Cavanaugh. Ironically, Cavanaugh was associated with the more conservative wing of the Democratic party, but he was able to overcome the business community's support of Mayor Louis Miriani and win the mayoralty election of 1963. Cavanaugh moved quickly to solidify his support among blacks and liberal whites.[16]

The relationship between blacks and predominantly white UAW leadership in union politics has been equally complex. While the vast majority of black workers have been relatively complacent in union politics, during the 1960s a strong insurgent movement developed, led by black radicals. The League of Revolutionary Black Workers strove to heighten class consciousness in Detroit factories, particularly at Dodge Main, with some success. The league died when its leadership cadre split up. Sociologist James Geschwender, in his analysis of the league, suggested that the league "is more likely to have been a significant harbinger of things to come than it is to have been a passing epiphenomenon."[17] The prophecy seems to have been hollow; unlike the Great Depression, which stimulated militant unionism in the automobile industry, the hard economic times of the late 1970s and 1980s seem to have had a chastening effect on black union insurgency.

In 1960, blacks made up 29 percent of the city's population, which was mostly concentrated in two sprawling ghettos. The improved economy of the 1960s and the intensified white flight from the city after the 1967 racial disorders meant that a far wider variety of housing was available to blacks, and by 1980, blacks were living throughout the city proper. In 1970, Detroit's population was 44 percent black; by 1980, it was 63 percent black.

In 1973, black state senator and former labor activist Coleman A. Young defeated Police Commissioner John Nichols in a bitterly fought, racially polarized election by a razor-thin margin. At the same time, a change in the city charter increased the mayor's power in making appointments and in financial affairs, simultaneously reducing the power of the common (now city) council. Armed with increased formal powers, acute political skills, and the enthusiastic support of the black community, particularly its poorest segment, Coleman A. Young has become the strongest mayor in the city's history.

Young's policies have consistently echoed three themes: increasing opportunities for blacks in the city's thoroughly reformed bureaucracies, forging linkages with private-sector elites in order to accomplish economic-development objectives, particularly in the downtown business district, and working closely with state and national officials to maximize the flow of intergovernmental funds to the city. Clearly the success of these aims depended on the cooperation of individuals outside of the city, and Mayor Young has earned a reputation as a master coalition builder. His early support of Jimmy Carter gained him a special relationship with the Carter administration. Young also had close ties with the administration of Republican Governor William Milliken, so much so that Milliken's Democratic opponent in 1978 accused Young of keeping down the Democratic vote in Detroit. Young has also worked closely with the city's business community on various civic projects.

DETROIT'S EVOLVING POWER STRUCTURE

At the turn of the century, Detroit's industrial power structure was almost exclusively white, Anglo-Saxon, and Protestant. Oliver Zunz's study of the 133 largest industrial employers in 1900 found the new industrial elite to be 71 percent Republican, 87 percent Protestant (almost all Episcopalian, Congregational, or Presbyterian), and 85 percent Anglo-Saxon. Interestingly, many had only recently settled in Detroit, and most were founders or cofounders of the manufacturing firms they headed.[18]

Although the great transformation brought about by the automobile changed the sources of wealth, it did not, it seems, change the base of this private power structure. In a study of the Detroit economic elite in the early 1970s, Lynda Ewen reported a tight-knit elite whose wealth was based on manufacturing, commerce, and banking and which was characterized by a great deal of intermarriage.[19] Neither Zunz nor Ewen, however, examined explicitly the linkages between politics and this economic elite; therefore these studies tell us little about the relationship between private elites and public power.

Other studies do, however, suggest substantial linkages; they also indicate that independent power derives from control of institutions in the public sector. Moreover, these studies provide evidence of separate constituencies and interests in the two domains. Thomas Anton and Bruce Bowen report data that suggest a pragmatic working relationship between the private and political decision makers in Detroit. In a survey of ninety-two members of the economic elite in 1975, 63 percent reported that they spent half or more of their working time on public issues. The attitudes of these individuals were characterized by pragmatism rather than ideology.[20] Anton concludes that "Detroit's concentrated and highly-organized institutional structure produces a small group of elite leaders who easily exchange information and opinions among themselves."[21]

The most interesting modern study of the Detroit power structure was conducted by the *Detroit News,* under the supervision of sociologist Charles Kadushin. The *News* assembled a list of major Detroit organizations in business, banking, government, law, community affairs, the media, religion, sports, the arts, labor, medicine, society, and wealth, and among retired executives. The top individuals in the organizations thus isolated were listed; they numbered some twelve hundred. The seventy-five individuals who appeared most often (usually across sectors) were interviewed, and an additional forty whose names were frequently mentioned by the initial seventy-five were also interviewed. The forty-seven most powerful individuals were those mentioned most frequently in a variety of circumstances.[22]

Kadushin writes that the power structure is

> composed of two groups linked by some common members. The first group is composed of the rich, the socially elite and the commercially important people of Detroit. This group includes auto magnates, former board chairmen, bank presidents, top retail merchants, heads of local utilities. . . . The second group is composed of people from working-class backgrounds and it holds resources not of things, but of people. Politicians, labor leaders, lawyers, ministers and other professionals form this group. . . . But what may be unique to Detroit is the fact that the second is also well connected to the first (or "elite") group. This is both the result and the cause of coalition policy-making in Detroit.[23]

THE AUTO INDUSTRY AND CIVIC PROJECTS

Seldom have the leaders of automobile companies taken the lead in civic affairs in Detroit, but when they do intervene, the results tend to be dramatic. Henry Leland of Cadillac spearheaded the city's municipal-reform movement, but, in general, the executives of General Motors have not been noted for their involvement in community affairs. The Ford family is much more active; it has endowed many cultural projects, in particular the symphony and the art museum.

The most spectacular civic accomplishment, however, of Henry Ford II was Renaissance Center, a hotel and office complex on the Detroit River. Ford was committed to a major project on the river, and he acted as the entrepreneur in putting together the investment package. This was not an easy matter, because most of the investors did not view the project favorably. Of the fifty-one corporations that invested in the original plan, thirty-eight had strong ties to the automobile industry.[24] Ford Motor Company itself invested one-third of the total.

More recently, General Motors, after making a corporate decision to keep its headquarters in Detroit rather than to move to New York, has committed funds to projects in the New Center area. Both commercial and residential projects have been initiated. The residential projects, which have been directed at restoring older houses and apartment buildings directly north of GM's world headquarters, met with some opposition from neighborhood groups. The city, however, has been solidly behind the project and has helped by writing applications for federal grants and by committing community-development funds to the area.

SECTORAL CENTRALIZATION

Robert Dahl, in his path-breaking study of urban power in New Haven, Connecticut, wrote: "Industrial society dispersed, it did not eradicate political inequality. . . . The political system of New Haven, then, is one of *dispersed inequalities.*"[25]

The best evidence from the city that felt industrial transformation most strongly is contrary to this. In Detroit, rather than dispersing power by creating new forms of political resources, thus allowing new groups to gain access to the political system, industrialization swept away the variegated, diverse, small-scale social structure and replaced it with a unitary system. No longer could an individual achieve upward mobility within his ethnic community; a single system of social stratification had replaced the cross-class ethnic communities. Social cleavages were no longer rooted in ethnic diversity; class, and later class and race, were Detroit's social fissures. It became much harder for the individual entrepreneur to establish himself in the manufacturing sector; he had to join the large-scale corporation to achieve success. In government, too, a structure that reflected urban diversity had been replaced by a unitary structure. No longer could politics serve as a balancer of ethnic interests; the municipal-reform success of 1918 had ensured that.

It would be a mistake, however, to assume that industrialization had replaced pluralism with an elitism in which the economic notables dominated politics and government. Quite the contrary. By forging deep, reinforcing divisions in society, this industrial revolution had solidified power within a limited number of sectors. If industrialists were powerful because of their large-scale organizations, so was labor, whose organizational structure had to follow the contours of the oligopolistic corporate structure. Government, in the hands of individuals whose backgrounds and organizational interests not infrequently were at variance with the captains of industry, was better organized to deal with the heads of corporations than were the neighborhood-level politicians and interest groups. Power in the church was increasingly centralized, with the parish priest becoming less a neighborhood entrepreneur and more a small part of a religious bureaucracy that was organized on a metropolitan scale.

Increasingly, the important political agreements are being forged among leaders who represent a very limited number of economic and political sectors, each of which has different interests and constituencies. Business, labor, government, and, to a far lesser extent, the church: these are the participants in politics. It is a politics of large scale; it works (to the extent that it can be said to work) because leaders in each sector can impose settlements on other actors within his sector with minimal need to engage in internal bargaining. The touted "coalition building" that has occurred in Detroit is possible because only the leaders need to agree; the hierarchical arrangements within sectors negates the need for expanding the bargaining beyond the sector's leaders.

In the automotive industry, market pressures and the enormous problems of meeting federal regulatory standards have increased the tendency toward centralized decision making and policy control. Chrysler has traditionally been led by "strong-willed, authoritarian individuals, and decisions have been made by one person alone."[26] Since its founding, Ford had, until the retirement of Henry Ford II, always been headed by a member of the Ford family. As a consequence of his equity position in the company, Henry Ford II continues to wield a critical influence in corporate decisions.

At General Motors, all major policy decisions are made at central headquarters. Over the years, headquarters has assumed more of the decision-making functions in the corporation; for example, all personnel and labor-relations matters were centralized in 1937. In the past, however, the company's belief in internal competition to promote productivity allowed a considerable amount of discretion for division management. This discretion has been severely circumscribed in recent years, because of corporate standardization programs and the demands of federal regulatory standards.[27]

Similarly, union power has become increasingly centralized, with local automobile-union workers generally following policies that emanate from the United Automobile Workers' Solidarity House in Detroit. Only a national union could deal effectively with corporations as large as the automobile companies. As importantly, the modern pattern of collective bargaining became firmly established in the GM/UAW agreement of 1948. After a lengthy strike in 1945/46, both the company and the union wished to avoid another round of bitter labor strife. The agreement provided for the industry's first multiyear contract, a cost-of-living formula, agreement in principle that pay raises had to be tied to increases in productivity, and an understanding of the "private" nature of the bargaining process.[28] This contract established the unwritten norms for collective bargaining that prevail in the automobile industry, and it contributed substantially to the national, centralized power that is enjoyed by Solidarity House.

GOVERNMENTAL FRAGMENTATION

Coalition building among sector elites fails most often because government is the most fragmented sector. In 1918 there were no suburbs to speak of in Detroit. Today Detroit is home to only about 27 percent of the area's residents. The modern tendency to reimpose special agencies and districts has also affected metropolitan government (or the lack of it) in Detroit. Hence city/suburban divisions have appeared on issues of transportation, water and sewerage, taxation, and economic development.

In their study of ten cases of public decision making in the Detroit metropolis during the 1950s, Robert Mowitz and Deil Wright were most struck with the pluralistic governmental system in operation. The dispersion of governmental power into a multiplicity of general-purpose and special governmental units made the accomplishment of metropolitan goals difficult but not impossible. Indeed, when the differences of interest are negotiated to produce solutions, the resulting changes "strengthen rather than weaken the pluralistic governmental structure of the metropolis."[29] To these authors, the resulting system of fragmented public power, with negotiation and adjustment on important civic projects, implies a pluralistic power structure. "The success with which the various competing organizations and groups have prevented power from becoming concentrated in the hands of a ruling elite makes it unlikely that the pluralistic power balance will be significantly tipped in the future."[30]

While the Detroit metropolis today remains as governmentally fragmented as ever, certain changes over the last twenty-five years now operate to make metropolitan cooperation more difficult. Detroit is both poorer and blacker in relation to its suburbs than it was in 1960. Indeed, in that year, a number of Detroit neighborhoods were in the highest income quartile for the metropolis. The aggressive style of Mayor Young and the racial consciousness of suburban whites have contributed to problems in interjurisdictional cooperation. Today, the mayor of Detroit represents an entirely different constituency from the majority of his suburban counterparts, not just a different governmental jurisdiction.

The resulting governmental power configuration is both fragmented and dispersed. Local governments in the Detroit metropolis increasingly represent not just geographically distinct jurisdictional interests but critical social groupings as well. Jurisdictional boundaries today reinforce basic social divisions more than they did a quarter of a century ago, when the city itself was more diverse. This fragmentation weakens the ability of governments to negotiate among themselves and with the representatives of the giant manufacturing corporations that dominate Detroit's economy.

SECTARCHY

This characterization of power in Detroit is admittedly based on a limited number of studies and our own nonsystematic observations. Nevertheless, none of the terms that are currently being used to describe the configurations of community power quite fit the description of sectorally organized power that we presented above. Pluralism connotes a dispersion of power and an openness to groups that fits only part of Detroit's power configuration, the governmental sector. Even this characterization may better fit relations among governments than within them. On a number of civic projects, both Mayor Young and his predecessors have been able to forge a community consensus—the Renaissance Center is the premier example.

The logic of pluralism implies that power relations are shifting and unstable, and resulting public policies follow the contours of changing political coalitions. In Detroit, power is far more structured than this. Elitism stresses stability and concentration of power, as do we, but it relegates the power that is rooted in elections as secondary and posits a unity of purpose among members of the elite that does not seem to be warranted in the modern industrial city.[31]

We suggest the term *sectarchy* (from the Latin *sectare*, "to cut") to describe this system of sectoral power.[32] We hesitate to propose this new term, less out of deference to current terminology than to the use of the related term *polyarchy* by such scholars as Robert Dahl and Charles Lindblom. Lindblom, for example, has defined polyarchy as a set of decision rules for choosing political leaders through an electoral system. He then goes on to examine the close connection between government and business in polyarchies.[33] We have substantial sympathy for this approach, but we feel that it fails to capture the notion that political power is based in the sectoral organization of the political economy. Government as well as private organizations in a polyarchy bring resources to bear in politics; elections ensure that at least part of the time, elected leaders will have interests different from those of the leaders of business and labor organizations. The size and scope of modern government ensures that political leaders will have resources to pursue these interests. In Detroit, peak bargaining among sectors is quite common, and it is in this format that major decisions are made—not within the councils of government alone. The difference between this structure and elitism, pluralism, or a polyarchy that is heavily dependent on market forces (as in Lindblom's model) is striking enough that a separate term is warranted. The likelihood that it exists elsewhere strengthens the case for the proliferation of terms.

THE ORGANIZATIONAL BASES OF URBAN POWER

The nature of Detroit's sectarchy is probably best appreciated by Mayor Young among all the major actors. In an interview in early 1984 he responded to a question concerning his apparent recent failure to "build coalitions." Young responded:

> The coalition I was successful in establishing when I first became mayor pre-dated the severe economic conditions that laid siege to this city and to the auto industry. And those members of the auto industry were so damn busy fighting to keep their companies' heads above water that they didn't have time for much else. In the meantime, there was almost a complete change in leadership.
>
> I was looking at a picture in my office just the other day. It was 1976, the third year I was in office, when Jimmy Carter came through here, running for president. And there was Pete Estes from General Motors, Riccardo from Chrysler, Ford from Ford, Leonard Woodcock from the auto workers' union, Jimmy Carter, and me. I'm the only one that's left.[34]

Young equated leadership with organizational position, and indeed, the bases for power in the industrial city are organizational. When one leaves his position in the organizational structure, he leaves most of his political power behind. It is indeed these "command posts," in the words of C. Wright Mills, that confer power.[35] As Andrew Hacker has noted, "Members of [the] elite are easily replaceable; in many cases it is impossible to distinguish an officeholder from his predecessor or successor."[36] Thomas Dye has also focused on the key role of institutional position in power configurations.[37]

These key command posts, which are so important in theories about institutional elites, are in the hands of people who, because of their positions in the political and economic systems, have very different interests to pursue. Politicians hail from very different backgrounds than do businessmen, and they clash with businessmen on a number of important issues. Union leaders, who are representative of a distinct economic interest that is often different from either business or government, are nevertheless frequently consulted formally on major policy initiatives and are able to contribute to civic projects by depicting them to their members in a favorable light. Not infrequently, members of the business community themselves hold differing opinions on civic projects, with local commercial interests seeing the situation differently from the way in which multinational automobile companies and their suppliers see it. (A special case of this was Henry Ford's advocacy of the Renaissance project, with Ford, the local advocate, lobbying the other automotive companies and Ford's own suppliers directly and strongly for investment funds.) Nevertheless, on at least major issues that involve all sectors, representatives of each sector negotiate with leaders from other sectors, secure in the knowledge that they will not be undercut by intrasectorial divisiveness.

The result is either a very structured form of pluralism or a fairly open system of elite rule, depending on one's perspective. Major decisions that affect urban policy are often made in forums in which representatives of the major sectors are in direct contact with one another. Usually these forums, always bringing together representatives of government, labor, and business, are established in order to "solve problems." Examples include Detroit Renaissance, which is a group of business and government leaders that convenes to promote downtown revitalization; the Economic Alliance of Michigan, an association of business and labor that works on economic policy concerns; and New Detroit, the nation's first "urban coalition" of blacks, business, labor, and government, which was established after the 1967 civil disorders to promote black economic progress.

This pattern of sectarchy does not imply that other traditional forces in urban politics are impotent; far from it. *Within* the governmental sector, on issues of concern only to governmental officials, such groups as public-employee unions, bureaucrats, and neighborhood groups do influence city policies, and these policies are important for the development of the region. But where the sectors meet, a pattern of bargaining at the peaks emerges.

Peak bargaining does not include all urban issues; rather, it incorporates the current concerns of participants. (As one former radical organizer commented to us, "I finally see that Henry Ford doesn't care how Detroit distributes its community development block grant funds.") It is not even clear that, in the aggregate, issues that are "peak bargained" are more important than those that are handled through more traditional channels. Peak bargaining does seem to encompass expensive capital projects and issues of current high salience, however.

A major issue is whether this system of peak bargaining is biased toward the economic elite. It is possible that the sectarchy of the industrial city yields results that generally favor the upper economic strata. Clarence Stone has identified the differing bases of power of public officials and private elites and has concluded that the economic elites are disproportionately powerful because the politicians rely on them for support for public projects.[38] And Charles Lindblom points to the "privileged position" of businessmen because they provide the economic livelihood of the community.[39] Paul Peterson argues that a special relationship emerges between public and private officials when the community's export industries are involved.[40] It is exactly this issue—the relative influence of public officials and corporate leaders in real decision-making situations involving the manufacture of automobiles in Michigan—that we examine in the rest of this book.

4

The American Automobile Industry
under Pressure

On 4 January 1980 an era ended when Chrysler Corporation finally closed the doors on its assembly plant in Hamtramck, Michigan, throwing three thousand Detroiters out of work and costing the city of Hamtramck some $2.6 million in property taxes.[1] The place that Hamtramck Assembly, once known as Dodge Main, holds in the history of industrial democracy is matched by few other factories. In 1914, Dodge Main produced its first automobile, a Dodge touring car, which sold for $785.[2] By the 1920s, Dodge Main was a fully integrated automotive-production complex; component parts were built and assembled on the site. The massive reinforced-concrete structure, over eight stories tall in places, contained more than five million square feet of floor space and covered more than 120 acres.[3]

By modern standards, Hamtramck Assembly was terribly inefficient. It was one of several "first generation" multistory assembly plants that characterized automobile manufacture until the mid 1920s, when it became clear "that horizontal movement of materials was more efficient than vertical movement."[4] The assembly line snaked over several floors, a far cry from today's one-story linear assembly plants. Its utility bills ran almost three times those of comparable linear plants. Such a plant was not long destined for the modern world, a premier example of the inefficiencies of the industrial "built environment" in America's northern center cities. Indeed, it remained in use as long as it did only because Chrysler, the poorest of the "big three" automobile manufacturers, lacked both the capital to replace it and the intense competitive pressure to force such replacement.

Yet Dodge Main represented both the great promise and the cruel realities of industrial America. Its work force was, by the early 1960s, thoroughly integrated. Older Polish-Americans worked side-by-side with younger blacks, Appalachian whites, and Arabs, sharing together the rigors of that creature of time-and-motion engineers, the assembly line.

The site of major labor unrest throughout its history, Dodge Main had been the main target of revolutionary organizing among Detroit's active radical community during the late 1960s and early 1970s.[5] Just across Joseph Campau Boulevard clustered the bars and restaurants that served kielbasa and *boombas* of beer to hungry workers as they left the plant in the middle of the afternoon. To the north of the plant lay the little suburb of Hamtramck, entirely surrounded by Detroit, an area of tight-knit Polish families and small bakeries, butcher shops, and restaurants where Polish is heard almost as much as English. To the south, east, and west of Dodge Main stretched the solid wooden two-flats of working-class Detroit. Once populated heavily by Polish families, these neighborhoods had become by 1980 American hybrids. Older Polish families coexisted with blacks, Appalachians, Albanians, and Arabs, mirroring the composition of Dodge Main's work force. While these neighborhoods had become substantially more black over the years, the main wave of black migration had by-passed them, allowing some relief from the pattern of "invasion and succession" that has characterized racial change in most Detroit neighborhoods. Life centered on the factory, as it had for almost seventy years.

During a recession, companies close their least-productive facilities first. This has the effect of raising productivity overall, thus putting the company in a better position to withstand the increased competitive pressures associated with slack demand. As demand for automobiles decreased during the spring and summer of 1979 from the peak year of 1978, Chrysler announced that it planned to close Dodge Main in July of 1980. The announcement was greeted with great bitterness by the workers, many of whom had spent their working lives in the plant. Between July and December 1979, as automobile sales declined, Chrysler reduced Dodge Main's work force from 5,200 hourly workers to 2,475 by eliminating one of the two assembly lines and by eliminating a shift and slowing the remaining line.[6] This action failed to adjust production to the rapidly falling demand for automobiles, and Chrylser closed Dodge Main for good six months earlier than planned.

The fates of Dodge Main, Poletown, and GM's new Detroit assembly plant were inextricably intertwined; the former two had to be demolished to make way for the third. But the fate of the three was more fundamentally linked. Ironically, the same economic forces that stimulated General Motors to announce its decisions to build new assembly plants in Detroit and Orion Township forced Chrysler to close its obsolete facility in Hamtramck.

THE AUTOMOBILE INDUSTRY UNDER PRESSURE

The 1970s had been both the best and the worst for America's domestic automobile producers. The decade had included the best year ever for sales; in 1978, domestic producers sold over 13 million passenger cars, busses, and trucks in the United States. Moreover, the total market that year for motor vehicles was the largest in history, with 15.4 million vehicles sold in the United States. That year capped three years of unprecedented growth in the industry.

Yet the decade of the 1970s had certainly not brought entirely good news to Detroit. The OPEC oil embargo in 1973, after the United States had supported Israel in the 1973 Yom Kippur War, had thrown the economy into a steep recession, and the automobile industry suffered greatly. Domestic car and truck sales fell from 12.6 million units in 1973 to 9.6 million in 1974, a 24 percent decline. Sales continued to fall to 9.3 million units in 1975.

The oil embargo brought home to Americans the realization of just how fragile the American high-energy life style was; it also brought higher gasoline prices and queuing at filling stations, both of which were consequences of short supply. Events in the faraway Middle East had doomed the all-purpose American road cruiser, which had dominated the domestic market since the early 1950s.

THE CHALLENGE OF THE IMPORTS

The oil crisis also permitted the smaller imported automobile to achieve a permanent niche in the giant American transportation market. The inability of domestic manufacturers to build a competitively priced small car has been the Achilles heel of American automotive manufacture since the late 1930s, yet there has always been substantial consumer demand for such a vehicle. The major reason for this inability is that dominant consumer demand had supported the production of the all-purpose road cruiser, and any attempt to produce a smaller automobile had run headlong into a basic fact of the automobile market: "Within reasonable size ranges, production costs did not decline as rapidly as price with declining car size."[7] By 1936, no major producer had a product aimed at the lower-price market. That year, Ford Motor Company built a smaller-sized prototype which was intended to capture that market segment. Its cost advantage was calculated at only $36 less than the full-sized models; therefore it was scrapped.[8]

The whole idea of a cheaper, smaller automobile was not resurrected until the late 1950s, when European, particularly West German, manufacturers began to exploit their labor-costs advantages and their careful attention to quality in the American market. The import share of the market reached 10 percent in 1959, and each of the "big three" domestic producers introduced a smaller model (Corvair, Falcon, Valiant) to compete with the imports. By 1962 the import share had dropped to 5 percent of the market, prompting Ford Motor Company to shelve its Cardinal, the small front-wheel-drive model that it had developed for the American market.[9]

A second wave of imports, which began in the mid 1960s, was much more firmly founded than was the earlier intrusion. American life styles had changed substantially over the decade; suburban living, working wives, and the continued deterioration of urban mass transportation made it desirable to have a second automobile. While the all-purpose road cruiser could serve well as a first car in an era of low energy costs, it was inappropriate as a second vehicle. Imports took 15 percent of the market until the Vega, the Pinto, and the Gremlin were introduced in the early 1970s.[10]

This time, the domestic producers were unable to beat back the challenge mounted by foreign competitors. Japanese manufacturers had aimed their products directly at the American subcompact market; indeed, the growth of the Japanese automobile industry is due almost solely to its ability to capture this segment of the American market with inexpensive, high-quality automobiles. By 1975, imports were capturing more than 16 percent of the market.

At this point, American manufacturers made a decision not to compete seriously in the subcompact market. American subcompacts were selling so poorly in 1976 that auto makers offered rebates for only one month into the new-model year. Oil prices had begun to decline, and the economy was picking up; in a growing market there seemed to be plenty of room for all. Imports were expected to capture around 15 percent of the domestic market permanently, but they did not seem to pose a threat in the down-sized V-8 sedan and the intermediate 6-cylinder market that had always generated the most profits for domestic manufacturers. Chevrolet's subcompact, the Chevette, had not been significantly improved since its introduction, but it continued to sell well over 400,000 in 1979 and again in 1980. Ford remained in the subcompact market with its Pinto, which was introduced in the early 1970s but was phased out early in 1980. Chrysler refused to enter the subcompact market of the 1970s, a decision that was to bring that company to the brink of financial collapse. With stable and declining gas prices, Americans seemed to be returning to their traditional preference for larger automobiles; in 1976 the standard and intermediate share of the market grew by more than 6 percent and remained constant throughout 1978. Stability, it seemed, had returned to the automotive industry.

DISASTER IN 1979; COLLAPSE IN 1980

Stability, however, was short-lived. In February of 1979, political unrest in Iran stopped the flow of oil from that nation. Although this affected only about 10 percent of the world supply, "this shortfall precipitated a scramble that drove spot market prices to $40 per barrel."[11] Americans were once again treated to lines at the gasoline pumps and steep rises in the price of fuel. As in 1973, the oil shortage plunged the American economy into a recession; this time, however, there was no quick rebound. The tight money policies of the Federal Reserve Board, beginning in the fall of 1979, ratcheted interest rates higher and higher, until the nation finally experienced a prime rate of over 20 percent late in 1981. Unemployment rose, with the manufacturing sector being hit especially hard.

The automobile industry was devastated. Each month, sales declined in comparison to the previous month's sales and to the identical period the year before. The brief economic upturn in 1980 left the automobile industry virtually untouched; sales declined steadily until an upturn established itself in the spring of 1983. At the end of 1981, in the middle of the recession and the worst year for the automobile companies ever, *Ward's Automotive Yearbook,* the industry's authoritative annual compendium, said: "The U.S. and Canadian car and truck industry stumbled, battered and bleeding into 1982 from the pummelling it absorbed in 1981 as production declined 1.7% to an 18-year low of 9.2 million from 9.3 million in 1980" (see figure 4.1).[12]

Some idea of the magnitude of the devastation in the automobile industry, as well as the rapidity of the fall, can be gleaned from the figures, which not only document the decline of the automobile industry but also reflect changes in consumer preferences from the larger models to the subcompacts. Domestic new-car sales for April 1979 were 11 percent below those for the preceding year, while imports had increased by 24.2 percent. Dealers' inventory figures documented changing consumer preferences: inventories of imports dropped from a 122-day supply on January 31 to a 58-day supply on April 30. Small domestic cars, such as Ford's Pinto, also experienced inventory reductions during this period, but inventories of full-sized models climbed steadily. Inventories of full-sized Pontiacs, for example, increased from a 44-day supply on 31 December 1978 to a 106-day supply on 30 April 1979.[13] Imports captured 20 percent of the market in 1979, up from 15 percent in 1978, and more than 25 percent in 1980 (see figure 4.2). As inventories reached record levels in May 1979, General Motors announced reductions of 20,000 cars and 10,000 trucks in its June production plans, and Ford reported reductions of 23,000 cars and 12,000 trucks in its July–September output plans.[14] In August, General Motors announced reductions in assembly-line rates at plants in Flint and Pontiac,

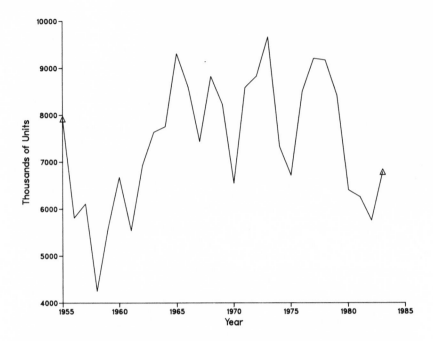

Figure 4.1. Sales of passenger cars by domestic manufacturers. Automotive sales
are very sensitive to changes in economic climate. Source: *MVMA Motor Vehicle
Facts and Figures '84* (Detroit: Motor Vehicle Manufacturers Association, 1984), p.
6.

which produced large cars, increases in small-car production at its Lords-
town plant, and the addition of a second shift at its Oklahoma City assembly
plant, which built the popular front-wheel-drive X cars.[15] Production
cutbacks continued throughout 1980, by the elimination of second shifts and
the reduction of assembly-line speeds. In an effort to stem the flow of red
ink, General Motors initiated dramatic cutbacks in April 1980, to a level 30
percent below that of the preceding year.[16] Sales of domestic cars in May
1980 reached their lowest level in twenty-two years.[17] Production of cars
and trucks in the Detroit area for the first four months of 1980 was 44
percent below that for the same period in 1979; Chrysler experienced the
largest decrease, 73.3 percent, while production dropped 54.7 percent in
the four General Motors plants assembling full-sized or luxury models.[18] By
November 1980, car output in Michigan had sunk to a record low of 26.2
percent of United States auto production.[19]

Late 1979 and early 1980 were also marked by the announcement of
plant closings, as automobile manufacturers coped with the deepening

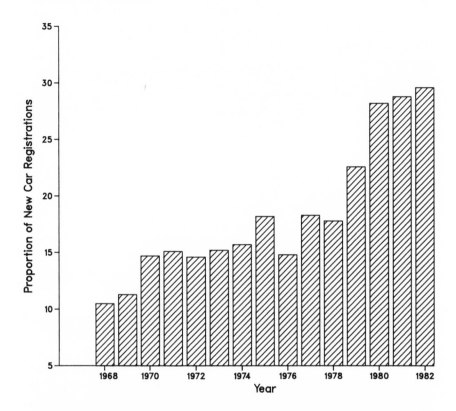

Figure 4.2. Penetration of the American automotive market by imports: foreign car registration as a percentage of new car registrations. Source: *MVMA Motor Vehicle Facts and Figures '84* (Detroit: Motor Vehicle Manufacturers Association, 1984), p. 6.

recession. Chrysler, the weakest of the "Big 3," reported in June 1979 that its massive Dodge Main assembly plant in Hamtramck would close at the end of 1980 production, eliminating an estimated 2,200 to 4,000 jobs.[20] April 1980 brought the announcement that a Chrysler stamping plant in Detroit, which employed 1,270 workers, would be closed by the end of the year.[21] A month later, Chrysler reported plans to close its Lynch Road plant in Detroit and its V-8 engine plant in nearby Windsor, Ontario, by the end of June.[22] In July, *Ward's* reported that Chrysler's Huber Avenue foundry in Detroit would close by January 1981 and noted that seven Chrysler plants, five in the Detroit area, had closed since July 1979.[23]

Production cuts and plant closings were accompanied by steadily increasing levels of unemployment and financial losses by auto manufacturers. In January 1980, 144,600 auto workers were on indefinite layoffs. By

February, the figure had jumped to 173,996, and 25 percent of the industry's blue-collar work force was on indefinite layoff. By May, indefinite layoffs totaled 211,350, surpassing record levels set during the 1975 recession. Layoffs continued to climb in June, to 237,850, representing 30.5 percent of the industry's hourly workers, and reached 250,050 in July. Not until October did indefinite layoffs fall below 200,000. The layoffs extended into the network of suppliers who are dependent on the automobile industry; fully one-third of the work force in auto-related supplier industries was on indefinite layoff in May of 1980.[24]

Management and stockholders were also feeling the effects of declines in production. All domestic automobile manufacturers were awash in red ink in 1980, with a combined loss of almost $4 billion. In 1979, General Motors' stockholders had watched their company's profits drop to their lowest level since the 1975 recession; the next year the corporate giant lost three-quarters of a billion dollars. Severe cutbacks and aggressive capital spending to improve its product line allowed GM to post a modest profit in 1981.

If things were rough at General Motors, they were approaching disaster at Ford and Chrysler. Ford managed to accrue a loss of over $1.5 billion in 1980. Only the solid performance of the firm's overseas operations prevented the loss from being twice as large. Ford posted another record loss of over $1 billion in 1981. Chrysler was faring even worse. The company, which had been unable to make money in the boom years of the late 1970s, was rapidly acquiring a reputation for shoddy workmanship. Between 1974 and 1981, Chrysler had made a profit in only two years, 1976 and 1977, and the 1977 profit was but $163 million. In 1979 the company lost over $1 billion; in 1980 it set the all-time record for losses among American corporations: $1,709,700,000.[25] Only a federal-government loan guarantee and the aggressive entrepreneurship of Chrysler's Chairman Lee Iacocca saved the company from bankrupcy.

THE INDUSTRY'S STRUCTURE

The American automobile industry in the 1970s was not organized to adapt to the new pressures that it faced. The industry is highly concentrated, both in the United States and world-wide. Moreover, the industry had developed a concentrated structure early in its evolution. By 1923, Ford had cornered 50.3 percent of the market, and Ford and General Motors were manufacturing 71 percent of the cars sold in America. In the late 1920s General Motors overtook Ford as the industry's leader. For the next fifty years the market structure remained virtually unchanged: three major automobile manufacturers, virtually unchallenged by foreign manufacturers, were focusing on the dominant American consumer demand for comfort and convenience rather than on economy and quality in the product.[26]

Henry Ford had cornered the automobile market with his philosophy of standardization, quality, and low prices. The earlier technological ferment in Detroit was replaced by the cautious policies of large-scale corporations. Yet the decade of the 1920s was critical in the development of the modern industry structure.

In 1919, just over 1.6 million automobiles were sold in America. In 1929, almost 4.5 million were sold. The auto makers would have to wait until 1949 to exceed that total. Yet hidden below these totals were profound changes in the nature of the market that the manufacturers faced. First, the market in which Henry Ford's manufacturing philosophy was so successful no longer comprised primarily first-time buyers; it consisted mostly of replacement buyers. Second, the closed-body car added significant costs to the manufacturing process and made it possible to build automobiles that were far more comfortable. This technological innovation made possible the "full line" of automobiles, from the cheapest necessity to the luxury sedan, an idea pioneered by General Motors.

General Motors not only pioneered the "full line" of automobiles and selling to a differentiated market; corporate leadership there also first grasped the importance of the model changeover in combating the growth of the replacement market. One student of the development of automotive-industry structure has commented:

> The rise of the annual model change to combat the replacement market ultimately resulted in a significant change in the structure of the industry. . . . The fixed investment in the production of a specific model now had to be depreciated completely in one or at best two seasons, where previously the cost of the design, tool, and dies would be spread over a period of several years. Firms with large annual sales thus had a significant cost advantage over their smaller rivals.[27]

The increased costs associated with model changeover and the closed-body car did not result in increased concentration in the industry. It was already highly concentrated. But these events foreclosed the possibility of the entry of independents and the capture of a large market segment by them; henceforth they were limited to speciality markets.

Perhaps more importantly, the "full line" and the model changeover established General Motors as the market-share leader in the industry. Ford continued to hold to his strategy of standardization, quality, and low price, a philosophy that was not well suited to the replacement market. His response to the General Motors challenge was to lower the price of his automobiles, down to $290. In 1926, nevertheless, Ford's share of the automotive market had dropped to 25 percent.

Throughout the reduced sales of the 1930s and the boom of the postwar era, the industry's structure remained stable. The "big three"—GM, Ford, and Chrysler—together divided about 80 percent of the market. Several independents held on until the 1950s; after that, only American Motors was able to compete as a minor automobile producer. There was virtually no import penetration of the market until, as we noted above, the "first wave" of imports during the late 1950s.

Because automobiles are expensive and postponable purchases, traditionally the industry has been highly cyclical. It falls first, and further, in a recession than do other durable goods; it rises first, and sails higher, than do other products in a recovery (see figure 4.3.). This makes it very difficult for independent producers to survive recessions; it also means that a great deal of money is to be made in boom times. This cyclical nature has also produced grave problems for governments that rely on the automobile

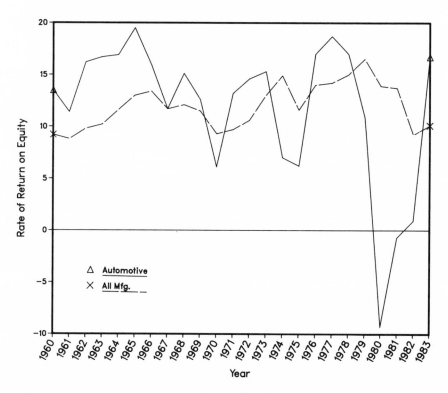

Figure 4.3. Profits of the automotive manufacturing industry after taxes (in percentages). Profits in the automotive industry are considerably more volatile than profits in manufacturing generally. Source: Robert Crandall, "Import Quotas and the Automobile Industry," *The Brookings Review* 2 (Summer 1984).

industry for revenues; as we shall see, they have a tendency to overexpand in good times and to be forced into extremely painful reductions during recessions.

Between 1959 and 1969, profits in the automotive industry exceeded those of manufacturing in general; thus the traditional instability had less of an effect during these years. After 1969, however, automotive profits, and the industry generally, became highly unstable relative to manufacturing in general. As figure 4.3 shows, six times in fourteen years the profits in the motor-vehicle industry shot higher or dropped lower than profits in manufacturing in general.

MATURE MARKETS

The automobile market is what economists term "mature." This means that technological innovation plays a relatively limited role in the struggle for competitive advantage and that cost considerations play a very large role in the struggle.[28] Because technologies are settled and well understood, they may be easily copied. Hence, in a mature market, firms are continually vulnerable to competition from manufacturers, especially foreign manufacturers, who can exploit a cost advantage, and, in particular, a labor-cost advantage.

In the mature, oligopolistic market of automobile manufacture, "technological diversity gives way to standardization. Innovation, even if significant, alters only a small aspect of the basic product. . . . Economies of scale guarantee a product unlike the fluid 'job shop' of the early years. Work-flow is now rationalized, integrated, and linear; skilled labor is now replaced by highly specific 'dedicated' equipment."[29]

It is unclear, however, whether maturity is a consequence of the limited potential for technological innovation or whether it is a consequence of the organizational structure of the market. Oligopolies breed caution, not innovation. As GM's President Alfred Sloan said, it was "not necessary to lead in design or run the risk of untried experiment."[30]

What large firms in mature markets are good at is coordination. The typical automobile is an assembly of more than ten thousand basic parts; the modern internal-combustion engine plant houses the most complex manufacturing process devised since the dawn of the Industrial Revolution. Like all plants involved in automobile production, it is highly specialized and capital intensive, and it is oriented toward rapid production of a standardized product. Coordination of this inherently complex process, in conjunction with the production of the "full line" of automobiles, occupied most of management's attention in the mature automobile market for the thirty-five years after World War II.

THE PUBLIC CORPORATION

In 1965, consumer advocate Ralph Nader, a David in the world of Goliaths, challenged the cozy corporate world of automobile manufacture with his attack on Chevrolet's Corvair in his book *Unsafe at Any Speed*. When Congress accepted the idea that consumers and citizens at large ought to be protected from the decisions made in the corporate board rooms of private concerns, a new set of demands was placed on the automotive industry. Henceforth, public demands from governmental agencies would supplement, and not infrequently contradict, the demands of consumers in the marketplace. By the late 1970s, two professors of business at Harvard University could write that "traditional market forces are now supplemented by strong external pressures for technological innovation to meet national policies and plans for energy conservation, environmental protection, and improved product safety."[31] Safety regulation began in 1966; standards for exhaust emissions, in 1968; and fuel economy regulations, a decade later. Robert Crandall rates these regulations as successful, but not without costs: he estimates them to have added almost $2,000 to the price of an automobile in 1981. Moreover, the safety and emission regulations caused declines in quality and fuel efficiency just as a wave of Japanese imports was reaching the country.[32]

The rapidity with which Congress passed the initial safety regulations, after the revelation that General Motors had authorized an investigation of Nader following the publication of his book, taught the industry the importance of politics and public image. Not only did the new regulatory environment channel a great deal of capital into product development in the public interest; it also infused a large dose of caution into an already cautious industry. According to an analysis of corporate decision making, federal regulation was one of two major external influences on the decision-making process in the 1970s (the other was loss of share of the market).[33] Regulation had made automotive manufacture vastly more complicated, and the companies themselves had helped to create the political environment that made this possible.

A REVOLUTION ON FOUR CYCLINDERS

The halcyon days of 1976–78 provided a period of record sales, record profits, and a decline in the challenge from the imports. Yet in hindsight, the industry's basic structure had been radically altered by the 1973 oil embargo and the tightening net of federal regulations. In the days ahead, the industry would face rapidly declining total sales and dramatically increasing import penetration of the smaller-car market. Only an aggressive, innovative strategy would meet the challenge, and only the executives of General Motors perceived, albeit dimly, the extent of the necessary changes. The anemic sales of subcompacts and the boom in sales for full-sized and intermediate cars during these years lulled manufacturers into lethargy; Chrysler boasted of being the home of the gas guzzler, while Ford's front-wheel-drive vehicles were years from production. General Motors, however, propitiously introduced its X-body front-wheel-drive cars in the spring of 1979, on the heels of the Iranian unrest. Ford's and Chrysler's "world car" entries into the market came a year and a half later, in the 1981 model year.

Some idea of just how propitious GM's X bodies were can be gleaned from their sales figures. In 1978 Chevrolet Division sold over 600,000 full-sized Chevrolets; in 1979, 450,000; and in 1980, only 250,000. By 1980 the subcompact Chevette and the Citation (Chevy's X body) each sold more than the full-sized Impala; Citation was the most popular car in America in 1980. The introduction of the X bodies allowed General Motors to survive the coming recession with only one year of losses; the other manufacturers suffered massive losses for years.

A CAPITAL RESPONSE

Down-sizing and conversion to front-wheel-drive vehicles are expensive—far more expensive than the traditional process of model changeover. In response to the challenges of the new marketplace, the domestic automobile manufacturers made massive commitments in capital spending to effect the change. Capital spending, in constant dollars, climbed to record highs during the late 1970s (see figure 4.4). Given the profit margins during these years, this is probably not surprising; patterns of capital expenditure tend to follow economic cycles. When large profits are available, at least some of them get plowed back into enterprise as capital improvements. What is surprising is the continuing commitment of the domestic manufacturers to their capital-spending programs during the severe recession of the early 1980s. In the recessions of 1970/71 and 1975/76, capital spending in constant dollars fell substantially. In 1980 and 1981, it continued to rise, although all auto makers were forced to cut back sharply on their original planned expenditures as the recession deepened.

General Motors responded to the 1979 crisis aggressively. The company announced a $40-billion five-year plan of capital spending through 1984, which would enable the company to produce more than six million front-wheel-drive cars world-wide by 1983.[34] The capital-spending program implemented an even-more-dramatic corporate commitment: *all* models in *all* General Motors divisions were to be changed over to the smaller, lighter

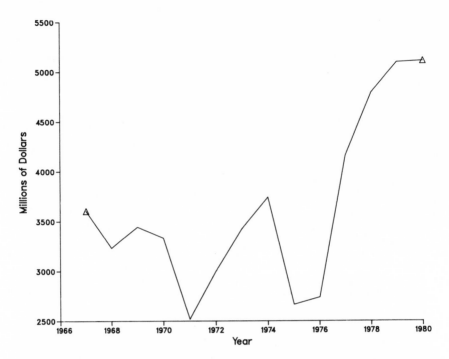

Figure 4.4. Capital expenditures by American automotive manufacturers, in constant dollars. Record capital spending continued well into the recession. Source: *MVMA Facts and Figures '82* (Detroit: Motor Vehicle Manufacturers' Association, 1982), p. 65.

front-wheel-drive vehicles. In the minds of GM's corporate planners, the day of the "full line" of automobiles was almost over; the new day of the "world car" was dawning. As the recession deepened, only General Motors continued its capital spending at record rates, and its percentage of total capital spending soared from less then 65 percent to more than 95 percent. The corporate decision was being cast in concrete.

INVESTMENT AND THE "BUILT ENVIRONMENT"

About two-thirds of the capital-spending program was targeted for real-estate acquisition, plant construction and modernization, and new equipment; the rest was earmarked for the special tools necessary for constructing the new models. Of the $40 billion, $32 billion was earmarked for the United States; in 1979 the corporation was on the verge of effecting a major change in the "built environment" of industrial America.

As early as January 1980, reports were circulating that General Motors planned to build or renovate as many as five car-assembly plants for production of front-wheel-drive vehicles; the Chevrolet assembly plant in St. Louis and the Pontiac assembly plant in Pontiac, Michigan, were mentioned as "prime candidates" for replacement. These plans were confirmed two weeks later with announcements that new three-million-square-foot assembly plants would be built near St. Louis and Pontiac. Simultaneously, Ford announced plans to spend $3.5 billion in 1980 on capital facilities, of which $2 billion would be spent in the United States. Details of GM's overseas expansion plans were released in late February 1980: the construction of five new plants (three in Spain, one in Austria, one in Northern Ireland) and the expansion of one existing facility (near Belfast, Northern Ireland).[35]

GM's massive program of plant construction was the result of a corporate decision in the late spring 1979 to replace the company's oldest, least-efficient assembly plants. In addition to the plants in St. Louis and Pontiac, those in Fairfax, Kansas, and in Baltimore, and the Detroit Cadillac Assembly and Fisher Body Fleetwood plants were targeted for replacement; Flint Buick was also seriously considered for retirement. All of these plants were multistory "first generation" plants; two were converted World War II bomber plants. Production of front-wheel-drive vehicles required changes in plant design which were difficult to accomplish in the older multistory plants; moreover, such plants contained longer assembly lines, and therefore more time was required for a vehicle to pass through a line. General Motors was also concerned about the cost of bringing the old plant into compliance with new levels of stationary-source pollution which would be required by clean-air regulations scheduled to go into effect by 1983. This deadline, as well as slumping big-car sales and increased demand for more fuel-efficient models, resulted in an initial scheduled completion date for the new plants of mid 1982 (for production of 1983 models), slightly more than two years after the corporation's announcement of its plans.[36]

CONCLUSIONS

Several analysts have argued that the decline in the American automobile industry reflected international economic trends and the changing role of the United States in the world economy. More than one analysis at the time questioned the need for major automotive capital investment, given the declining demand for American automobiles and the loss of competitive advantage to foreign manufacturers.

Nevertheless, in 1979 the domestic automobile industry committed itself to a massive capital-spending program that, if totally implemented, would change both the capacity of the automotive industry and the built environment of industrial America. General Motors alone was embarking on a $40-billion investment program designed to counter the inroads of the imports. In doing so, the corporation explicitly ended its "full line" strategy and concentrated on the "world car." All models would be down-sized and changed to front-wheel drive. Nevertheless, the import percentage of the American market climbed steadily until the imposition of "voluntary" import quotas on Japanese automobile manufacturers by the Reagan administration in 1981. Then, as gasoline prices stabilized, the industry faced increasing demand for its large, rear-wheel-drive models once again. General Motors put its "world car" plans on hold and continued to manufacture its popular large models. Whatever the final result, the late 1970s and early 1980s have proved to be an era of change in the American automobile industry unlike any period since the 1920s.

The plant-replacement strategy of the automobile manufacturers struck hard at American's center cities. Almost invariably a plant targeted for closure was located in a center city: Detroit, St. Louis, Flint, and Baltimore. Almost as invariably, replacement plants were to be located in exurban "greenfields." Such was the economics of the situation. The older multistory plants were located in cities out of necessity: access to transportation networks and labor markets was essential. Now center cities were filled up; little available land remained for building the linear one-story plants that were most efficient for the modern production process. Moreover, now labor was mobile: workers could come to the plant, so that plants did not have to go to the workers. And both land and taxes were cheaper in the countryside.

Political decisions, however, frequently combine in strange ways with the dictates of economics. While economics was critical in the decision of the automobile manufacturers to close aging plants and to build new ones in the face of intense competition from foreign manufacturers, economics cannot entirely explain the decisions concerning the location of these facilities. As we shall see, political considerations intervened.

PART 2

THE DECISION AT MILWAUKEE JUNCTION

5

General Motors Searches for Sites

To the executives on the fourteenth floor of General Motors' headquarters in Detroit's New Center area, the critical decisions they face concern strategies for product development and capital investment. Each product must meet the twin goals of satisfying market demand and meeting the federal government's regulatory standards. The company's significant others, then, are its competitors in the marketplace, on the one hand, and the federal government, particularly the relevant regulatory agencies and Congress, responsible for setting standards, on the other. From the perspective of the corporate board room, decisions that do not impinge directly on the nature and cost of products or on regulatory standards are of a distinctly secondary nature.

These secondary decisions often have major impacts on the cities in which GM facilities are located and on the workers and their families whose livelihoods are dependent on the corporation. Where to construct facilities, which facilities to close in the face of declining demand, whether to modernize or rebuild—all are decisions that have major geographical impacts. Because governments are above all geographical entities, they can be dramatically affected by such locational decisions in the private sector. Because they rely heavily on property taxes to finance their operations, local governments can be affected most severely of all.

DECISION MAKING AT GENERAL MOTORS

General Motors is a closed corporation. Key executives have all worked their way up the corporate ladder at General Motors, with most being groomed in staff positions and in the divisions before joining the top corporate management. Corporate philosophy opposes hiring executives from outside the organization, and the average length of service of members of the executive committee is more than thirty years.[1]

Alfred P. Sloan, Jr., was with General Motors for more than forty-five years; from 1923 through 1946 he was chief executive officer of the corporation. Under Sloan, two major management principles were developed: the decentralized operating system and management by committee. "These were not the creation of a single inspired moment, but the result of a long process of development in dealing with a fundamental problem of management, that of placing responsibility for policy in the hands of those able both to make the decisions and to assume the responsibility."[2] Decentralized management meant not only substantial discretion on the part of division heads (Chevrolet, Pontiac, Cadillac, Buick, Oldsmobile, and GMC) but also internal competition that requires divisions to bid on company projects. However, central headquarters always retained substantial control not only over general policy direction but also over product development, engineering, and even styling. Moreover, all assembly plants other than the five "home" plants that were operating when the corporation was formed are run by the Assembly Division, established in the 1960s, rather than the traditional divisions. A separate real-estate division, Argonaut Realty, is responsible for acquiring property. With corporate decisions to standardize the product line, even more central control was instituted, further removing responsibility for policy from the traditional divisions.

Sloan's second management innovation—management by committee— permeates corporate decision making from decisions on corporate policies, to financial planning, to product development. The system assures that no project is approved solely by one individual. Several disgruntled GM executives have criticized the system as being conservative, slow, and stifling of innovation, but GM believes that it helps to avoid major product blunders.[3]

The most powerful committees are the Corporate Executive Committee, which decides what products and programs to recommend to the board of directors, and the Finance Committee, which determines the projects that it will recommend to the board for capital funding. These two committees held four members in common in the late 1970s, when the company approved major changes in product strategy and capital investment: Thomas A. Murphy, chairman; Elliott Estes, president; Richard Terrell, vice-chairman; and Roger Smith, executive vice-president, financial staff.[4]

DECISIONS ABOUT LOCATIONS

It was competition—pure, simple economic competition—that stimulated General Motors to decide to invest massively in its production facilities in 1979. Changed conditions in the demand for automobiles offered an exceptional opportunity for Japanese manufacturers to increase their share of the vast American automotive market after the spring of 1979, and they proved to be able entrepreneurs in exploiting the advantage that the Iranians had provided to them. Domestic manufacturers responded with an unprecedented capital-spending program, a program that at General Motors, at least, survived the severe economic downturn of the early 1980s.

While the capital-investment strategy of General Motors was prompted by economic considerations, the specific mix of new facilities and remodeling of existing facilities and the geographic dispersion of the new facilities were not. In both cases a complex mix of standard economic forces, governmental regulations, union contractual obligations, internal company politics, and external political considerations molded the decisions. Yet the pattern of location of facilities had the potential of dramatically affecting citizens and governments both by creating jobs and by contributing to the property-tax bases of localities. Hence this private decision, shaped by both economics and politics, was likely to have important impacts far beyond corporate headquarters.

While much has been made in the popular press and in the academic literature about the shifting of jobs and industry from America's industrial crescent (an area stretching from Boston to Milwaukee, going no further south than Cincinnati) to the Sun Belt, new automotive assembly plants in the Sun Belt were not likely. Japanese innovations in inventory control, in which parts are delivered directly to the assembly line, thus eliminating inventory storage and control problems, made necessary the location of parts plants near to assembly plants. In the new competitive environment, domestic manufacturers quickly saw the wisdom of such an arrangement. Since a single parts plant may serve several assembly facilities, the entire logic of the inventory-control system dictated geographic concentration in the industry. Moreover, the new emphasis on quality control, again forced by foreign competition, meant that manufacturers were very reluctant to abandon the skilled labor of the Midwest.

Hence the industrial crescent enjoyed significant initial advantages in the corporation's search for sites. Cities, however, suffered a significant disadvantage: the limited availability of land, higher costs of acquisition, and higher taxes there made them vulnerable to decisions about relocation. One key issue, then, in the struggle for locational advantage hinged on refurbishing versus replacing older, central-city plants.

THE RECONDITIONING ISSUE

While many of GM's plants were inefficient from the standpoint of producing front-wheel-drive models, the decision to replace rather than to recondition these plants was not automatic. Major modifications were necessary in the assembly process because the front-wheel-drive cars employed integral body frames instead of the separate body-frame design used on earlier vehicles. In some cases, the facilities were so inefficient that only replacement would suffice; in others, plants could be improved but at a cost that exceeded the cost of replacement. In Detroit, in Pontiac, in Kansas City, and in St. Louis, replacement was chosen; in Baltimore and in Flint, reconditioning was chosen. The Flint Buick plant, originally slated for replacement, became the object of vigorous politics both within the company and between the company and the city of Flint.

While the intrinsic inefficiency of production in the assembly plants was foremost in the minds of GM executives in determining the replacement/reconditioning mix, air-pollution regulations were also important. Beginning in 1983, the Clean Air Act mandated new levels of pollution controls for stationary sources. A company analysis indicated that bringing existing assembly plants into compliance would cost $3.5 billion. In the spring of 1979, corporation executives decided to combine the air-pollution upgrading program with the program for front-wheel-drive production, thus effectively accelerating plant replacement by two years (originally scheduled in a ten-year product-improvement plan written in 1974.)[5] This decision was stimulated by the success of imports in the American market and allowed the announcement of the $40-billion capital-improvement program, which received extensive coverage in the media.

The particular mix of new and reconditioned facilities, then, was a function of market conditions, production inefficiencies, and governmental regulation. The cost of utilities, which was considerably higher in older plants, was not a major consideration; these costs run only about 2 percent of production costs.[6]

FACTORS OF SITE SELECTION

A considerable body of literature has developed analyzing the factors that influence corporate decisions in regard to locating facilities. Generally, businessmen are concerned with the stream of operating costs they face over the lifetime of facilities, and the lack of available space to expand existing facilities. Very seldom do governmental tax policies or governmental policies designed to lower the cost of capital, such as industrial-revenue bonds, play an important role in the decisions that corporation executives make in regard to relocation. These are simply too minor in the long-run costs associated with a new facility.[7]

Several years ago the Survey Research Center at the University of Michigan conducted a survey of Detroit-area businesses to ascertain the causes of industrial exodus from Michigan. The study indicated an increasing concern with wage rates, which were ranked as the most important factor in decisions about plant relocation. Wages were third most important in 1961; seventh in 1950. Other factors mentioned as important were transportation costs, availability of skilled labor, distance to customers, and state and local taxes.[8]

The "big three" of site selection at General Motors are (1) land costs, (2) the available labor pool, and (3) transportation costs.[9] Moreover, an added factor during the accelerated capital-investment program was timeliness; originally the new assembly plants were to be finished in 1982 in time for the production of 1983 models.

While none of these major factors directly involves public-sector incentives, it would nevertheless be a mistake to conclude, as some of the plant-location literature has done, that public intervention is unimportant. The reason is that a variety of public policies have an indirect effect on plant costs. For example, if a city underwrites land-clearance costs, it can become more attractive in the competition for corporate capital investments. Moreover, such public regulatory actions as clean-air requirements can, as we noted above, influence corporation decision making. Real-estate taxes, however, do not seem to play a key role in decisions about sites; hence, state and local policies designed to attract plants by reducing or abating real-estate taxes may be more questionable.

Certain facets of the layout of automotive assembly plants have a great influence both on the corporate location decision and on the community's responses to those decisions. Maximization of assembly efficiency requires a one-story plant, of approximately three million square feet, with a serpentine assembly line and access to a main rail line. In the new plants, parts would have to be shipped by rail to the assembly site, where rail cars would be put together into a train that would carry the parts needed for each shift into the plant in the order in which they would be used. This inventory system required extensive rail "marshaling yards," and the length of the rail cars dictated a minimum turning radius for the rail loop into the plant. The consequence of these requirements was that plant sites had to be rectangular in shape and had to encompass from 450 to 500 acres. In addition to the assembly building and rail yards, each site had to include a power plant, parking lots, storm-water treatment and retention facilities, storage areas for completed automobiles, and space for landscaping, to minimize the visibility of the plant to surrounding areas.

Two considerations about labor costs influenced the GM site-selection process. First, a location near an existing facility that is slated for closure allows the full utilization of the trained work force. In the second place, collective-bargaining agreements with the UAW require that workers have the right to transfer to new facilities and that they be paid relocation benefits to a new plant that is more than fifty miles from an existing facility. Transfer rights however, are complex; the skills mix for new facilities can be substantially different from that of older ones. The city of Detroit's chances for attracting the new Cadillac assembly plant that was scheduled to replace the aging Fleetwood facilities were considerably enhanced by the negative publicity that General Motors received when it located a new assembly plant in Wentzville, Missouri, just under fifty miles from the St. Louis facility that it replaced.

THE SITE-SELECTION PROCESS
AT GENERAL MOTORS

Procedures for site location at General Motors are standard, at least at the initial stages of review. A site-selection task force, administered by the company's real-estate division, Argonaut Realty, undertakes the review. In keeping with the company's committee philosophy, it includes representatives from real estate, plant engineering, industry/government relations, labor relations, personnel, public affairs, the corporate staff, and the division that is seeking a new facility (in this case, the Assembly Division). This committee makes recommendations to the involved division and to the company's Financial Committee and to the Executive Committee of the corporation. The affected division prepares a detailed financial analysis of alternative sites, using primarily land, labor, and transportation costs. However, taxes, the impact on governments, utilities, and public relations are also considered. Results are forwarded to the corporate Executive Committee for final decision.

Site review went relatively smoothly for most of the new assembly plants. In St. Louis, seven sites inside and outside of the city were studied before the rural Wentzville location was chosen. Three sites, including one in Sarnia, Ontario, Canada, were considered for the Pontiac replacement plant prior to selection of the undeveloped area in Orion Township. Replacement of assembly plants in Fairfax, Kansas, and Flint, Michigan, was also considered early in 1980. In each of these cases, several sites were reviewed, and options were acquired on property, but these options were allowed to expire as both economic conditions and corporate strategies dealing with them changed.

THE BARGAIN AT THE PEAK

On 29 September 1979, General Motors' chairman, Thomas Murphy, invited Detroit's Mayor Coleman Young and Michigan's Governor William Milliken to a meeting in his office. Murphy wanted to brief the two political leaders on the deteriorating state of the automobile industry, and he wanted to fulfill perfunctorily an earlier promise that he had made to allow the city of Detroit to bid on the next GM facility. GM wanted to replace its Cadillac transmission line, located at its Detroit Cadillac/Fleetwood Complex. According to Michigan law, any company that is receiving economic-development benefits from a Michigan community as a consequence of relocating from another community must have the approval of that community. Murphy felt that obtaining the approval of Detroit would be no problem, because the company, as usual, was considering sites in Michigan (in the Detroit suburb of Livonia) and out of state (primarily in Indiana). This strategy of site selection had several advantages: it allowed full considera-tion of engineering, transportation, and labor-force aspects of the proposed facility in a variety of settings; it decreased land speculation; and it allowed maximum leverage in extracting benefits from state and local officials. The threat of moving out of state was almost always enough to gain the acquiescence of the community that would be losing the facility, even if the company might have to tolerate some posturing on the part of the city council.

When Murphy presented his need for the land, Young almost immedi-ately leaned forward and asserted: "You knew we couldn't do that. When you ask us to do something, and you give us 24 hours, you know up front that we can't produce. When will the day be when you come to us and say, 'Here are our plans; let's sit down and plan together.' "

Murphy was put on the defensive by Young's blunt criticism of a standard GM tactic for dealing with local communities. By offering them the opportunity to bid on facilities with only a moment's notice, the company could claim that it had given the home community the chance but that no land was available. The mayor of Flint characterized this as the "purple horse approach": "Bring me a purple horse in twenty-four hours and I'll give you $100." (GM was to use the same approach in moving to relocate facilities in Pontiac and Flint, and had already done so in St. Louis.)

Murphy offered to consider Detroit seriously for the next plant: "I'll tell you what I will do. The next plant—the next facility—the next time we do something major, we're going to give you guys a shot at it. We're going to let you guys participate, but you will have to move quick."[10]

The offer was not an idle one. GM had already begun to explore sites for its soon-to-be announced capital-spending program to produce front-wheel-drive cars and to modernize its aging assembly facilities. Corporate executives had scheduled Detroit's inefficient Cadillac/Fleetwood complex for replacement in the future. Murphy's offer would ultimately result in a $600-million investment in the city of Detroit by General Motors, but it would also require over $250 million of public investment and the largest urban land-assemblage and clearance program in United States history.

THE DETROIT DECISION

Locating a site for the Cadillac/Fleetwood replacement plant proved to be difficult. Initial site review had begun in the summer of 1979, but by early 1980 no acceptable site had been found. There were few suitable sites within fifty miles of the existing facility that simultaneously satisfied the conditions of size, transportation access, and timeliness. Sites in the city were initially rejected because they lacked the necessary rail access or would have required the removal of so many homes and businesses that General Motors' construction deadlines could not be met.

In April of 1980 General Motors' chairman, Thomas Murphy, formally asked Detroit's Mayor Coleman Young to join in a combined effort to locate a suitable site in the city of Detroit. A committee of GM representatives and city officials carried out the site review, but the alternatives that were considered were limited by GM's refusal to compromise its plant-engineering decisions: the site would have to be 500 acres in size, be approximately rectangular in shape, have access to a long-haul railroad and freeways, and be available within a short period of time. Of secondary importance were criteria developed by city officials: the number of housing units, businesses, and institutions that would have to be destroyed should be minimized; the age, condition, and economic viability of these structures should be considered; the potential for environmental harm should be minimized; historical properties should be preserved to the greatest extent possible; and viable industrial and commercial areas should not be disturbed.[11]

The city/company joint committee reviewed the sites that had already been studied by the company and added several more potential locations, for a total of nine (see figure 5.1). First priority was given to old industrial corridors as potential locations, both because of city policies aimed at recycling them and because such sites filled GM's requirements of rail access and ready availability. Unfortunately, after the first round of reviews, the committee "could not make any of them work."[12]

NINE SITES; NINE REJECTIONS

Each of the nine sites had significant disadvantages in terms of GM's specifications (and the city's, but these were clearly secondary). The site

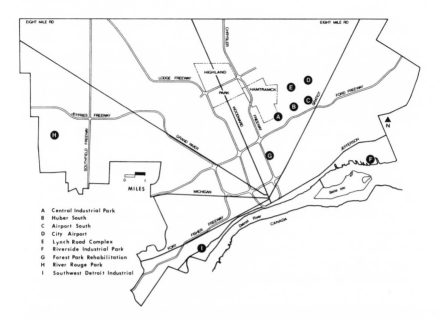

A   Central Industrial Park
B   Huber South
C   Airport South
D   City Airport
E   Lynch Road Complex
F   Riverside Industrial Park
G   Forest Park Rehabilitation
H   River Rouge Park
I   Southwest Detroit Industrial

Figure 5.1. Proposed alternative sites for General Motors' Detroit Assembly Plant.
Source: City of Detroit Community and Economic Development Department.

that ultimately was chosen, the Dodge Main/Central Industrial Park site spanning the border between Detroit and Hamtramck, had the advantage of containing "a significant number of vacant parcels," especially the vacant Dodge Main plant. Residential areas were described as "somewhat blighted," with "approximately one third of each block containing abandoned parcels." Other advantages were listed as access to railroads and freeways, correct shape, and the presence of some of the necessary infrastructure for the plant.[13] Major problems with this site included the extent of required relocation of residents and businesses and the difficulties in finding a new location for the headquarters of the city's Public Lighting Commission. Another potential problem was that two municipalities would have to participate in development of this site, which would complicate decision making.[14] This site was the second most expensive, at a cost of $112 million, not including costs of acquisition and relocation in Hamtramck, largely because of an estimated property-acquisition cost of $42 million.[15]

The second-choice site included two Chrysler Corporation facilities, both on Detroit's east side. These, unlike Dodge Main, were still in operation, although there were sound reasons to believe that they might soon close. This site was desirable from the city's perspective because it would involve the reuse of industrial property. Other advantages were that it had excellent rail access, it was located adjacent to other industrial facilities, and it currently had heavy industrial land use. However, it lacked direct access to a freeway and would require the demolition and relocation of economically vital and essential industries. In addition, potential expansion was limited by the presence of a cemetery, rail lines, and a major arterial thoroughfare.[16] Use of this site would have required less relocation than the Dodge Main site, but costs of acquisition, relocation, demolition, and site improvement were nearly as high, being estimated at $96 million.[17]

Three other potential sites were located in Detroit's aging east-side industrial corridor. Two of them had the desired access to freeways but none had the necessary access to a main rail line, which was stipulated by GM. One of these sites included most of the Detroit City Airport, which handled 179,000 flights in 1979, primarily by small commercial and private planes. The only advantages of the City Airport site were reductions in acquisition time and costs and in the lesser extent of residential relocation, because the city owned much of the property. Two adjacent sites would have required more-extensive residential and commercial relocation, although both residential areas were characterized by blight and deterioration. Both, however, did satisfy GM's criteria in regard to size, shape, and freeway access, but they lacked rail access.[18]

Only one other alternative site met the requirements of size and shape. This site, a major park on the city's western boundary, was, like the City Airport, readily available without any relocation and only a small amount of demolition, making it one of the least expensive sites; it lacked freeway access, but it was accessible to a main rail line. However, its use would have required the relocation of the Rouge River, at a cost of close to $30 million, and would have eliminated 500 acres of badly needed parkland.

Three other sites—two small industrial parks and an urban-renewal area—were much too small and had extremely limited potential for expansion. Their primary advantage was that they had been cleared and were, therefore, readily available at a relatively low cost. None of these sites seems to have been seriously considered.

QUICK TAKE

At this point the site-selection process was back to square one. All of the potential sites had been rejected, for one reason or another. Then Detroit's director of community and economic development, Emmett S. Moten, Jr., initiated a reexamination of the area around Dodge Main in light of recent action by the Michigan Legislature. On 8 April 1980 the legislature had completed action on Public Act 87 of that year. That act, which came to be known as the "quick take law," allowed municipalities to acquire title to property before reaching agreement with individual owners on a purchase price. The act responded to experiences in urban-renewal and other redevelopment projects in which negotiations over the price of a few parcels of land had delayed and often sabotaged the implementation of a project. Previously, owners could block governmental action by obtaining an injunction in circuit court; if the parties could not agree on a purchase price, the court would impose one. Court backlogs, up to five years in Wayne County Circuit Court, meant that there were incentives for owners to hold out for large settlements.

The "quick take" law meant that the land around Dodge Main could be assembled quickly enough to meet General Motors' deadlines. Without it, Poletown would have survived, and Detroit would not have gained an assembly plant. Review of the site was completed in early summer; in a public hearing on July 8, residents of the area that was to become the Central Industrial Park learned that their homes and businesses were to be demolished.

PUBLIC POLICIES FOR ECONOMIC DEVELOPMENT

The burden that government assumed by undertaking the development of the Central Industrial Park was enormous. GM agreed to "construct and complete an assembly plant by May 1, 1983," only if the site was delivered to the company in sections, beginning on 1 May 1981 and continuing through 1 June 1982. For this property GM would pay $18,000 an acre, for a total of $11.5 million, far less than the costs of acquisition and demolition but far more than a comparable "green field" site in an undeveloped rural area. The cities of Detroit and Hamtramck would have to raise over $200 million to clear and prepare the site. They would have to coordinate the relocation, demolition, and construction of certain public infrastructure improvements required by GM.

This was made possible by certain enabling statutes enacted by the state of Michigan during the 1970s. While the "quick take" act was the keystone that made the project feasible, the rest of the economic-development arch was already in place.

Critical to the project was Public Act 338 (of 1974, as amended in 1978), Michigan's Economic Development Corporation Act, which authorizes the formation of municipal economic-development corporations (EDCs), specifies their powers, stipulates the provisions that must be included in plans for EDC-sponsored projects, and outlines the procedures to be followed in the preparation and adoption of such plans. As the basis for the powers granted to EDCs, the Economic Development Corporation Act cites the need for programs to alleviate and prevent unemployment and to encourage industrial and commercial location and expansion and defines these powers as public purposes. These powers include the construction of development projects, the acquisition of land for project sites, the borrowing of money and the issuing of revenue bonds to finance the project or the acquisition and improvement of a site, and the entering into agreements with firms or corporations for the sale or use of development projects. Municipalities may acquire property and transfer it to an EDC for use in a project, and may "lend, grant, transfer or convey" funds (including funds received from the federal or state government) to an EDC. Proponents of the act describe it as giving EDCs a flexibility that municipalities lack. Critics have suggested that it has contributed to a loss of accountability because EDCs are not bound by the "rules of the game" of either the public or the private sector. The legislation, however, does specify the roles to be played by the EDC, local public agencies, local governing bodies, and citizens' district councils in the project area in the preparation and adoption of project plans. Essentially, these procedures involve a transfer of policy-making responsibilities to the EDC, thus formalizing the participation of the private sector in the formation of public policy; EDC boards of directors must have a minimum of nine members, no more than three of whom may be city officials or employees. The constitutionality of P.A. 338 was challenged by the Poletown Neighborhood Council, an organization of citizens who were opposed to the Central Industrial project, but the law was upheld by the Michigan Supreme Court.[19]

Although P.A. 338 authorizes local governments to acquire land for development projects and to transfer it to EDCs, neither municipalities nor EDCs could assemble land quickly for a major urban project until P.A. 87 was adopted. Allowing municipalities to acquire title to property before reaching agreement with individual owners on a purchase price gave them increased flexibility in regard to economic development; it also could be used to deprive citizens of property without immediate just compensation. Agencies are required to establish "just compensation" for a piece of property and to submit to the owner a "good faith offer" to purchase the property for that amount. If an agency is not able to reach an agreement with the owner for purchase, it may file a complaint in the county circuit court, asking the court to determine just compensation for the acquisition of the property. Title to the property is vested in the agency as of the date of the filing of this complaint unless a motion to review the necessity of acquisition has been filed. The legislation, however, sets forth very narrow grounds for such challenges: for acquisition by a public agency, "the determination of public necessity by that agency shall be binding on the court in the absence of a showing of fraud, error of law, or abuse of discretion." The procedures in P.A. 87 were first used in the Detroit GM

project, but they have applied to "all actions for the acquisition of property
. . . under the power of eminent domain" since 1 May 1980.

In the letter of intent to Detroit's city officials, GM had made
construction of its plant in Detroit contingent upon the establishment of a
plant rehabilitation district and the granting of the "maximum allowable tax
abatement" under the provisions of Michigan P.A. 198 (of 1974, as
amended in 1978). P.A. 198 authorizes local governments to reduce
property taxes on new industrial facilities by one-half for up to twelve years
and to freeze the assessment of a replacement facility at the level of the
"obsolete industrial property" it is replacing, also for a period of up to
twelve years. The legislation allows for the establishment both of plant-
rehabilitation districts and of industrial-development districts, but is unclear
on their relationship to replacement facilities.

General Motors, in seeking the establishment of a plant-rehabilitation
district, was asking that the assessment on its new Detroit assembly plant
be frozen at the level of the old Fleetwood and Cadillac assembly plants. The
company ultimately received a 50 percent tax reduction for a new facility
rather than a freeze for a replacement facility. This change in designation
resulted in a doubling of the property taxes for the first twelve years of
operation of the new plant. In Orion Township, where there was no
obsolete GM facility within the municipal boundaries (it was three miles
away, in Pontiac), GM applied for and received the 50 percent, twelve-year
reduction. Because P.A. 198 provides that facilities receiving abatements
must not have a "primary effect of mere transfer of employment" among
governmental units of the state, consent of the city of Pontiac had to be
obtained prior to approval of the abatement by the Orion Township board. In
the context of both requests for tax abatements, previously veiled threats of
corporate relocation became explicit, making public officials reluctant to cast
a negative vote. If a corporation were to move to another state, of course, it
would not need any such permissions.

Another means of manipulating taxing power is through *tax increment
financing,* which allows increased property-tax revenues from a development project to be pledged to repay the costs of a project or to be
committed to encouraging additional development in the project area. Public
Act 197 of 1975 granted Michigan municipalities the power to establish tax-
increment-financing authorities (TIFAs) to finance development in central
business districts. Expansion of the utilization of tax-increment financing for
neighborhood revitalization and other economic-development projects was
provided by Public Act 450 of 1980, adopted by the Michigan Legislature on
15 January 1981 in the context of growing uncertainty about the availability
of federal funds for the Detroit GM project under the Reagan administration.

This legislation, which was drafted by the law firm that represents the Detroit EDC, authorizes municipal governing bodies to establish TIFAs and allows them to select a TIFA's board. Several options are provided for such a board; but in Detroit the EDC board was designated to serve as the TIFA board. A TIFA board has the power to formulate and implement the development plans for areas under its authority, including the acquisition, rehabilitation, and demolition of property and the preparation of sites and the construction of buildings. To finance these activities, it may issue revenue and tax-increment bonds, which rely on tax increments from development projects. The use of tax-increment funds is based on a tax-increment financing plan, which essentially turns over to the TIFA all taxes on the difference between the assessed value of all real and personal property in a designated development area before development and the assessed value after development. Details of how these revenues will be used must be included in the plan, which must be accompanied by a development plan and must be approved by the local governing body. County commissioners and school boards, whose tax revenues would be affected by this reduction in funds, must be given information about the TIFA plan and may comment on it, but they have no voting power. In the case of the Detroit GM project, which straddles the border between Detroit and Hamtramck, the TIFA plan provides for sharing revenues between the two municipalities and pledges that the bulk of project revenues for thirty years will be applied to repaying federal loans used to cover the costs of preparing the site.

The Detroit GM project would not have been feasible without all of these state policies as well as extensive grants and loans from the federal government. In Orion Township, most development costs were paid by GM, with only a tax abatement being granted. Detroit's mayor and development director were familiar with the state's enabling legislation and with federal funding opportunities when they agreed to engage in site review for the project; they could not have committed themselves to the project had they not thought that the state and federal programs would provide the city with the legal and financial capacity to carry it through to completion.

ALL OR NOTHING

Because of the number of structures that would be demolished, both city officials and community groups raised the issue of the appropriateness of General Motor's "green field" plant specifications in downtown Detroit. Why did so much land have to be taken? Could the neighborhood and the plant coexist with some minor modifications in the plant's design? Even if the need for a one-story linear plant were granted, was the huge parking lot really needed? Could roof parking be used, or could a special parking structure be built? Could the rail yards be built off the site?

Each alternative was quickly rejected by the corporation. First, the size of the assembly plant itself was determined by the length of the assembly line, which could not be shortened without reducing the capacity and efficiency of production. Second, because parts for assembly would be stored on site in rail cars—which could then be made up into trains of one hundred cars, containing all parts needed for one assembly shift, that would bring parts into the assembly plant—rail storage and marshaling yards were needed on the site (although some rail yards were located off the site in Orion Township). Third, the length of the rail cars determined a maximum curvature in the railroad tracks on the site, which, in turn, determined the size and configuration of the site. Fourth, parking structures, according to both General Motors and city of Detroit officials, were rejected because they require additional time and cause traffic jams when large numbers of cars enter and exit at changes in shifts, thus resulting in high levels of air pollution. Roof parking is technically difficult because there are numerous fans, vents, and other openings on the roof of the plant, and it would create some of the same traffic and pollution problems as would a parking structure. Rooftop parking would have added from $20 to $25 million to the cost of the plant, in addition to the cost of redesigning the roof ventilation system, and would have saved only 232 residential units, which would have been sandwiched between the Edsel Ford Freeway and the plant's access roads. Moreover, GM officials contend that roof parking is prohibited by regulations of the state fire marshal (see fig. 5.2).

The reasoning of the corporate planners was clear enough: as long as adequate sites outside of the city could still be found, there was no reason to compromise plant design, especially when substantial modifications saved so little of the neighborhood. If the green-field plant could not be built downtown, then it would have to be built somewhere else. The new competitiveness of the industry meant that it was dangerous to accept any modifications that might interfere, even marginally, with plant efficiency. Hence, every suggested modification was summarily rejected by the corporation, and indeed, most of the suggested modifications were really not feasible. Green-field plant designs are not incompatible with urban America; but it is urban America that must change, not the plant design.

CONCLUSIONS

The new economic competition from the subcompact imports was caused by changes in the price and availability of oil. The response of the

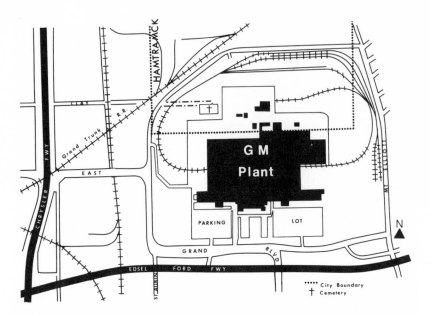

Figure 5.2. Layout of the Central Industrial Park project. Rail marshaling yards are north of the plant; truck marshaling yards are just to the west. The storm-water retention pond is to the southwest of the cemetery, which was granted an easement. Dodge Main was located in the upper quarter of the project area, primarily in Hamtramck. The Poletown neighborhood stood at the southern and southwestern parts of the project area. See also figs. 10.1 and 10.2. Source: City of Detroit Community and Economic Development Department.

domestic manufacturers was massive reinvestment. While this would seem to be a straightforward result of competition, this is not really the case. Reinvestment was one option; diversification was a second. This second strategy has been followed by domestic steel companies to a substantial extent.[20] In 1980, General Motors had $6.8 billion in working capital; $3.6 billion in governmental securities, other marketable securities, and cash; and only $1.9 billion in long-term debts.[21] Clearly, the acquisition of nonrelated companies was one possible strategy; such conglomerate acquisitions swept the American business community during the early 1980s as reinvestment strategies seemed to be less profitable in the face of lagging demand. An acquisition strategy would have run counter to traditional ways of doing business in Detroit, but these were not normal times.

If reinvestment was not a foregone conclusion, the tactical deployment of resources was even less certain. Most of General Motors' capital expenditures went into retooling the assembly lines and into the parts-manufacturing operations, but substantial expenses went into building new facilities and refurbishing old ones. The particular mix of reconditioning and replacement had significant impacts on communities; effects were far less traumatic in the case of reconditioning. In this case, property-tax revenues would be retained and loss of jobs would be minimized (although increased automation and "robotics" in the facilities meant considerable loss of jobs even in the case of reconditioned plants).

The replacement option raised the stakes of the decision about location. Each replacement implied a plant closure and a loss of tax base and jobs; each implied a major investment in a community. Just where these investments were made was of vital importance to communities but was a minor consideration to corporate decision makers. Normally site-selection procedures were handled as an internal corporate matter. In the case of the search for a site to replace the Cadillac assembly and Fleetwood body plants, however, Detroit city officials were invited to join in the search process. The company's image had suffered considerably because of its decision to relocate its St. Louis facility, a decision that apparently had caught city officials by surprise. By including Detroit officials in a search for a suitable city site, criticism could be defused if no site could be found. Moreover, GM had recently relocated a transmission facility to a nearby suburb. Under Michigan laws a property-tax abatement for a replacement facility cannot be granted by a municipality unless the municipality that is losing the facility agrees. The city of Detroit agreed but received a pledge that GM would search diligently for a Detroit site in future relocations.

A Detroit site that would fill GM's plant-engineering requirement and timetable was found only because of the Michigan Legislature's passage of Public Act 87 of 1980, the "quick take" law. This law made possible the rapid acquisition of property under eminent-domain procedures. Other economic-development legislation passed during the 1970s, especially that enabling communities to establish economic-development corporations, also facilitated the project. These statutes acted as a funnel; they did not provide the public-sector financing, but they did allow public effort to be focused on the project. These acts made possible a Detroit response but did not ensure it.

6

The Bureaucracy in Action:
Meeting General Motors' Timetable

Once the bargain between the city and the company had been struck, an air of intense crisis pervaded the decision-making process. Deadlines imposed by General Motors were inflexible, and much had to be done. If all parts of the project's planning and implementation process did not proceed smoothly, the project would be doomed. City officials had to acquire nearly seventeen hundred pieces of property, relocate more than thirty-five hundred residents, demolish fifteen hundred residential and commercial structures, and complete the site preparation in less than eighteen months. Moreover, the process was complicated enormously by the need to obtain financing immediately and the need to secure waivers of certain federal requirements relating to urban renewal and air quality.

The necessity of meeting extremely tight deadlines meant that opponents of the project did not need to halt the project completely; a delaying strategy would suffice. With the competitive pressures facing GM, it was unlikely that any major relaxations of the original deadlines would occur. Indeed, as opposition to the project solidified, major strategies were centered on symbolic protest and delay.

However, the crisis atmosphere, the cold competence of city officials in piecing together the financing, relocation, and site-clearance plans, and the deteriorating state of Detroit's economy all contributed to the city's ability to accomplish what was demanded of it. In addition, the political skills of Mayor Coleman Young and the entrepreneurial skills of Emmett Moten, the director of Detroit's Community and Economic Development Department (CEDD), were critical elements in successful completion.

Many city officials who were involved in the project openly speculated that GM's inflexible site criteria and stringent deadlines were set in the expectation that the city would not be able to meet them. This would have allowed the corporation to build the plant elsewhere and yet would have enabled it to claim that it had offered Detroit the opportunity to participate in the project. This was a not uncommon GM strategy, employed for public-relations purposes. Such speculation added to the sense of urgency surrounding the development of the project, as a mistake could lead to cancellations.

In this chapter we sketch the complexities of the project-planning process and the delicate nature of the necessary financial arrangements. Finally, we show how the city intervened, with substantial success, to nullify neighborhood-based opposition to the project through a generous and expansive relocation plan.

WAIVING THE REQUIREMENTS

General Motors' timetable for the project required that the city receive waivers of federal requirements related to the submission of an Environmental Impact Statement (EIS) for the project, which was required in Title I of the Housing and Community Development Act of 1974 and Section 102(2) of the National Environmental Policy Act (NEPA) of 1969. Pursuant to the implementing regulations for NEPA, an Emergency Request for Alternative Arrangements was submitted to the Federal Council on Environmental Quality on 10 September 1980, requesting a waiver of the requirement for withholding the release of federal funds pending completion of the EIS. Granting of this request would allow the city to obtain the federal-loan money needed for acquisition and relocation costs by the time the project plan was adopted; adoption of the plan, in turn, was a prerequisite to a GM commitment to carry out the project.

The emergency request emphasized the deadlines set by GM: that the city must have title to the site by 1 May 1981 so that GM could begin construction in time for the plant to be completed by August 1983. In order to meet this deadline, the city claimed, a commitment of federal funds for land acquisition was needed by 1 October 1980, before the EIS could be completed. To justify the need for the project, the city provided information on the declining job base of the cities of Detroit and Hamtramck and the unemployment rates in those cities, layoffs of city employees, cutbacks in city services, lowering of ratings of city bonds, reductions in the tax base of both cities, and increases in the number of residents receiving welfare. Construction of the GM plant, according to the request, was essential "to address the city's emergency financial condition and the economic state of emergency that has been declared by the Governor of Michigan."[1] Acting with the speed characteristic of policy decisions related to the project, the council granted the waiver, stipulating only that the EIS process be completed prior to the start of project construction.[2]

Because the Dodge Main facility was eligible for inclusion on the National Register of Historic Places and because other structures in the area had potential historical significance, review by the Advisory Council on Historic Preservation was necessary in order to consider "feasible and prudent alternatives to avoid or satisfactorily mitigate" adverse effects that the project would have on these structures.[3] The review concluded that no feasible and prudent alternatives existed and that the project should proceed, with certain stipulations. These included documentation and preservation of artifacts from Dodge Main, the conducting of an archaeological survey of the area and of studies to determine National Register eligibility for the Poletown neighborhood surrounding the project, and should eligibility be established, the carrying out of measures to preserve the characteristics of the area that contributed to its eligibility.[4]

THE IRRELEVANCE OF IMPACT ANALYSIS

The EIS submitted by the city examined the Central Industrial Park project, comparing it to alternative sites and to the alternative of having no project. The bulk of the document was devoted to analyzing the economic, social, and physical impacts of the project. The statement included a complete examination of neighborhood development and social composition, a study of all structures in the project area, an assessment of the project's impact on the Detroit economy, on air quality, and on traffic patterns. Not surprisingly, the analysis, which was coordinated by planners from the city's Community and Economic Development Department, was favorable to the project.

This analysis, complete as it was, had no influence on project planning. The draft EIS was not completed until 15 October 1980, two weeks after Detroit's Economic Development Corporation had approved the project plan and two months after the City Council had authorized the application for the initial "Section 108" loan from the Department of Housing and Urban Development (HUD). The process of planning the project proceeded simultaneously with the process of impact analysis, with the former affecting the latter, but not vice versa. While it was technically possible for the environmental analysis to result in the rejection of the project, given the commitment of city officials and state government to the project and the political connections between Young's administration and federal officials, this was highly unlikely. There were significant reasons to doubt whether the project would proceed, but these reasons concerned (1) financial arrangements, (2) local political opposition, (3) potential legal challenges, and (4) the strictness of GM's deadlines, rather than the environmental analysis. At base, the environmental impact analysis was a meaningless charade.

PLANNING THE PROJECT

The planning of the project involved three major elements: the preparation of physical plans for the project, the piecing together of the necessary financial commitments, and the developing of a relocation plan for area residents and businesses. Complete physical and financial plans were required by the state of Michigan under its economic-development legislation (P.A. 338). The planning for relocation was required by HUD under the Uniform Relocation and Real Property Acquisition Act of 1970, which had been passed to stop abuses by local governments that were conducting urban-renewal projects.

To promote the necessary cooperation in planning and implementing the project among city, state, and federal officials, as well as General Motors, the city established several task forces. An "executive task force," which included officials from Detroit, Hamtramck, the state of Michigan, General Motors, and Turner Construction Company, the construction manager for the project, met weekly to identify problems and to work out solutions. In so doing, they often worked with the representatives of eighteen city departments who formed the "city task force." CEDD's director Moten and staff members from CEDD's property acquisition, development, and relocation divisions participated in both of these groups, whose membership changed as the project progressed. The task forces met weekly throughout the various phases of the project, switching to biweekly meetings early in 1982, when construction of the plant was well under way. Another task force of federal officials from HUD, the EDA, and the Department of Transportation, chaired by Assistant Secretary Robert Embry of HUD, helped Moten and his staff in arranging federal financing.[5]

The planning of the project was complicated by the involvement of two municipalities, by the accelerated pace required by GM's deadlines, and by the corporation's requirements in regard to physical site, which had been developed for rural sites and were difficult to impose on an urban area. Coordination between Detroit and Hamtramck was achieved through the task force, through the mediating role played by a representative of the governor's office, and through Hamtramck's ceding a "lead role" to Detroit's CEDD, whose involvement in planning was primarily in the areas of financing and relocation. As one GM official put it, the city's role was that of "site provider": its responsibilities were determined by the need to acquire the property, to relocate residents and businesses, and to provide

GM with a cleared site in five phases (generally starting at the northern boundary of the site and proceeding to the south), beginning in May 1981 and concluding on 1 June 1982; financing arrangements were dictated by the need to have funds available quickly for acquisition, demolition, and relocation.

The planning of the project began before GM had made any written commitment to build the plant. Such a commitment was conditional on the satisfaction of a lengthy list of site criteria contained in a letter from GM's chairman, Thomas Murphy, to the chairmen of the Detroit and Hamtramck EDCs, dated 8 October 1980 (after the EDCs had approved the project plan); less specific criteria had been set forth in earlier discussions between GM, Young, and Moten. Murphy's letter also requested that the EDCs accept the site criteria by 31 October 1980 and that by November 30 GM would receive a draft of a development agreement which would describe "conditions for satisfaction of the site criteria and . . . the financing methods, procedures and timing required to complete the development of the site."[6]

THE PHYSICAL PLAN

The physical plan was largely determined by specifications formulated by GM for other assembly plants (in Oklahoma City and in Wentzville, Missouri), with some modifications for the slightly smaller Detroit site. The plant complex would include a main assembly building to house body, paint, service, trim, cushion, chassis, and final process operations; this would be divided in the center by double rail docks and would have a small one-story section for personnel operations, data processing, hospital services, and cafeteria. Also on the site would be a powerhouse, a pumphouse and waste-treatment complex, parking lots for three thousand cars, truck haul-away and rail-marshaling areas, and a pond for the retention of storm water. Rail access, storage for several hundred rail cars, and the construction of a railroad bridge was to be completed by Conrail.

In addition to these privately financed facilities, the following "public improvements" were to be provided: the construction of a ring road around the site, alterations to exit and entrance ramps of the Ford Freeway, alterations to peripheral roads, the removal or alteration of utilities in the project area and realignment of them on the periphery of the project area.

The city's most significant contributions to the project plan were: (a) the preparation of a financial plan, based on cost estimates for the acquisition and demolition of property, the relocation of residents, and the preparation of the site (derived from experience with other projects and the initial relocation surveys) and on projected public and private sources of revenue; (b) the preparation of a description of exiting land use and zoning and of zoning changes necessary for the project; (c) the formulation of plans for the relocation of residents and businesses in the project area. Of particular significance in regard to policy were the financial and relocation components, because they implied significant modifications in and the reinterpretation of federal policies in order to complete the preparation of the site in accordance with GM's schedule.

THE FINANCIAL ARRANGEMENTS

As cost estimates and available revenue sources changed, arrangements for financing the project underwent several revisions from the plan that had originally been presented. The changing financial picture is documented in tables 6.1, 6.2, and 6.3. Table 6.1 presents the initial funding plan, developed in the project plan during the fall of 1980. Shifts in sources of funding were already evident two months later in the figures presented in the EIS. Table 6.2 indicates the financial picture in the spring of 1981, and table 6.3 shows CEDD's figures a year later. The figures graphically illustrate the changing sources of funds for the project and indicate the high degree of speculative financing that was involved. All versions of the financial plan centered on the extensive use of intergovernmental grants and loans, and all were premised on close relationships between Detroit officials and state and federal agencies. Moreover, the city had to produce funding commitments immediately, so that the acquisition of property could begin as soon as the project plan had been approved by the City Council. Reliance on loans necessitated repayment plans, which also underwent changes as anticipated future revenues from federal grants declined.

The major supplier of funds was to be the federal government, in particular the Department of Housing and Urban Development, through a Section 108 loan, an Urban Development Action Grant (UDAG), and Community Development Block Grant (CDBG) funds. Other key sources listed in the plan were the federal government's Economic Development Administration, the Environmental Protection Agency, state and federal road funds, state rail funds (in the form of grants and loans to Conrail), and a vague category of "other grants and land sale revenue."[7]

SECTION 108

Most HUD funding was through the Section 108 loan-guarantee program established by the Housing and Community Development Act of 1974 and amended in 1977. This legislation authorized the secretary of HUD to guarantee loans to governments for the acquisition or rehabilitation of

TABLE 6.1
PROJECTED COSTS AND SOURCES OF REVENUE,
CENTRAL INDUSTRIAL PARK PROJECT, OCTOBER 1980

Costs	
Acquisition	$ 62,000,000
Relocation	25,000,000
Demolition	35,000,000
Roads	23,500,000
Rail	12,000,000
Other preparation of the site	38,700,000
Professional services	3,500,000
Total	$199,700,000
Sources of Funding	
HUD Section 108 loan	$100,000,000
HUD Urban Development Action Grant	30,000,000
Economic Development Administration	30,000,000
Economic Protection Agency	6,870,000
State road funds	38,700,000
State rail funds	17,800,000
State Land Bank loan	1,475,000
Urban Mass Transportation Administration	1,364,000
Community Development Block Grant	2,025,000
Other grants and revenues from the sale of land	72,941,000
Total	$301,175,000
Less funds for the repayment of loans	− 101,475,000
Net financing	$199,700,000

SOURCE: Central Industrial Park Project Plan, 30 Sept. 1980, p. 11.

property, up to a maximum of three times the annual Community Development Block Grant allocation. Detroit's allocation was approximately $60
million in 1980, so it was authorized to borrow up to $180 million.

Loan guarantees require that the local government enter into a
repayment contract with HUD, pledging block-grant funds as security for
the loan and, at the discretion of the secretary, pledging the tax increments
from assisted projects toward the repayment. Interest rates on the loans
are determined by the secretary of the Treasury; at the time that Detroit
applied for its loans, the rates were around 15 percent. The initial 1974
authorizing legislation explicitly prohibited the issuance of loan guarantees
that would "benefit, in or by the flotation of any issue, a private individual or
corporation."[8] This passage was deleted in the 1977 renewal legislation, in
order to allow more flexibility in the use of funds. The project would have

TABLE 6.2
FINANCIAL ARRANGEMENTS, CENTRAL INDUSTRIAL PARK PROJECT, SPRING 1981

SOURCE	AMOUNT	STATUS AS OF 30 APRIL 1982
Committed Funds		
HUD Section 108 loans	$100,000,000	secured
HUD Urban Development Action Grant	30,000,000	contract in progress
Block grant	5,522,000	secured
State and federal road funds	25,570,000	secured
State Land Bank	1,425,000	secured
Water and Sewerage Department	10,870,000	bonds to be issued by city
Revenues from sale of land (General Motors and Consolidated Rail Corporation)	7,970,438	agreed to
Total	$181,357,438	
Uncommitted Funds		
Economic Development Administration	$ 7,500,000	applied for
Urban Mass Transportation Administration	1,364,000	not applied for
Total	$ 8,864,000	

SOURCE: Central Industrial Park Development Agreement, 30 Apr. 1981.

been impossible without this change, which had been aimed at facilitating housing programs.

As of July 1980, HUD reported that twenty-four projects in twenty-three cities were being funded in part with Section 108 loans. Fewer than half of these projects involved commercial or industrial development. Most of the projects were on a small scale, but Detroit had initiated the nation's first large-scale use of Section 108 when the city received a $38-million loan guarantee for its Joe Louis arena and parking garage in 1978. This pledging of community-development funds toward risky downtown development was controversial at the time; however, this aspect of financing received limited attention during the uproar surrounding the Central Industrial Park project. Media coverage and debate in the City Council focused almost exclusively on the drama surrounding relocation and the demolition of the neighborhood and ignored the implications of the problematic and arcane financial underpinning.

Access to the Section 108 loan funds was essential to the initial implementation of the project, for these funds ensured that the city would be able to pay for the expenses of acquiring property and of relocation, pending the awarding of other grants. During the late summer and early fall

TABLE 6.3

SOURCES OF REVENUE FROM THE PUBLIC SECTOR AND PROJECT COSTS
OF THE DETROIT GENERAL MOTORS ASSEMBLY PLANT, APRIL 1982 (IN $ MILLION)

SOURCE	TOTAL	ACQUISITION	RELOCATION	DEMOLITION	ROADS	OTHER SITE PREPARATION	PROFESSIONAL SERVICES
HUD letter of credit	65.000	60.1124				4.8876	
HUD Urban Development Action Grant	30.000		16.009	10.000		3.991	
HUD Section 108 loan	35.000	33.567		1.433			
Community Development Block Grant (HUD)	8.522	0.400	2.450	3.000			2.672
Economic Development Administration	15.000			9.300		5.700	
Urban Mass Transportation Administration	1.364	0.901	0.363	0.100			
State road funds	32.660	4.530	1.570	0.700	25.3356	0.5244	
State Land Bank	1.425						1.425
Interest on income from program[a]	2.400	2.400					
Income from the program[b]	11.470	11.470					
Income from sale of fixtures[c]	1.000	1.000					
Totals	203.841	114.3804	20.392	24.533	25.3356	15.103	4.097

SOURCE: City of Detroit, Community and Economic Development Department, 9 Apr. 1982.

[a] From funds put in an escrow account during property-condemnation proceedings.
[b] From the sale of property to General Motors, Conrail, etc.
[c] From the sale of fixtures from businesses that were relocated from the project area.

of 1980, numerous meetings took place between HUD officials in Washington and Detroit's Mayor Young and CEDD's director Moten and members of their staffs to develop details of the application. Moten appeared several times before the City Council to report that he could not provide that body with a final written loan application because specific aspects of the repayment schedule were still being "worked out with HUD." Moten's association with HUD's Secretary Moon Landrieu when Landrieu was mayor of New Orleans facilitated the progress of the negotiations. Moreover, several other responsible HUD officials had previously been associated with Young's administration. Speed was of the essence, not only because of GM's deadlines but also because it was becoming apparent that Carter would not be reelected, and a commitment on the loan was needed before his administration left office.

On the basis of initial estimates of cost, CEDD's staff proposed borrowing $60.5 million for the project through the Section 108 loan program. Authorization to apply for the loan was granted by the City Council in August, and federal approval came in early October. By this time, revised cost estimates in the project plan indicated that more money would be needed, and a $100-million figure was included in the project plan for Section 108 loans. This necessitated additional authorization from the City Council, which came on October 24, one week before the council formally approved the project. At this time, CEDD's financial planners also presented a repayment schedule for each loan, covering a six-year period, at 12 percent interest. Repayment sources were identified as land sales of $27.2 million ($6.2 million from GM, $15.2 million from state and federal departments of transportation, and $5.8 million from Conrail for railroad right of way), approximately $51 million in block-grant funds (unidentified federal grants obtained during the life of the project would be used to replace these block-grant funds), and approximately $51 million in state contributions on behalf of the city of Hamtramck. The additional $39.5 million in Section 108 funds was approved by President Reagan's HUD secretary, Samuel Pierce, on 25 February 1981, making a total of $100 million available in loan guarantees under this program.

A LETTER OF CREDIT

The city, however, intended to rely primarily on an alternative financing mechanism which would save the interest costs that would be incurred if the Section 108 money were spent. A procedure known as a letter of credit allows the city to draw upon committed but unspent block-grant funds from current and past years to pay for project costs. Approximately $60.5 million was available from this source in October 1980. Should the block-grant funds drawn upon for the project be needed for other block-grant projects, Section 108 loan funds or other available grant funds would be used to repay the letter-of-credit account. In November 1980, letter-of-credit funds were put into escrow accounts amounting to $47.5 million for acquisition costs and $3.5 million for relocation costs.

AN URBAN DEVELOPMENT ACTION GRANT

Urban Development Action Grant (UDAG) funds were a logical source of revenue, according to financial planners in the CEDD, because the UDAG program is based on the principle of using public money to stimulate private investment. The UDAG program was established by the 1977 amendment to the Housing and Community Development Act to aid distressed cities in alleviating economic and physical deterioration; eligibility standards are based on the age of housing, incomes, the out migration of population, and stagnation or decline in the tax base. Selection criteria for applications, in addition to the relative degree of physical and economic distress, include a city's past community-development performance, the program's impact on problems of low- and moderate-income persons and minorities, the impact on physical or economic deterioration, financial participation by other public or private entities, the impact on the neighborhood in which the project is to be located, and the feasibility of accomplishing the program "in a timely fashion within the grant amount available." The legislation also stipulates that the grants be made only where "there is a strong probability that the non-federal investment in the project would not be made" without the grant.[9] Although not specifically stated in the legislation, the premise of the program is that private investment in UDAG-aided projects will be substantially greater than public investment will be (a concept that is referred to as "leveraging"); the desirable ratio is considered to be about four private dollars to one public dollar.[10] As of October 1980, Detroit had received $73.9 million in UDAG money for fourteen projects. Private investment in these projects totaled $376.6 million.

Detroit applied for a $30 million UDAG grant for the project prior to approval for the project plan in late October 1980, and it was planned that the city of Hamtramck, in which part of the project area is located, would make a similar application. Although the requests were twice the size of the largest UDAG grant that Detroit had previously received, it was anticipated that the double application would raise the necessary $30 million. In December, however, questions were raised about Hamtramck's eligibility because of a 1968 lawsuit involving the illegal removal of blacks through urban-renewal projects, which precluded that city from receiving funds from the UDAG program. Negotiations to settle the suit, which had been inactive for several years, were resumed, and an agreement was worked out which lifted the ban on UDAG funds.[11]

No commitment from HUD was forthcoming in the waning days of the Carter administration. In early February 1981 the future of the entire UDAG program, and Detroit's grant in particular, were put in jeopardy because of budget cuts made by the Reagan administration. Opponents of the project were briefly encouraged, but on February 11, Michigan's Governor William Milliken announced that the $30-million grant to Detroit had been approved. Although this action was indicative of cooperation with the new administration, it is significant that the Republican governor, rather than Detroit's Democratic mayor, made the announcement.

COMMUNITY DEVELOPMENT BLOCK GRANT

Community Development Block Grant (CDBG) funds were utilized both for short- and long-term project financing and were pledged as security for the Section 108 loan. On 17 July 1980 the City Council authorized the reprogramming of $1.5 million of Detroit's block-grant funds from other projects for use on appraisals, relocation surveys, and other early planning activities. In November 1980, $51 million in committed but unspent block-grant funds were placed in escrow accounts to cover the costs of acquisition and relocation, through a letter of credit. April 1982 figures listed expenditures of $8.522 million in CDBG funds.

THE ECONOMIC DEVELOPMENT ADMINISTRATION

It was expected that another major source of funding would be the EDA; a total of $30 million in EDA funding was identified in the project plan. EDA funds have been used for a variety of development projects in rural and urban areas. The agency's goals include the promoting of economic development in depressed areas, the improving of development planning, the alleviating of short-term economic problems through countercyclical measures, and the redressing of the negative effects of federal economic policies. EDA grants have tended to be concentrated in small cities and rural areas, and those which have gone to large cities have tended to be relatively small (in the $2 million to $5 million range). CEDD planners anticipated receiving EDA money in several annual installments. These revenue estimates were later revised in the context of the Reagan administration's cuts in the program. By April 1981, CEDD was budgeting only $7.5 million from EDA (which had already been committed), but a year later, figures were presented to the City Council listing $15 million in EDA funds.

THE ENVIRONMENTAL PROTECTION AGENCY

The initial financial plan projected revenue of $6.87 million from the Environmental Protection Agency (EPA) for work on water and sewer lines. Six months later, CEDD's revenue projections had replaced the EPA grant with the sale of $10.87 million in Detroit Water and Sewer Department bonds. Revenue estimates released in April 1982 included neither of these funding sources but showed larger amounts for CDBG and EDA.

ROAD AND RAIL FUNDS

Another fluctuating amount of revenue was that to be obtained from state and federal road funds, which would be used for the construction of the ring road around the plant, alterations to freeway exits and entrances, and relocation payments to persons and businesses that would be displaced by the road construction. Initial estimates in the project plan were $38.7 million. In the development agreement dated 30 April 1981, $25.57 million in state and federal road funds are listed as being secured; revenue figures presented to the City Council in April 1982 indicated $32.66 million in state road funds.

The project plan listed state rail funds of $17.8 million among the public revenue sources, but at the time the development agreement was adopted, these had been shifted to the private sector, as a contribution from Conrail. Neither the development agreement nor the April 1982 figures specify any of the "other grants" mentioned by the project plan; the April 1982 figures listed revenue from land sales as $11.47 million.

TOTALS

As of April 1982, these sources, along with a small grant from the Urban Mass Transportation Administration, revenue from the sale of businesses that did not relocate, and income on the funds in the escrow account, totaled $203 million in public-sector contributions of funds to the project. Of this, over $150 million had come from federal programs, primarily through HUD grants and loans, and over $30 million from the state of Michigan. Unspecified amounts of future state funds to be received by the city of Detroit were pledged toward the repayment of the Section 108 loans. Detroit's contributions included the income from interest, from the sale of property and fixtures, and the time spent on project planning and implementation by hundreds of city employees (for which no specific dollar figure can be calculated). It should also be noted that nearly 50 percent of the public-sector revenues were derived from loans, a consequence of the accelerated timetable for the project, which allowed insufficient time to apply for grants, and, quite probably, of the anticipated election of Ronald Reagan, under whose administration reductions in urban-grant programs could be expected. The heavy reliance on federal loans required commitments for repayment which had a long-term impact on city revenues derived from the project and on the use of federal and state grants. The Reagan administration's grant cutbacks and the lowering of Detroit's bond ratings to below investment grade in 1980 began to squeeze the city's Community Development Block Grant funds by 1984, the first year for repaying the Joe Louis Section 108 loan. The inability to refinance the loans meant that CDBG funds would have to be used to make the repayments.

COSTS

Like funding, cost estimates were revised substantially during the course of the project (compare tables 6.1 and 6.3). At the time that the project plan was written, expected project costs were categorized as follows: acquisition, $62 million; relocation, $25 million; demolition, $35 million; roads, $23.5 million; rail, $12 million; other site preparation, $38.7 million; and professional services (e.g., appraisers, attorneys), $3.5 million. Cost projections were based on the city's experience with other projects and on information gathered in an initial survey of all the residents and businesses in the project area, which was conducted by CEDD's relocation staff in July 1980. It is difficult to pinpoint exactly the additional costs that were imposed by the accelerated pace of the project—for example, overtime by demolition and site-preparation workers, bonuses to encourage the quick relocation of area residents, and generous payments for the acquisition of property and for replacement housing for residents. GM's stringent requirements in regard to site preparation, including the removal of all utilities and the complete removal of demolition rubble, also contributed to the cost of the project. GM and its construction contractor, neither of whom had had any experience with building a plant on a cleared urban site, were particularly concerned about the removal of all previously existing materials, stipulating, for example, that all substructures (foundations and basements) be completely removed to a depth of ten feet. Because of the difficulty of doing this for a structure the size of Dodge Main, CEDD officials on the task force were able to negotiate an exception to this requirement. Finally, the city's cost estimates excluded interest charges on loans, and thus understated the total public costs of the project.

PLANNING FOR RELOCATION

Mimimum requirements for relocation services and benefits are established by the Federal Uniform Relocation Assistance and Real Property Acquisition Policies Act of 1970. Additional benefits and special procedures were established by the city for the Central Industrial Park project, partly to expedite the clearance of the area and partly in response to concerns articulated by area residents and by the Citizens District Council, which was established under state economic-development legislation.

In addition to the benefits available under the Uniform Act—replacement housing payments of up to $15,000, for homeowners, rental assistance or assistance of up to $4,000 with downpayments for tenants and the payment of moving expenses for residents and businesses—the plan established a $1,000 bonus for residents and businesses that would move within ninety days of receiving a Notice of Displacement. Provision was also made to compensate home owners for higher interest rates on new mortgages through a lump-sum payment, which was calculated so that payments on that portion of a new mortgage equal to the balance on an old mortgage did not exceed the payments on the old mortgage. In negotiations with the Citizens' District Council, an additional payment to home owners whose property taxes increased as a consequence of relocation was incorporated in the plan. The relocation budget was based on the assumption that all residents and businesses would be eligible for the maximum allowable benefits, for a total relocation cost of $25.75 million (later reduced to $20 million).

Plans for relocating the residents included contacts with realtors, making rehabilitated HUD homes from CEDD's inventory available for purchase on a priority basis, moving homes from the project area to another site, priority for tenants in newly constructed subsidized units, priority for public housing, rental of HUD homes, and rental referrals from management companies. A task force was established to identify and solve relocation problems of businesses, and CEDD attempted to provide referrals and assistance in securing public and private funding from the reestablishment of businesses. Somewhat later, CEDD established a supplemental grant for certain businesses if they reestablished within one year of displacement.

The relocation staff made a serious effort to be generous in its payments for moving expenses and replacement housing in order to expedite the clearance of the area. This was also the intent of the bonus program. CEDD was not generous in waiving eligibility standards for the various benefit programs, because it was seeking to prevent transients from moving into the area to collect benefits. Inflexibility on this point was the subject of complaints at public meetings, along with the higher mortgage costs and taxes and the impact that relocation had on elderly citizens.

Additional benefits were provided in response to citizen concerns about costs, but psychological and emotional impacts were not really addressed. The only special provision for the elderly in the project plan was "special consideration to barrier-free dwellings."[12] According to relocation staff members, social and psychological problems were referred to the Neighborhood Services Organization (NSO). A consultant, University of Michigan gerontologist Dr. Leon Pastalan, was hired to assist the NSO staff and to formulate responses to the special needs of senior citizens. Pastalan later prepared a report on the reactions of senior citizens to relocation, which concluded that most of them were quite satisfied both with their new homes and with the way in which they had been treated by relocation workers.

Other "mitigation measures" were proposed to alleviate the negative impacts of residential and business relocation. For residents, these included (1) efforts to change negative attitudes toward HUD houses, (2) working with residents on an individual basis to provide information on procedures and benefits, so as to reduce uncertainty, (3) establishing a Citizens' District Council (CDC) to determine "citizens' feelings, needs and frustrations,"[13] (4) utilization of the CDC and such community institutions as churches to provide citizens with information about the project and with opportunities to react to project decision making, (5) efforts to avoid moving senior citizens during severe winter weather and to minimize disruption of the school year for families with children, (6) efforts to provide those residents who wished to relocate into a neighborhood that had other residents from the project area with referrals that would allow them to do so.

Mitigation strategies for businesses included (1) assistance in obtaining relocation financing through the establishment of procedures to facilitate loans from the Small Business Administration (SBA) and the development of block-grant funding for rehabilitation loans; (2) obtaining listings from commercial/industrial realtors and CEDD's Industrial and Commercial Development Division, and information on city-owned buildings from CEDD's Real Estate Division to maximize relocation resources in Detroit and Hamtramck; (3) establishment of special procedures by the Michigan Liquor Control Commission and by Detroit's Buildings and Safety Engineering Department and the Zoning Board of Appeals to speed up the issuance of licenses and permits and the granting of waivers for relocating businesses.[14]

THE ACQUISITION OF PROPERTY

CEDD's acquisition staff began to make site visits to the project area and to prepare estimates of acquisition costs in May 1980, prior to the approval of the project plans. In August and September, appraisals of individual pieces of property were performed by forty-three independent fee appraisers who were hired by the city. Official acquisition notices and formal purchase offers were prepared, to be mailed to property owners as soon as the project plan was approved.

Members of CEDD's acquisition and real-estate-sales staffs were trained to serve as negotiators to work out settlements with the approximately 80 percent of the area's property owners who eventually accepted the city's original offer or who negotiated a higher acquisition price without going to court. Due to the volume of transactions and the tight schedule of the project, four private title companies, rather than the city's Law Department, acted as escrow agents and provided the title work for closings.

Property acquisition was also facilitated by changes in relevant HUD regulations. In earlier projects, HUD had required that each piece of property be appraised before and after funding had been approved and that there be an on-site inspection by a HUD representative prior to approval of the project. The revised regulations that applied to the GM project relied upon the monitoring of a random sample of appraisals by HUD auditors and upon meetings with appraisers to make adjustments.

By January 1981, according to the head of CEDD's real-estate division, Russell Chambers, 65 percent of the city's offers had been accepted, by 808 residential, 63 commercial/industrial, and 12 institutional owners. Nearly 80 percent of the court challenges to the city's offers came from owners of commerical or industrial property, reflecting the vagueness of HUD regulations on reimbursement for the acquisition of such property. CEDD records on moving claims indicate that more than 40 percent of the area's residents moved in April, May, and June of 1981 and that a total of more than 70 percent had left the area by the end of June.

Most businesses—more than two-thirds of those that relocated—also stayed in Detroit, but nearly one-third of the area's businesses discontinued operations. Businesses were eligible for the same $1,000 relocation bonus as residents and, under the Uniform Act, for reimbursement for moving expenses and the "fair market value" of buildings and permanent fixtures. A number of larger businesses challenged city awards in the circuit court; smaller, marginal businesses, which were unable to afford a challenge or to relocate with the money that they received from the city, closed down. In July 1981 the city established a program of supplemental grants of $6,950 as compensation for losses from the disruption of business for those businesses that reestablished off the site within a year of displacement.

Several businesses received substantial settlements in circuit court. Reinterpretation of HUD regulations on payment for movable and immovable fixtures was a consequence of these decisions, adding significantly to acquisition costs. Another expense for the city from these awards stems from P.A. 87's requirement that property owners who successfully challenge city offers be reimbursed for attorney's fees, up to one-third of the increase in compensation awarded by the court.

RELOCATION STRATEGIES AS PAYOFF

As should be clear from the above discussion, the city's relocation strategies were carefully planned and were extraordinarily expensive.

Special relocation incentives added more than $2 million to the cost of the project. Grants for residents were particularly lucrative. Owners not only received generous condemnation estimates for their homes; they also received full benefits payable under federal guidelines and special bonuses for prompt action. Special arrangements were made to facilitate residential relocation. Offers to business owners, however, were far less generous.

The generosity toward residents was designed to avoid neighborhood-based opposition to the project. Businesses, of course, were not likely to engage in sufficient mobilization to delay the project significantly and were more likely to utilize litigation to resolve disagreements; hence, they received a far different treatment at the hands of the city's relocation staff. The strategy was, by and large, successful. While significant neighborhood opposition did arise, in the form of the Poletown Neighborhood Council, its appeal to residents was undercut by the generosity of the city in its relocation offers.

One interesting unanticipated consequence of the city's relocation generosity has been the demands that residents whose property has been condemned for other projects have made for equal treatment. When the city refused these demands, owners challenged their awards in court.

CONCLUSIONS

The typical American urban-renewal project is invariably characterized by delay upon delay as deadline after deadline is missed, reestablished, and missed again. In the case of Detroit's Central Industrial Park project, however, there was no possibility that urban renewal could proceed "as usual." General Motors had made its offer and had stood firm on its deadline. Ironically, it was the corporation that delayed the originally announced August 1983 start-up date. Declining demand for front-wheel-drive automobiles and changes in quality control had caused revisions in production schedules that altered the opening date of the new plant. Nevertheless, in the view of GM officials in 1980, delay in capital investment in the front-wheel-drive program was tantamount to capitulation to the challenge of the foreign manufacturers.

GM's inflexible deadlines meant that project planning and implementation had to proceed with little margin for error. It was a massive undertaking, and Detroit city officials proved to be up to the task. Waivers of federal requirements for impact analysis had to be obtained, physical plans had to be developed, major changes in the zoning ordinance and other city laws had to be made, relocation strategies had to be devised, coordination among various agencies at three levels of government had to be forged, and above all, financing had to be arranged. Any "glitches" in progress on all fronts simultaneously could well spell doom for the project. Indeed, several city officials speculated that GM had been so flexible in order to be able to reject a Detroit plant location without experiencing harm to its public relations similar to that in the move of an assembly plant from St. Louis to Wentzville, Missouri.

By October of 1980, project planning had proceeded satisfactorily enough that GM formally committed itself to building an assembly plant in Detroit. By late October the project plan was approved by the City Council, and early in 1981 most major problems with financing had been ironed out. A thorough and expensive relocation strategy was developed to nullify potential neighborhood opposition.

Three elements contributed to the success of the project: the competence of city bureaucrats, the entrepreneurial skills of CEDD's director Emmett Moten and Mayor Coleman Young, and the political connections between Young's administration and Carter's administration. Moten's past association with HUD's Secretary Moon Landrieu smoothed negotiations with federal officials over the financing plan, while Young's unwavering support for President Jimmy Carter meant that federal officials were virtually unanimous in their support for the project.[15] Young had been an early supporter of Carter in 1976, and several members of Young's administration had taken positions in Washington after Carter was elected. City bureaucrats efficiently developed and later implemented the project plans with a minimum of the bureaucratic delay that is almost legendary in big cities.

Hovering in the background was the solid backing that Young enjoyed with the Detroit electorate. This popularity provided the mayor with a cushion of power that allowed him to move decisively in project planning and even more decisively in maneuvering his program through the City Council and in dealing with opposition to the project.

7

The Trappings of Democracy

With the adoption of the project plan by Detroit's Economic Development Corporation in September of 1980, the city was ready to proceed. Yet the niceties of local democracy, as well as the specifics of the economic-development enabling legislation, dictated that the residents of the project area be consulted and that a full and frank consideration of the plan be undertaken by the City Council.

Thus, in September, success was far from assured. Indeed, a new phase had begun, one that had significant potential for derailing the project. From now on the project had to be scrutinized by bodies that had varying degrees of decision-making authority, any of which could cause a significant delay or even the termination of the project. In the final analysis, however, these bodies failed to challenge the project seriously or even to raise meaningfully the significant issues of financing and long-term benefits to the city.

THE ECONOMIC DEVELOPMENT CORPORATION

Detroit's Economic Development Corporation (EDC), the official sponsor of the Poletown project, also acted on behalf of the Hamtramck EDC, in accordance with a formal agreement between the two communities.[1] The municipalities acted under state enabling legislation that permitted such agreements.[2] The arrangement provided that Detroit would receive two-thirds and Hamtramck one-third of the project revenues after certain administrative and project costs had been paid.[3] The City of Detroit would both do most of the work on the project and receive most of the revenue.

109

The membership of Detroit's EDC is drawn solely from city officials and businessmen. In 1981 the members of the EDC's board of directors, of which the mayor is chairman, were George E. Bushnell, Jr., a partner in the law firm of Bushnell, Gage, and Reizen; Albert T. Hastings, director of real-estate property management for General Motors Corporation; city council-man Nicholas Hood; Robert E. McCabe, president of Detroit Renaissance, an organization of elite businessmen committed to downtown redevelopment and responsible for the Renaissance Center; the director of Detroit's CEDD, Emmett S. Moten, Jr.; Dr. William F. Pickard of McDonald's franchise; Daniel S. Voydanoff, a vice-president of the National Bank of Detroit; and Robert E. Winkel, president of Crowley's, an area department store. There were no representatives of labor, the neighborhoods, or small business.

The GM project is the largest in which the EDC has been involved. Its other activities in the period 1979 to 1981 included: the issuance of EDC revenue bonds totaling about $30 million, which were used to assist the expansion and renovation of the facilities of twelve firms employing a total of thirteen hundred workers; the preparation and marketing of an industrial-park site in the east-side Conner industrial corridor; and working with government officials and businesses in the administration of Urban Development Action Grants.

Although composed predominantly of representatives of the private sector, the EDC is granted quasi-public powers. It may construct, improve, and maintain projects and may acquire land for project sites; it may borrow money and issue revenue notes to finance all or part of the cost of the acquisition, purchase, construction, or improvement of a project site; it may lease or sell part or all of the project to a person or to a corporation; it is responsible for designating a project area and for preparing a project plan.

Notes and bonds issued by an EDC constitute nonguaranteed debt for the municipality in which it operates. Nevertheless, like municipal bonds, they are tax exempt. Although EDCs cannot directly take private property, because they lack the power of eminent domain, a municipality may acquire private property and transfer it to its EDC for use in an approved project, and this "taking, transfer, and use shall be considered necessary for public purposes and for the benefit of the public."[4] Funds for the administration of the Detroit EDC are set aside in the city's application for Community Development Block Grants; funds for EDC projects come from the sale of bonds and, through the city, from state and federal grants and loans.

The board of Detroit's EDC was also designated as the board of directors for the tax-increment financing authority that was established for the project. In this capacity, its powers included the preparation of economic analysis; the formulation and implementation of plans for the revitalization of designated development areas; the acquisition, demolition, relocation, and rehabilitation of property in development areas; the preparation of building sites and the construction of public facilities; the borrowing of money and the issuing of bonds.[5] It was responsible for preparing a tax-increment financing plan for approval by the City Council and for reporting annually to the council on the status of that plan.

The EDC, both in its role as project developer and tax-increment authority for the Central Industrial Park project, was little more than the ratifier and legitimizer of decisions that were made by the executive departments of the city of Detroit. Project plans were developed in the negotiations (to the degree that they could be called that) between Mayor Young and development director Moten and their counterparts at General Motors. The details of the project, including the formulating of financial and relocation plans, the carrying out of the acquisition of property and relocation activities, and the coordinating of the actions of the interdepartmental, intergovernmental, and city/GM task forces, fell to the professional staff of the Community and Economic Development Department (CEDD). The EDC was completely reliant on analyses and decisions made by the CEDD's staff. Chaired by Mayor Young, with Moten and Young's City Council ally Nicholas Hood as members, the EDC was not a public/private partnership; it was simply a vehicle to get around certain limitations on municipal government in the sphere of economic development. It is not too strong to characterize the businessmen on the EDC as tools, albeit willing tools, of the Young administration.

THE CENTRAL INDUSTRIAL PARK
CITIZENS' DISTRICT COUNCIL

Michigan's economic-development legislation authorizes municipal governments to establish citizens' district councils for project areas, but it leaves the final decision on establishment, as well as the composition of the body, to the discretion of the municipality.[6] On the recommendation of the CEDD, Detroit's City Council established the Central Industrial Park Citizens' District Council (CDC). The City Council also agreed to most of the CEDD's recommendations in appointing members to the CDC but added a few members on the advice of the City Planning Commission, an advisory body to the council.

The membership of the Central Industrial Park CDC included six owners of businesses in the project area, four representatives of institutions located in the area (two churches, a hospital, and a public school), and twelve residents. Because they were appointed by the city, most of the members initially favored the project, but a few known opponents were included among the original nominees in order to avoid accusations of bias. The views of the opponents has little influence on the CDC's actions.

Although the EDC is required to "consult with" the CDC and the CDC is required to submit recommendations to the City Council, the CDC is only an advisory body, and its failure to approve a project plan would not prevent the City Council from adopting that plan. State statutes do not explain what is meant by consultation; in this project, it was interpreted as staff attendance at CDC meetings to answer questions, but not to solicit citizen opinions. Dependent as they were on the information provided by these experts, CDC members were not equipped to participate as equals in the preparation or implementation of the project plan. In addition to information, the CDC may, upon request, receive "technical assistance" relevant to the preparation of the project plan; minimum compliance with this requirement was provided by staff attendance at meetings of the CDC.

Despite its inability to obtain relevant technical information, the Central Industrial Park CDC, under Act 338, was required to notify the City Council of its recommendations concerning the project plan. When these recommendations were forthcoming, CEDD's staff raised numerous technical and legal objections to their requests. Lengthy negotiations were required to resolve these disagreements so that the City Council was not forced to choose between the conflicting views of an administrative agency and a citizens' organization. During these negotiations, CDC representatives were able to secure from city staff some concessions, which were included in the revised project plan adopted by the City Council.

Discussions of recommendations for the project plan took the form of a dialogue between CDC members and CEDD's director of community development, Thomas Cunningham, with comments being interjected by attorneys who represented area businessmen. CDC proposals included the establishment of tax abatements and low-interest mortgages for relocated residents; the expediting of court hearings for residents who contested the city's offers for their property; the moving of homes; the payment by the city of attorney's fees for those who contested the city's offers; the stipulation that any increased award by the court should not be deducted from payments for relocation; not forcing people to move in cold weather; giving area residents priority in demolition and construction jobs for the project; and the providing of waivers of zoning regulations for businesses such as taverns to facilitate their relocation. CDC incorporated these and other suggestions into a set of specific recommendations for action by the CEDD.

Several of the recommendations were strongly opposed by the CEDD on the grounds that relevant state and federal legislation did not permit or require such measures. These recommendations included (1) that each property owner be provided with a copy of the city's appraisal for each piece of property, (2) the assurance that increased awards for acquisition resulting from court settlements should not be deducted from awards for replacement housing, (3) provision of a $1,500 "dislocation allowance" to home owners whose property taxes increased as a result of relocation, (4) the extension of the rent-free period after the city's acquisition of property in the case of senior citizens and handicapped persons, (5) provision of four relocation referrals to residents and businesses (instead of the two required for residents only by HUD regulations), (6) the establishment of task forces, composed of equal numbers of representatives from the city and the CDC, to handle such specific issues as house moving and zoning waivers.

Negotiations between the CEDD and the CDC continued until and throughout the day when the City Council took its final vote on the project plan. Several council meetings were devoted to hearing each side's position, reasons for disagreement, and reports on compromises that had been reached since the previous discussion. Debate continued into the evening at lengthy CDC meetings, with CEDD's Cunningham attempting to explain his department's positions and to mediate disagreements. CDC members, with the exception of the minority who opposed the project, were strongly committed to their recommendations, and they threatened to withdraw their support of the project plan if these recommendations were not incorporated as amendments to it. While the CDC's role was only advisory and while its approval was not necessary for the adoption of the plan, its lack of support would have put the City Council in the awkward position of opposing the official representatives of the project area if the council were to vote to approve a project plan that was not endorsed by the CDC. Members of the City Council, whose choices were limited to approving or rejecting the project plan, grew increasingly irritated at being used as what one member called a "forum for dialogue" between the CEDD and the CDC.

Eventually, with the deadline for the council's approval just hours away, the CEDD agreed to provide copies of appraisals, to incorporate the $1,500 allowance for higher taxes, and to extend the rent-free period (and eligibility period for relocation bonuses) for senior citizens, the handicapped, and others who had demonstrated "good faith efforts" to move. Compromises were accepted by both sides on the issues of referrals (three instead of the four proposed by the CDC) and task forces (the CEDD agreed to the concept of task forces but not to granting them final authority in resolving grievances). The issue of whether relocation awards would be reduced in cases of increased court-ordered payments for acquisition was not resolved, and no statement on it was included in the plan. The CEDD's relocation officials later reported that they had computed payments for replacement housing on the basis of the city's acquisition offer and the cost of comparable housing. The CEDD required clients whose awards were to be determined in court to sign an agreement that they would reimburse the city for the amount of the increase if their acquisition payments were raised by the court; HUD regulations and the Uniform Relocation Act, the CEDD claimed, did not permit anything else. The CEDD's eventual acceptance of the CDC's recommendations was facilitated by the fairly minor nature of most of them but was also compelled by the approaching deadline for the adoption of the project plan, which was needed for GM's commitment and for applications for funding.

Opponents of the project raised more major criticisms of the plan at meetings of the CDC and at a City Council hearing on the project, which was conducted jointly with the Advisory Council on Historic Preservation and was required because the project involved the amendment of the city's Master Plan, an application for a Community Development Block Grant, and an application for an Urban Development Action Grant. At meetings of the CDC, the objections of those few members who opposed the project were generally ignored by the chairman, a strong supporter of the project. The views of citizens who attended the meeting were set aside for the last item on the meeting's agenda; by this time, many citizens had left. After the CDC had adopted the revised plan, the inadequacy of the revisions was vehemently criticized by one of its officers, who also served as cochairman of the Poletown Neighborhood Council, which represented opponents of the project. During the "citizen concerns" portion of the meeting, he delivered an impassioned monologue denouncing the lack of discussion of such alternatives as economic diversification, the development of labor-intensive industries, or regional multi-governmental strategies. He was cut off by the CDC's chairman, who ruled him out of order on the grounds that he was not expressing a "citizen concern" and ordered him to leave the meeting.

Lack of consideration for citizen concerns also characterized the evening meeting of the City Council that was devoted to the project. The meeting was held at a high school several miles from the project area, occasioning criticism from some residents, although the CDC provided bus transportation. The meeting featured nearly three hours of presentations by GM and city officials and lengthy commentaries by representatives of historic-preservation agencies. As at the meeting of the CDC, citizen comments were the last item on the agenda. By this time, many citizens had gone home, and City Council members, conspicuously seated in the front of the auditorium, were paying little attention to the proceedings. Each citizen was allotted five minutes, and those who exceeded the time limit were ruled out of order by the council's president, Erma Henderson, who chaired the session.

At this point, neither CDC members nor opponents of the project raised questions about the financing of the project. (Several months later, a study prepared for the Poletown Neighborhood Council by members of Ralph Nader's support staff did raise such questions.) The CDC's primary interest was in improving the treatment and benefits for individuals who were being relocated; the opponents were mainly interested in revising the project plan so that fewer homes would be demolished and in obtaining funding for the revitalization of the remainder of the neighborhood.

COUNCIL POLITICS

Under the City Charter of 1918, Detroit's ward system was abolished and a smaller nine-member council, elected on a nonpartisan ballot from a city-wide district, was substituted. Considerable tension between the council and the mayor has characterized Detroit politics since that time. A 1973 revision of the charter increased the power of the mayor relative to the council, giving the mayor full budgetary powers and a line-item veto. Nevertheless, tensions between the mayor and the council remain high, with both being jealous of its powers relative to the other. Since 1973 the mayor has clearly had the upper hand. One indicator of this is Young's general position on having his department heads testify before the council: they are generally forbidden to do so, even in the face of a council subpoena. Moreover, Young has almost always had enough council support to prevent overrides of his vetoes, which he has used liberally in budgetary matters. During the 1970s and the early 1980s the council has been divided between a black majority of five and a white minority of four, with blacks generally being more supportive of the policies of Young's administration.

The small size of the council has meant that council members have been dependent on city-wide interest groups for electoral support and, consequently, have been less concerned about particular neighborhood-based interests. In council elections by far the most important endorsement is that of the UAW; Democratic congressional-district organizations, other industrial unions, and municipal unions also endorse candidates. Among black organizations, the Shrine of the Black Madonna's Black Slate is most important, and the Shrine is closely associated with Mayor Young. Other black churches provide a forum for the expression of black opinion but are circumspect about making direct endorsements. Young himself has generally refused to endorse candidates directly, but he did provide strong support and thinly veiled endorsements for two council members in 1981, both of whom were elected.

Council politics, as a consequence of electoral arrangement, tend to center on city-wide groups and on city-wide issues. Nevertheless, neighborhood groups are vocal in the city, and the council has adopted the role of speaking for these interests. In the allocation of Community Block Grant funds, the council has wanted more money for neighborhood projects, often opposing Young's focus on downtown development. Young, however, has consistently vetoed the council's changes in his budget, and the council has not been able to muster the votes to override his vetoes. Generally, the council has advocated neighborhood interests as a whole, with council members seldom acting as proponents for particular neighborhoods.

This pattern continued in the politics surrounding the Central Industrial Park project. While council members expressed concern on several occasions about the settlements that residents were receiving, most members were supportive of the project itself. Only the radical councilman Kenneth Cockrell voted against the project at any stage, and he did so consistently, producing a series of 8 to 1 votes on the various measures. He did so on ideological grounds rather than on the basis of considerations of neighborhood interest, however.

THE CITY COUNCIL ACTS ON THE PROJECT PLAN

State enabling legislation grants the City Council fairly extensive formal responsibilities in economic-development projects. These include: (1) the approval of the mayor's appointments to the EDC board; (2) the conducting of a public hearing on the project plan; (3) the approval or rejection of the project plan, including financial arrangements; (4) the establishment of district-area boundaries for the project; (5) the establishment of a citizens' district council, if the City Council determines that one is necessary, and the approval of appointees to that council.

These formal requirements set forth essentially a legitimizing function for the City Council: in each case, action by the council ratifies a recommendation from an administrative agency, giving the views of the experts the approval of a democratically elected body. In carrying out these responsibilities, Detroit's City Council assumed an active, if not an influential, role. From the time that it was informed of the project in July 1980 until it adopted the project plan in late October, the council scheduled numerous discussions of the project during its regular meetings, as well as several special meetings that were devoted exclusively to the project. These sessions involved the close questioning of EDC and CEDD officials and the examination of the recommendations of the CDC in regard to the project plan. Throughout this period the council received advice from the staff of the City Planning Commission, which provides the council with advice about various proposals presented by executive agencies. The planning commission's ability to present independent recommendations was limited, however, by its dependency on executive agencies for information and by the tight time schedule that had been imposed by General Motors. This time schedule also prevented the council from giving careful study to the planning commission's recommendations and often forced it to act on the basis of very little information or with very little understanding of the available information. The council's discussions, then, seem to have served mainly a symbolic function, creating the impression that the council was conducting an independent review and careful study, when, in the end, its votes simply ratified the proposals of the executive branch.

Council action was also necessary for the granting of a tax abatement and for the establishment of a tax-increment financing plan. Council discussions on these issues also demonstrated the lack of information and the time constraints under which that body was required to act. Applications for the UDAG grant and for the HUD Section 108 loans also had to be approved by the council. Although council members occasionally expressed reservations, they voted 8 to 1 in favor of all these proposals. Each approval contributed to the momentum of the project and was used to justify subsequent actions. For example, CEDD officials who requested that the council establish the tax-increment financing authority emphasized that this action was required by the Interlocal Agreement with Hamtramck, which the council had approved the previous year.

Most of the council's energies were directed at securing the well-being of neighborhood residents and at attacking the perceived arrogance of GM. How the city would pay for the project did not overly concern the council members, nor did the relationship between benefits flowing from the project relative to its costs to the public sector. Although several council meetings were devoted to explanations of the financial arrangements, these arrangements were complex and hard to understand. Moreover, the financial applications, which the council had to approve, came to the council piecemeal, many of them before the final approval of the project plan. A week prior to voting on the project plan, the council approved several resolutions dealing with various aspects of financing the project: the authorizing of two loans of $1.4 million each from the Michigan State Housing Development Authority and the EDC; the accepting of the contract for the initial $60.5-million Section 108 loan and authorizing the use of funds from the city's block-grant letter-of-credit account; the authorizing of an additional $30.5-million Section 108 loan; and the authorizing of an application for a $30-million Urban Development Action Grant. The piecemeal approval of financing prevented a comprehensive review of financial arrangements. It also increased the dependence of the council on the CEDD's economic-development experts.

Doubts were expressed by the staff of the City Planning Commission about the availability of state funds, but the primary area of concern both of the planning commission and of the council was the letter-of-credit arrangement. Both feared that this would result in the transfer of funds from ongoing projects funded by block grants. A resolution prepared by the staff of the planning commission stipulated that the council receive "for its review and approval" a list of each block-grant project from which it was proposed that funds be drawn, as well as the amount of funds to be transferred. Officials of the CEDD explained that funds would be drawn from a bank account and that specific projects could not be identified; they objected to the council's becoming involved in the spending of block-grant funds on individual projects. By an 8 to 1 vote the council adopted the resolution that authorized the use of the letter-of-credit account, subject to the previously stipulated conditions. Other elements of the financial package were approved by the same vote, despite evident confusion on the part of council members about what they were voting for. This confusion would arise again when the council voted on a tax abatement for the project in April 1981 and when it approved a tax-increment financing plan in April 1982.

Approval of the financing package that had finalized some earlier financial agreements—namely, the authorization of federal loans and the transfer of block-grant funds—and contributed to the momentum of the project by continuing a sequence of policy decisions in which each action was justified by a previous one. The major decision of approving the project plan was accomplished with little resistance because it was the next logical step in the sequence of events. Approval of the project plan also concluded the City Council's involvement in project policies until it was called upon to adopt a tax abatement six months later.

MAYOR YOUNG'S ROLE

The weakness of the City Council and of the Citizens' District Council contrasted sharply with the leadership role that Mayor Coleman Young assumed. In Young the City of Detroit had an aggressive and talented black leader. He came to political awareness through the rough-and-tumble politics of the UAW, where he was known as an able, outspoken radical. He served in the Michigan Senate from 1964 through 1973, when he was elected mayor of Detroit in a bitterly fought, racially polarized race against the city's commissioner of police. Young's early years as mayor were characterized by considerable acrimony between the mayor, on the one hand, and Detroit's entrenched civil-service bureaucracy on the other. Relationships with the police were particularly rough. His strong advocacy of an affirmative-action program and his reversal of several longstanding departmental policies solidified opposition among police officers and their union spokesmen.

Throughout his first term in office, Young steadfastly cultivated the major elements of Detroit's power structure: his own black electoral coalition, the city's economic elite, union officials, and the state and federal elected officials and bureaucrats who could provide funds to a city that was experiencing increasing economic difficulty. When he was challenged in his 1977 reelection campaign by black councilman Ernie Browne, who was supported by police and fire unions, Young emphasized his ties with the Democratic administration of Jimmy Carter in Washington and the Republican administration in Lansing. "He Brings Home the Bacon" read his billboards, which were placed along all major freeways. Young's electoral organization, which was funded by contributions from unions, from businessmen, and from black organizations, crushed Browne and his very efficient support from the city's unions. Young was reelected once again in 1981, this time with only token opposition.

By the late 1970s Young was, for all practical purposes, unchallengeable. Socialist councilman Kenneth Cockrell, a long-time critic of Mayor Young's cozy association with business leaders and a mayoral aspirant himself, failed to file for reelection in 1981. Cockrell frankly admitted that a challenge to Young in the near future was simply impossible; therefore he returned to his law practice. Deeply disappointed were Cockrell's supporters, who gathered together for several years in an organization called the Detroit Association for Radical Economics (DARE). The possibility of a radical challenge to Young had disappeared, just as the conservative challenge had been thwarted four years previously.

Mayor Young was critical to the success of the Central Industrial Park project in three ways. First, and most importantly, his firm and deep popular support assured that opponents of the project would be an isolated minority and allowed Young almost unlimited room for maneuvering. It allowed him to act as the sole spokesman for the city's interest, a role that he performed with considerable skill. Young's uncanny ability to project an image of sweet reason on some occasions and that of a vicious stump speaker on others became a prime asset when it was backed up with the solid electoral support that he enjoyed. A vitriolic attack on consumer activist Ralph Nader, who intervened on behalf of opponents of the project, during which Young characterized Nader as a "carpetbagger," was leveled with no harmful effects to Young's local political support but with considerable to Nader's.

Some idea of the magnitude of Young's support in the Detroit electorate may be gleaned from a survey financed by the *Detroit Free Press* in late 1980. He enjoyed a 93 percent approval rating among blacks and 47 percent among white Detroiters. This translated into an overall approval of 72 percent.[7] Five years later, Young's positive rating had declined to a still-impressive 73.3 percent among Detroit's blacks but to 13.7 percent among whites.[8] In 1980, Young had the unequivocal backing of almost all blacks and the grudging admiration of a sizable minority of whites.

Young's support, which was strong among all blacks but was particularly vigorous among the poorest segment of the black community, and his ties with the union movement gave him a political base that was independent of Detroit's economic elite. This political base allowed him to counteract the charge that the project primarily benefited a private corporation. In every public forum he stressed the project's potential impact on the city's unemployment problem, thus raising the manipulation of the symbol of jobs to an art form. He also became actively involved in discrediting the opponents of the project by attacking the representativeness of the opposition Poletown Neighborhood Council. He continued his vocal attacks on the opposition by claiming that there was no particular ethnic character to the neighborhood and, hence, that there was no compelling reason to save a neighborhood that he referred to as deteriorating. Young always refused to refer to the neighborhood as Poletown, preferring the phrase "that ethnically mixed area that some people have labeled Poletown."

Young's other contributions to the success of the project were his extensive connections with Washington and Lansing and the competence of the officials whom he had assembled to implement his economic-development objectives. The director of the CEDD, Emmett Moten, acted as development entrepreneur, while a thoroughly professional project team was assembled by Young and Moten to carry out the project. While these factors were extremely important, Young's major contribution stemmed from his unassailable position as political leader. In classic form, this political support was translated into power in the particular instance of the Central Industrial Park project, which added further to Young's acclaim as a political leader.

CONCLUSIONS

In local politics, power matters. Detroit has long been characterized by a freewheeling entrepreneurial politics in which great projects are planned, often to be smashed on the realities of the economic circumstances and the political complexities of the city. If the great projects are to be completed, then the extensive mobilization of political resources and the skillful deployment of those resources are necessary. Opponents of change hold a built-in advantage, and only in exceptional circumstances can major change occur.

Once the city had accepted GM's offer, it was on its own in completing the project. While much has been made in some analyses of the "ganging up" of the city and the corporation on the helpless neighborhood,[9] in reality the corporation set the conditions that it wanted met and then withdrew from the fray. Even if one were to accept the view that the city was an instrument of the corporation, one is left with the issue of how city officials were able to succeed with no overt and scant covert help from the corporation. The endeavor was controversial, it was expensive, and it had to be accomplished in a short time. Everything operated against the success of the project.

Two issues of community power are raised here: one is whether the city acted as an instrument of the corporation in accepting the latter's demands and in carrying them out; the second is why the city was able to prevail in the more limited arena of implementing the project. If the city was an instrument, it was a very effective instrument.

While we shall return to these issues later, some comments are in order at present. In the first place, it would be a mistake to attribute any power whatsoever to the businessmen who were represented on the EDC. The EDC was a tool of Young and Moten and was completely reliant on staff from the CEDD, a city agency. The EDC played no part in the politics of Poletown.

In the second place, the city's designated neighborhood representative, the Central Industrial Park Citizens' District Council, proved to be as supportive of the project as city officials had hoped it would be. While the CDC displayed considerable feistiness in negotiating with the staff of the CEDD for specific benefit provisions, it was negotiating within a very limited arena. The strategy of the city to undercut potential neighborhood-based opposition by designating a CDC and by providing lucrative relocation benefits worked to limit the effectiveness of the project's neighborhood opponents.

Third, the City Council failed to serve as an arena for marshaling the opposition to the project. The council, although it was weakened by the 1973 change in the charter, possessed sufficient formal authority to block the project if it had wished to do so. Instead, it served primarily as a resource for the CDC in the latter's negotiations with the CEDD over the specifics of the relocation package. The council did not seriously consider the project's worth or the power of the corporation or the problematic financial arrangements. Rather, it served to force the CEDD to grant extra benefits to neighborhood residents because council members did not want to adopt the project plan in the face of opposition from the CDC. Members of the council expressed reservations about some aspects of the financing, primarily the siphoning off of funds from other neighborhood projects. Generally, however, the council deferred to economic-development experts from the CEDD on matters of financing the project. This meant that the council could not evaluate the costs and benefits of the project independently. Several council members decried the arrogance both of GM and of the heads of city agencies (who routinely refused to testify before the council), but they compliantly voted 8 to 1 for every aspect of the project.

While the members of the council were not equipped technically to debate the merits of the project, there was a further overriding political component to the noninvolvement of that body. Council members were not about to challenge the coalition of supporters that the mayor had assembled. The council had very limited range for maneuvering, and its members knew this.

Young and Moten held the keys to success. Young's electoral support, his access to state and national officials, and his union connections were all elements in a democratic steam-roller that crushed the opposition with ease. He was able to mobilize his support in the electorate by making repeated symbolic appeals to the need for jobs and sustained public attacks on the opponents of the project. While such public attacks carry with them the risk of backfiring by alienating public support, Young's unequivocal support within the black electorate protected against this. Indeed, his attacks probably served to promote a we-versus-them solidarity among Detroiters.

Young provided the necessary political resources and the skills to mobilize them, and Moten provided the technical expertise and the administrative ability to complete the project. Some years later, GM's chairman Roger Smith said, "As I look out my window and see that plant for 600 million bucks, I just know it wouldn't be there if it weren't for Coleman Young."[10] Young was impertinent enough to demand from GM the opportunity to compete for the plant and ruthless enough to push the project through to completion against considerable odds.

8

The Democratic Steam Roller: Poletown in Court

The council's resolution of 30 October 1980 approved the project plan, declared that the GM's plant fulfilled a "public purpose," and authorized the CEDD to proceed with acquisiton of the property. It also signaled the start of court proceedings. Under the "quick take law" (P.A. 87), passed just prior to the initiation of the project (see chapter 5), city lawyers would, within a month, file a complaint in Wayne County Circuit Court for acquisition of those pieces of property for which negotiated settlements on acquisition prices could not be reached. This would initiate the condemnation process, in which owners could file motions challenging the adequacy of their awards. A series of individual trials would be conducted to resolve disputed offers. Adoption of the plan also allowed area residents to file legal action against the city and the EDC.[1] Such a suit was filed immediately by the Poletown Neighborhood Council, and hearings commenced on 17 November 1980 in the courtroom of Judge George Martin of the Wayne County Circuit Court.

The suit charged that the city had abused its authority by not adequately considering alternative sites or plans and that the project did not constitute a "public purpose" because a private corporation would be the chief beneficiary of it. The suit raised important constitutional issues relating to eminent domain and questioned the authority that the state had granted to the city and to the EDC to determine the public necessity of projects.

THE CITY ADMITS ITS ROLE

Oral testimony given by city officials in the case was the first public admission of just how far city officials had gone to meet the requirements set down by General Motors and how unwilling the company had been to alter any of its initial specifications. The director of the City Planning Commission, which advises the City Council, described his group's minimal involvement in the planning of the project and in selecting the site; he observed that his staff had not conducted a thorough investigation because it had not been given assurance that anything it did would affect GM's conditions and because the time involved in such a study could have jeopardized the project's deadlines. Director Moten of the CEDD, whose staff had done most of the planning for the project, claimed that city officials had attempted to negotiate changes in GM's site critieria, but that the corporation had stood fast on them. According to Moten, these changes included less spacious parking and the use of the old Dodge Main power plant. GM's rejection of these changes, according to Moten, created a situation in which the corporation, like other developers, said, in effect, "this (site plan) or somewhere else." Other testimony described the added cost (to GM) of changes in the standard plan and the delay that would result from the development of alternatives; the implication was that these concerns would have led GM to build the plant elsewhere.

According to the testimony of Mayor Young, General Motors' chairman, Thomas Murphy, when he approached Young with the offer to build the plant, indicated that the company had received offers from "several states outside of Michigan."[2] Young emphasized the jobs that would be lost to the city of Detroit by the closing of the old Cadillac plant and the construction of a new facility outside of Detroit. Under cross-examination by Poletown's attorney Ronald Reosti, Young pointed out that the city had independently verified GM's need for the acreage involved in the project site, and he summarized the outcome of the site-review process. Young's desire to have the plant built is evident throughout his testimony: "This program is beyond a doubt the most important single program that has been undertaken since I became Mayor. . . . If we can assemble this land . . . and provide a strengthening industrial base for our state, . . . I think we can open up an approach for other northern industrial cities . . . to relocate and to reassemble and to attract industry."[3] From Young's perspective, the city's interests and GM's interests coincided, and "negotiations" involved merely the working out of details, not the resolution of major disagreements.

Moten's testimony also indicates acceptance of the corporation's terms: "We were given the criteria (for the plant site) by GM . . . and we looked at several sites in the city of Detroit. We tried to match their criteria based on the sites that we were looking at. . . . We also took into account the population base that we were dealing with . . . there would be potential relocation of people."[4] Later, under cross-examination, Moten suggested that some negotiation had been attempted: "We approached it as if we had as much negotiating power as possible to make sure that every element would be thoroughly examined . . . we wanted to get less acreage, the ability to accommodate parking and different modes than they were suggesting. . . . We tried our best with the restraints we had to negotiate the best possible parcel of land for this specific project."[5] Pressed by Reosti, however, Moten acknowledged that, in the end, GM's criteria had been accepted. But he added: "Developers state the criteria. It is not peculiar to this project." Reosti also questioned Moten at length about the city's efforts to convince GM to use an existing Dodge Main power plant, which eventually failed because, in Moten's words, "It deviated from their footprint," or prototype site plan, which had been used in other locations. The choice of GM's project plan or no project plan left little room for bargaining or compromise, and though neither Young nor Moten would explicitly admit this, the city was not in a strong bargaining position.

Young's testimony emphasized the serious fiscal problems being faced by the city, with repeated references to the deterioration of its economic base, the loss of jobs, the increasing unemployment, budget deficits, the layoffs of city employees, and cutbacks in city services. The city's attorney, Jason Honigman, explored these topics at length with the mayor, securing abundant testimony on the relationship between the topics and the public interest and public purpose that provide the legal basis for land acquisition under P.A. 338. The following exchanges are indicative of how Honigman introduced testimony that could be used to support the legality of the EDC's actions:

> Q. Is that, in your opinion, a public purpose to have your Detroit citizens have jobs available?
> A. I should think so. . . .
> Q. In what way is that a public purpose?
> A. To the degree that it is in the public interest to provide adequate services to our people . . . it is necessary to have a tax base, and the basic ingredient of a tax base is jobs and manufacturing. . . .
> Q. What about the need of the citizens to have adequate employment?
> A. . . . It is clearly in the interest of any society to have its citizens employed.[6]

Reosti continually raised objections to these questions as "leading" and forcing the witness to draw conclusions, but he was unsuccessful in preventing these comments from being introduced. Both Circuit Judge Martin and the majority of the Michigan Supreme Court accepted these arguments and used them to support their opinions on the legality of the project.

THE FINANCIAL WIZARD TESTIFIES

Attempting to weaken the city's claim to public benefit, Reosti questioned Moten closely on the methods of financing the project. Neither Judge Martin nor Reosti seemed to understand Moten's explanation of how the federal loan mechanisms operated. Reosti sought to demonstrate that the utilization of the loan would jeopardize current block-grant projects and that the city lacked the resources to repay the loans, but Moten's detailed responses served only to illustrate his more sophisticated knowledge of the complicated financial package and the operation of various federal programs. At one point, Moten asked, "Do you follow what I am saying, counsel?" Reosti replied, "Not really . . . up to that time I thought I followed you, but then you got away from me," and Judge Martin interjected, "You brought thirty million out of the air."[7]

These reactions were not atypical, according to others who have worked with Moten. A member of the City Planning Commission's staff described him as "disarming" and commented that "unless you keep probing, you do lose sight of your original question."[8] Moten's former boss, Moon Landrieu, described Moten thus: "A master of obscurity. When he went before city council down here and didn't have a rational explanation for something, he'd talk for a long time, and afterward, everyone would say, 'What did he say?' "[9] In the courtroom, as elsewhere, it was evident that Moten's contributions to the success of the project involved not only what he knew and said but also how he said it.

POLETOWN PRESENTS ITS CASE

Expert witnesses for the Poletown group introduced alternative site plans which would have required less demolition by changing the alignment of rail yards and by replacing parking lots with roof parking or parking structures. Had the city used independent analysts, instead of accepting GM's dictates, the Poletown attorneys argued, these alternatives might have been investigated. In addition to raising the issues of costs and delay, the Detroit lawyers attempted to undermine the credibility of the Poletown expert witnesses by questioning them extensively about their lack of experience in designing automobile assembly plants.

The close relationship between city officials and GM during the planning stages of the project was interpreted by the Poletown attorneys as evidence that GM, not the city, was both the initiator and the chief beneficiary of the project, which therefore served a private, rather than a public, purpose. The city's position was that the jobs and tax revenues to be generated by the project constituted public benefits that would far exceed any private advantages secured by GM.

Although early city documents on the project had asserted that it would create five thousand new jobs, this position had been sufficiently criticized so that the city's attorneys did not try to sustain it in court. Instead, they emphasized the retention of employment opportunities (the jobs at the Clark Avenue and Fleetwood plants would not be lost to another city or state if the new plant were built in Detroit) as constituting a legally recognized public purpose, and they stressed the number of spin-off jobs that would be preserved or stimulated by construction of the plant (estimates ranged up to twenty-five thousand, a generous multiplier factor). Involvement of GM in the project, they claimed, did not eliminate these public benefits; rather, it was necessary for the achievement of them. Previous court decisions, they asserted, had affirmed that the involvement of a private corporation was permissible in such instances.

In response, Reosti cited the definition of the limits of the power of eminent domain in the Michigan Constitution to support his argument that the GM project did not fall within this definition of public purpose: the Constitution did not authorize the use of eminent domain to benefit a specific industrial concern. Evidence introduced in the case, he claimed, demonstrated that the motivating factor for the project was to provide land to GM and that the provisions of the project plan were dictated by GM and served the interests of GM. These conditions, he claimed, amounted to turning private property over to a private corporation, in direct violation of the Michigan Constitution.

PUBLIC PURPOSES

The definition of what constitutes a public purpose or a public benefit in this situation is problematic. At issue in the court case were several questions: (1) whether the Poletown project served the public purposes enumerated by Act 338 (which include the alleviating and preventing of unemployment, the retention of local industries, and the encouraging of industrial enterprises in reconstructing, modernizing, and expanding in the state and its municipalities); (2) whether these purposes fell within the scope of the proper exercise of eminent domain under the state constitution; (3) whether the provisions of P.A. 87 (the "quick take" law) permit a public agency to define public necessity on its own, restricting the courts from judging on public necessity and limiting them to deciding whether the public agency's determination of necessity involved fraud, error of law, or abuse of discretion; (4) whether the actions of the city of Detroit in relation to the project constituted an "abuse of discretion" under P.A. 87. A separate question involved the Poletown charge that the city had violated Michigan's Environmental Protection Act by failing to consider the negative social and cultural impacts that the project would have and by failing to consider adequate measures for the mitigation of these impacts.

The final arguments before the circuit court provide some clarification of the confusing and closely interrelated issues of public necessity, public purpose, and the abuse of discretion. Reosti, arguing on behalf of the Poletown organization, asserted that the city, by accepting GM's site criteria, by inadequately evaluating alternative sites and site plans, and by acting on the basis of insufficient information on financing and tax abatements, not only had abused its discretion but had also failed to exercise any discretion. Its actions, he charged, set a dangerous precedent for giving in to corporate demands. The influence of GM throughout the project-planning process, as well as the city's explicit objective of transferring the project site to the corporation, he further charged, clearly showed that the project did not serve a public purpose and that it represented an illegal use of the right of eminent domain.

Lawyers for the city and for the EDC countered that Reosti had failed to prove abuse of discretion and that, in fact, there had been an extensive review of alternative sites, there had been negotiation with GM, and considerable information had been presented to the City Council prior to the adoption of the project plan. Determination of public necessity, they contended, was delegated by P.A. 87 to the city and was a legislative function, not subject to judicial intervention. Development of jobs was recognized by P.A. 338 as a public purpose, and the involvement of a private corporation in carrying out this public purpose had been ruled permissible in a "long line" of cases, according to the EDC's attorney Eric Clay. The "public purpose" of providing employment was reemphasized by Detroit's attorney Jason Honigman. It was, he charged, "simplistic" to argue that GM, by getting use of the property, would receive all the benefits from the project. Honigman concluded by reminding the court of the time constraints that had been imposed by GM's requirement that the city have title to all property in the project area by 1 May 1981; he urged that the circuit court, as well as any later appeals court, reach a speedy decision.

Within the week, Judge Martin ruled in the city's favor, rejecting both the claim that there had been abuse of discretion and the claim that the project provided primarily private benefits. The Poletown Neighborhood Council immediately appealed Martin's decision to the Michigan Supreme Court, which heard oral arguments from both sides on 3 March 1981, in the presence of a delegation of seventy neighborhood residents. As they had in the circuit court, both sides pressed for a speedy decision; city officials were especially concerned about this because on February 20 the Supreme Court had issued an injunction that prohibited the city from acquiring property in the area, from sending notices to the residents to vacate their property, and from beginning any new demolition until the court had decided the case.

THE SUPREME COURT CLEARS THE PATH

The Michigan Supreme Court, in a 5 to 2 decision issued on 13 March 1981, ruled that the taking of property for economic development could serve a public purpose and, therefore, that P.A. Act 338 did not violate the Michigan Constitution. The court also ruled that the Michigan Environmental Protection Act did not protect cultural, social, and historical institutions. In the majority opinion, the court noted that its role in the determination of public purpose was limited, because the Michigan Legislature in P.A. 338 had declared that projects of this type must serve an essential public purpose. This purpose—the alleviating of unemployment and the revitalizing of the economic base of the community—far exceeded the benefits to GM, according to the majority opinion. In other cases, the court suggested, the public benefit might not be so clear and significant, and the court might hesitate to sanction such projects.[10]

The two dissenting justices, however, concluded that "the proposed condemnation clearly exceeds the government's authority to take private property" and expressed concern that the court's ruling could set a precedent for "the most outrageous confiscation of private property for the benefit of other private interest without redress." A month later, Justice James Ryan, a Republican who was reputed to be the court's most conservative member, filed an unusually lengthy separate dissent.

JUSTICE RYAN FINDS A CONTROLLING HAND

Ryan prefaced his discussion by noting the speed with which the case was "submitted, argued, considered and decided." He observed "how easily government, in all of its branches, caught up in the frenzy of perceived economic crisis, can disregard the rights of the few in allegiance to the always disastrous philosophy that the end justifies the means."[11] He then reviewed the economic conditions in Detroit and GM's plans, which were used by the city to support its argument that its taking of the property was within the bounds of eminent-domain powers. He concluded: "Thus, it was to a city with its economic back to the wall that General Motors presented its highly detailed 'proposal' for construction of a new plant in a 'green field' location in the city of Detroit . . . as both General Motors and the city knew at the outset, no such 'green field' existed."[12] The search for a site, Ryan emphasized, was shaped by criteria specified by GM: "Behind the frenzy of official activity was the unmistakable guiding and sustaining, indeed controlling hand of the General Motors Corporation. The city administration and General Motors worked in close contact during the summer and autumn of 1980 negotiating the specifics for the new plant site. . . . The corporation conceived the project, determined the cost, allocated the financial burdens, imposed specific deadlines for clearance of property and taking title, and even demanded 12 years of tax concessions."[13] Ryan concluded that what he saw as an unjustified extension of the eminent-domain power by the majority opinion was the consequence of "the overwhelming sense of inevitability" associated with the case, which he attributed to "the coincidence of interests of a desperate city administration and a giant corporation willing and able to take advantage" of an opportunity and to the "team spirit chorus of approval provided by labor, business, government and the news media."[14]

OPPONENTS TRY FEDERAL COURT

The decision of the Michigan Supreme Court signaled the resumption of activities in regard to the acquisition and demolition of property and contributed to an escalation of the depopulation of the neighborhood. By June 1981, records of the CEDD's relocation division indicate that over half the population had left the area. Nevertheless, some opponents continued to challenge the project, filing suits in the United States District Court several days after the state's supreme court had issued its decision. These suits charged that (1) the city had violated the National Environmental Protection Act by inadequately examining smaller plant sites in an Environmental Impact Statement (EIS) before choosing the plant site, (2) the federal government had acted improperly in releasing the $60.5-million Section 108 loan before an EIS had been prepared, and (3) HUD had improperly delegated to the city the role of preparing an EIS.[15] These charges were dismissed by Chief Judge John Feikens in late April, after three weeks of testimony by architects, engineers, area residents, and preparers of the EIS. These suits were characterized by Mayor Young as having a "nuisance character."[16]

The objective of the opponents of the project was to demonstrate that the city had not considered alternative site plans which would have allowed the preservation of the residential portion of the area. Lawyers for both the city and the EDC and Judge Feikens questioned what qualified their expert witnesses to comment on the site plan, claiming that although they were architects, their lack of experience in designing auto assembly plants disqualified them. Leonard Hostetter, director of facilities engineering for GM, who was chairman of the corporate task force involved in planning the new assembly plants and a member of its site-selection task force, was brought in to explain GM's site requirements. Hostetter testified that the Detroit site was the smallest of its new sites for assembly plants and that the corporation had made some compromises in adapting its prototype site plan to it. Specifically, he described how the layout of buildings had been determined by the shape and size of the site, by the turning radius of the rail tracks that would serve the plant, and by concern with providing for expansion. An additional factor was the presence of old industrial foundations and basements in the northern portion of the site which, he said, dictated an avoidance of heavy foundations in that area. Hostetter criticized an alternate plan that had been prepared by architect Richard Ridley. Ridley's plan included a parking garage, but Hostetter defended the use of surface lots, citing maintenance and security problems with parking decks. Decks, he said, would add $20 million to the cost of the plant and would interfere with traffic flow during changes of shifts, but he acknowledged that decks had been used at one GM facility. However, he said that different arrangements of the basic site design had been attempted for other sites and for this site and that no other feasible, efficient arrangement existed. Testimony by a Conrail representative further criticized the Ridley plan, specifically pointing out that the off-site location of the rail marshaling yards was infeasible (yet this was later done in Orion Towship).

Judge Feikens, in explaining his decision, emphasized both the infeasibility of the alternate proposals and the sufficiency of the evaluation of alternatives in the Environmental Impact Statement and noted the city's need for the economic benefits that the plant would provide.

Although several individual suits that challenged the necessity of the project remained to be decided by state courts, Feiken's decisions essentially concluded the legal challenges to the project. Unable to save their neighborhood, opponents then focused on preventing the demolition of Immaculate Conception Church, an issue that moved the locus of action from the courtroom to the streets and to the media.

CONCLUSIONS

Courts are frequently attacked for being a major source of delay and of frustration to the will of the majority, an important component of the "deadlock of democracy."[17] Yet in all of the various suits that were brought in regard to the Central Industrial Park project, the courts moved with unusual speed. While the typical case in Wayne County Circuit Court can take three to five years to reach the trial stage, hearings began on the Poletown case two weeks after the case was filed. In December 1980, less than two months after the case was filed, all testimony had been taken, and Judge Martin had rendered his decision. On 20 February 1981 the Michigan Supreme Court agreed to hear the case (by-passing the intermediate Court of Appeals because of the pressures of time), heard oral arguments on 3 March, and rendered its decision only ten days later. United States District

Judge John Feikens almost as summarily dismissed the contentions that the federal environmental laws had been violated. As a consequence the city was able to meet GM's deadline of 1 May 1981 for the acquisition of title to all pieces of property in the project area.

The possibility of legal sabotage of the Central Industrial Park project had been effectively limited by the Michigan Legislature's passage in the spring of 1980 of the "quick take" law (P.A. 87), which allowed the city to take title to property before reaching agreements with owners on a purchase price. While owners could still challenge the city's offer in court, they could not hold title to the property after it had been condemned. Hence, opponents of the project had to attack the project frontally, alleging that state and federal statutes and state constitutional provisions had been violated.

For all the courts' haste, the legal issues raised by the opponents of the project were not trivial. Public Act 338 (the economic-development legislation) had limited the role of the courts in determining what was a public purpose and had defined the alleviating of unemployment and the retaining of industries as constituting public purposes. Nevertheless, the issues of the legitimate scope of eminent domain and the extent of private versus public benefits had to be determined by the court. As Justice Ryan put it, "In the case before us the reputed public 'benefit' to be gained is inextricably bound to ownership, development and use of the property by one, and only one, private corporation, General Motors, and then only in the manner prescribed by the corporation."[18]

The basic issue before the courts, then, was whether the project provided enough public benefits to justify the taking of private property from one set of owners and conveying it to a second set of owners (GM and Conrail). A majority of the justices of the Michigan Supreme Court answered in the affirmative; a minority stridently disagreed.

There is, however, a second issue. The opponents of the project were a tiny minority within a city whose citizens overwhelmingly supported the policies of Mayor Coleman Young. While most citizens knew little about the specifics of the Central Industrial Park project and some had not even heard about it, they could understand jobs, and they could understand the necessity of supporting the mayor. Indeed, because of the lucrative property settlements and relocation benefits being offered by the city, the opponents of the project were probably a minority within the project area. It is likely that the Citizens' District Council, the city's "front" organization in the neighborhood, more correctly represented majority opinion in the project area than did the opposition Poletown Neighborhood Council. Had the court ruled against the city, it would have performed its classic role of protecting minority interests. To do so, it would have been necessary to override legislative intent, to set aside the determinations of public purpose by a legitimate municipal government, and to overrule majority opinion in the city (and probably in the state of Michigan). Evidently, that was too much for the court to take on.

The logic of Madisonian democracy is delay. Majority opinion is subject to a rush to judgment; courts, in theory, are to provide a high ground of reason in the flood tide of majoritarianism. The deteriorating state of the economy in Michigan ("The economy is in free-fall," commented the state's budget director, Gerald Miller) and the state's reliance on the automotive industry presented an urgency to economic-development policies that stilled any criticism of the Central Industrial Park project. The court, obviously, was not immune to this climate of opinion. Justice Ryan had a point when he accused his colleagues of caving in to the "team spirit chorus of approval provided by labor, business, government and the news media."

Yet it is also important to pay attention to subtleties here. A simplistic view of the corporation's acting contrary to democracy simply will not wash, because the elected democratic institutions and a majority of Detroit's citizens probably supported the project. The courts were not asked to intervene to halt an elitist bargain between the city and the corporation. They were asked to overrule the city's elected branches on behalf of a minority, and a small one at that. Though the city may have concluded a Faustian bargain, its citizens had not objected. If the city had acted as an instrument of capital, the working class heartily approved. To the extent that there was a majority opinion on the project, it was doubtless favorable, even though it had been mobilized by Young's symbolic appeal to the need for jobs during a recession that was matched only by the Great Depression. The court, nevertheless, faced a united front of supporters of the project, made up of state, city, and federal officials and reinforced by majority public opinion, which had been mobilized by the mayor's appeals.

9

The Politics of Tax Loss

In his testimony before the Wayne County Circuit Court, Mayor Young had justified the city's involvement in the Central Industrial Park project on the grounds of the new assembly plant's contribution to the city's tax base: "It is in the public interest to provide adequate services to our people. . . . [To do so] it is necessary to have a tax base, and the basic ingredient of a tax base is jobs and manufacturing."[1] Yet at the time when the mayor was appealing to the public interest in his attempts to bolster the tax base, city lawyers were drafting agreements that would asure that very little of the taxes on the increased value of property in the Central Industrial Park would flow to local governments. Moreover, the city was in the process of signing away property taxes that would have gone to other local governments—primarily the Detroit Independent School District and Wayne County.

Not only would GM receive a twelve-year, 50 percent abatement of property taxes, but a tax-increment financing scheme ensured that local governments would receive only $170,000 in "retained" taxes per year from the project area. This sum would be divided among six units of local government—the city of Detroit, the Detroit Independent School District, Wayne County, the Wayne County Intermediate School District, Wayne County Community College, and the Huron-Clinton Metropolitan Park Authority—even though General Motors would, according to city estimates, pay almost $8 million in property taxes in 1997 alone, the year when the twelve-year tax abatement would expire. The bulk of these tax monies would go to a tax-increment district, which would be responsible for repaying Detroit and Hamtramck for the project costs that these communities had incurred in regard to the Central Industrial Park project. Any surplus tax-increment funds would revert to the taxing bodies "unless the TIFA [Tax Increment Financing Authority] Board of Directors has determined by resolution to retain surplus tax increment funds paid under this Plan for other purposes in furtherance of the CIPP [Central Industrial Park project] development program."[2]

The politics of tax losses, then, contains two policy components. The first concerns the granting of a property-tax abatement; the second, the establishment of a tax-increment financing plan. The former has received much attention in both scholarly and popular literature, with most authorities being highly critical of programs that lower tax liabilities in order to retain or attract industries.[3] Far less attention has been given to the issue of tax-increment financing for industrial development.

THE TAX ABATEMENT

In his letter of 8 October 1980, GM's chairman, Thomas Murphy, had specified that Detroit and Hamtramck were to establish a plant-rehabilitation district and were to grant the "maximum allowable tax abatement" under Michigan law. On 2 April 1981, Detroit's City Council approved, not a plant-rehabilitation district, but an industrial-redevelopment district at the request of the CEDD's director, Emmett Moten.

Once again policy subtleties were important. The state of Michigan's enabling legislation for property-tax abatements allows municipalities to freeze property taxes on a replacement facility for twelve years at the levels of taxes on the facility that is being replaced. In an industrial-development district, on the other hand, the enabling legislation allows municipalities to grant a reduction in millage of up to 50 percent for twelve years.[4] Initial estimates suggested that the plant-rehabilitation approach would produce $4.3 million annually in taxes, while the industrial-development approach would yield $9.1 million.[5] Calculations presented to the City Council projected that GM would pay only $5.4 million annually in local property taxes under the industrial-development approach, and the tax-increment financing plan projected $6.8 million in 1985, declining thereafter.[6]

While all of this suggests the inexact science of tax projections, there was no debate on the projection that the industrial-development approach would yield more tax revenue than would the plant-rehabilitation approach. According to GM's Vice-President David Potter, the corporation revised its request out of concern for the city's financial plight. City officials, however, claim that they had negotiated the change with GM. In actuality, the parties were bound by a provision in the enabling legislation that required a plant-rehabilitation district to be contiguous to the existing facility.

CONFRONTATION AT THE CITY COUNCIL

The City Council's consideration of GM's request for a tax abatement presented the only forum during the history of the project in which representatives from the opposing sides faced one another in person. To opponents of the project, the issue was highly symbolic: the arrogant corporation was demanding maximum concessions from the destitute city, which was struggling desperately to balance a budget that had been stricken by the worst economic downturn since the 1930s.

During the council's initial discussion about establishing the industrial-development district, several members raised the issue of the city's desperate financial situation in an attempt to persuade GM to withdraw its request for a tax abatement. At the time the city was asking its residents to adopt an income-tax increase, was negotiating a wage freeze with city employees, and was cutting its services in order to offset its huge budget deficit. Members agonized over granting a multi-million-dollar tax reduction to a "financially healthy" corporation. In response to a request from Councilman Clyde Cleveland to "tell us one way or the other if you are or aren't going to build the plant without an abatement," GM's Vice-President Potter hedged. If the abatement were not granted, Potter said, "economic factors go against Detroit." Questioned by Councilman Jack Kelley, Potter responded that even with the abatement, GM's taxes were higher in Detroit than elsewhere. Without the abatement, Potter alleged, the corporation "would have to go back and rethink" its decision. Although Potter would not confirm a UAW claim that GM had plans to locate the plant in Alabama, he described the city as a supplier of land to the corporation, in competition with other localities. Potter claimed that even with the abatement, property-tax revenues for the city would increase (but his claim ignored the necessity of repaying the costs of the project). Moten also emphasized the increased tax revenues from the plant, noting that the project area was currently generating only $700,000 in property-tax revenues annually.

A City Planning Commission report that was prepared for the council recommended that the request to establish the industrial-development district be denied "because the need for tax abatement has not otherwise been demonstrated by the applicant, because various other generous public subsidies have already been committed to this project, and because of the city's current fiscal crisis."[7] Members of the Poletown Neighborhood Council (PNC) who attended the council hearing read a statement opposing the tax abatement, in which they pointed out that abatements were a relatively minor concern to GM and would not necessarily contribute to increased employment in the city. The PNC was less concerned with the merits of tax abatements than with exploiting the opportunity to derail the project. The council appeared to be uncertain about what action it would take and announced that it would postpone action on the request for two days.

Media reports on the next day reported that the council was deeply divided on the abatement issue, and Councilman Cleveland was quoted as saying that the council's vote on the issue would have been 4 to 4.[8] However, a day earlier than scheduled, the council voted 7 to 1 in favor of establishing the district. The threat that GM might reconsider its decision and might relocate the project figured importantly in the change. Cleveland was quoted as saying: "Emmett Moten said they had other offers. He said they had three real strong offers. He said they were backing off and that if we did not approve it, they would pick another site."[9] Council members had been subjected to intensive telephone lobbying by Mayor Young and by Moten, who told them that GM would pull out of the project if the abatement were not granted. Young also reportedly threatened political retaliation against those who opposed.[10] Opponents of the projects claimed that switching the day of the vote was designed to force a vote while the mayor's phone calls were still fresh in everyone's mind. The official reason for the change was that one council member would have been out of town the next day. The earlier vote, however, prevented another member, who was convalescing from an illness and who had planned to attend the session, from voting on the issue.

TAX-INCREMENT FINANCING

Less than one month after the confrontation over the granting of the tax abatement, Detroit's City Council quietly approved a legal agreement between Detroit and Hamtramck specifying the sharing of property-tax revenues from the new assembly plant. Absence of controversy did not imply an absence of importance, however, because this agreement required that future decisions of consequence be made.

The Interlocal Agreement adopted on 1 May 1981 was the third in a series of legal agreements.[11] The first, between the Detroit and Hamtramck EDCs, established an entity known as the Central Industrial Park Joint Venture, which was to be responsible for preparation of the site and its delivery to GM. This was followed by the signing of a Development Agreement between the Joint Venture and GM on 30 April 1981. Each agreement paved the way for subsequent decisions, but the tax-sharing agreement is of particular interest because it stipulated that tax-increment financing plans be enacted in 1982.

According to the tax-sharing agreement, initially Detroit and Hamtramck would each receive $1.7 million in tax revenues from the plant, with additional revenues pledged to repay the two cities for the costs of the project. After project costs had been repaid, Detroit would receive two-thirds and Hamtramck one-third of remaining tax revenues. Receipt of project revenues for reimbursement of project costs, however, was made conditional on the establishment of tax-increment financing plans by each city. The tax-increment plan was necessary to ensure long-term financing for the project.

The Detroit City Council's discussion of tax-increment financing was brief and was marked by misunderstanding of what this strategy entailed. Community and CEDD officials reminded Detroit's council members that this action was required by the earlier Inter-local Agreement, which they had approved, and that the city of Hamtramck had already established such an authority. Unanimous approval was given on 5 March 1982 to the establishment of a tax-increment financing authority and a tax-increment financing district for the project area, although details of the tax-increment financing plan were not available to the council.

The authorizing legislation provided several options for selecting a board of directors for the tax-increment financing authority.[12] Nevertheless, the council followed Moten's recommendation that the board of the EDC be utilized and that its executive vice-president, Jack Pryor, who had been in charge of EDC's involvement in the Central Industrial Park project, serve as the director of the tax-increment financing authority. The tax-increment financing plan, which had been adopted on 18 March by the EDC's board in its new role as the tax-increment financing authority, was approved by the City Council a month later, on 21 April.

ENABLING THE TIFA

Tax-increment financing is a method of financing by which property-tax revenues that are generated by economic growth in a project area are used to finance improvements in the area. The taxes that are generated by the value of property during a base year continue to flow to taxing jurisdictions, while the increment that is generated by economic growth goes to finance the improvements (or, as in the case of the Central Industrial Park project, to repay the costs of the project). The tax increment that is generated by growth is known as "captured" tax. The tax increment may be spent directly, or it may be used as collateral to finance tax-free bonds. Special development districts are established to administer the program.

In Michigan, tax-increment financing had been authorized for central business districts (CBDs) for several years, and a number of Michigan communities had in place their Downtown Development Authorities to administer CBD tax-increment schemes.[13] During the fall of 1980, lawyers from Detroit's CEDD helped to draft legislation that would extend tax-increment financing to development areas outside of the CBDs. The legislation was introduced by John Kelly, a senator from Detroit, and was adopted by the Michigan Legislature in January of 1981. Not surprisingly, the Central Industrial Park's Tax Increment Financing Authority was the first to be established under this legislation.

CAPTURING ALL OF IT

The state of Michigan had delegated to municipalities the authority to establish tax-increment financing districts and had limited to one the number of such districts per municipality.[14] This meant that the city of Detroit could make a major tax decision affecting all local taxing jurisdictions (this was also true of tax abatements). Moreover, the tax-increment financing legislation stipulated that the base, or initial, assessed value was to be the most recent assessed value of property in a project area, regardless of the progress of an urban-renewal project prior to the establishment of a TIFA.

In Michigan, assessed values are set when tax rolls are equalized on the first Monday of May. The TIFA for the Central Industrial Park project was established on 2 April 1982. The consequence of this is that the initial asessed value was set at slightly over $2 million, since the project area was almost entirely vacant at the time, due to demolition and clearing. Indeed, the 1981 State Equalized Value (SEV) for property in the project area "was all due to construction equipment and machinery."[15] Perversely, then, the taxes going to taxing jurisdictions would be based on construction machinery, and the Central Industrial Park project's TIFA would "capture" all the rest of the tax revenue generated by the assembly plant. In 1985 the TIFA would retain an estimated 97.6 percent of the total taxes generated. In 1997, when the tax abatement would expire, the taxing jurisdictions would still be receiving only 2.2 percent of total taxes generated (see table 9.1).

Pegging the initial assessed values at the most recent assessed value rather than at the most recent assessed value prior to clearance of the site had the effect of transferring a considerable portion of the cost of the project to other taxing jurisdictions. Indeed, of the 78.23 mills levied on property in Detroit, the city levies only 33 mills. Hence, the Detroit School District and other taxing jurisdictions were forced to help pay for the cost of the project, even though they had no formal voice in the establishment of the tax-increment financing plan. While there were no plans to use captured taxes as leverage for long-term financing to repay federal loans, the Detroit EDC

TABLE 9.1
ESTIMATE OF RETAINED AND CAPTURED TAXES, CENTRAL
INDUSTRIAL PARK PROJECT, FOR SELECTED YEARS

	BASE YEAR 1981	1985	1997
Captured Taxes	$ none	$6,849,800	$7,988,900
Taxes to be retained by:			
City of Detroit	71,400	71,400	71,400
Detroit School District	77,850	77,850	77,850
Wayne County	15,300	15,300	15,300
Wayne County ISD	2,350	2,350	2,350
Wayne County Community College	1,700	1,700	1,700
Huron-Clinton Metro Park Authority	550	550	550
Total retained	$169,150	$169,150	$169,150

SOURCE: Central Industrial Park Project Tax Increment Financing Plan, 18 Mar. 1982, exhibit A.

(with approval from the City Council) could (and later did) initiate such plans. The tax abatement had already been passed over the protest of the local jurisdictions; now they had been deprived of virtually all revenues from the project.

A comparison of the retained taxes that were projected in the tax-increment financing plan with the assessed values and taxes on property in the project area prior to the project indicates the magnitude of the loss. Project planners had estimated property-tax losses from demolition (over the estimated lives of the structures) to be $2,750,100 annually, based on the 1980 assessed valuation of $13,300,000.[16] While the assessed valuation (which by Michigan law is 50 percent of fair-market value) was projected to grow to more than ten times the 1980 assessed valuation because of the project, retained taxes amounted to considerably less than if the project had never taken place. Moten had indicated that the project area generated $700,000 in taxes, but the new plant would yield only $169,000 in retained taxes. The assessed valuation of the property in the project area would undoubtedly have declined steadily in the absence of the project. Nevertheless, the financial benefits to local governments, when examined in this context, are far less dramatic than they were originally presented as being by project planners. About the best that could be said for the project, in terms of its direct contribution to the tax base of the city, was that it would pay for itself.

"HIDDEN FUNCTIONS" IN TAX LOSS

Ironically, the Central Industrial Park project, which was touted as a vehicle for attracting a major addition to Detroit's tax base, will provide little in the way of new tax dollars. Even under the optimistic assumptions of the city's economic-development officials, the project will do well to allow the city to recover its investment and to repay the loans that it arranged. The 50 percent twelve-year tax abatement for the corporation and the tax-increment financing scheme that was designed to repay project costs to Detroit and Hamtramck ensure that very little tax money will be generated, in the words of Mayor Young, "to provide adequate services for our people."

While it is easy to focus on the "tax giveaways" to GM, other aspects of the politics of tax losses bear emphasizing. The first is that city officials were not overly concerned with the particular tax returns from the Central Industrial Park project. Rather, they conceived the project as contributing to the more general goal of economic revitalization. Economic-development policies, indeed, might be likened to an individual investor's investment strategy. While one would ideally like maximum returns on all investments, the important measure is the performance of the portfolio. City officials, of course, envisioned the CIPP as producing significant spillovers as suppliers and other manufacturers would also locate in the city because of the project.

Moreover, there was a highly symbolic component in the economic-development strategies of Detroit officials. The EDC's aim was to depict Detroit as a city that was attracting new industrial development, not just losing facilities to the suburbs and to the Sun Belt. To a considerable extent, image was more important than reality.

The second point is that the tax-increment financing plan served a dual purpose. First, it established a backup financing strategy for the project. If other sources, primarily the federal government's Section 108 loan program and other urban-revitalization programs, proved to be inadequate, the bonding capacity of the tax-increment district could be used to finance the project. This could be done because the "captured" portion of property taxes can be pledged as collateral for the issuance of tax-free municipal bonds.

The second function of the tax-increment plan was just as important. It provided a vehicle by which the cities of Detroit and Hamtramck could spread the costs of the project over all local taxing jurisdictions. Hence, Detroit and Hamtramck would not be in the position of themselves having to absorb the costs of the project, even though these communities were the only governmental units that had decision-making power with respect both to the tax-increment financing plan and the property-tax abatement.

CONCLUSIONS

The politics of property-tax loss raised three issues. The first and most obvious is that of private power in the public-policy process. As we have pointed out elsewhere,[17] corporate power in community politics is in part due to the ability of corporations to locate facilities in a variety of locales. During the City Council's debate on the tax abatement, GM's David Potter issued the thinly veiled threat of mobility if the abatement were not forthcoming. The city, he asserted, was a supplier of land to the corporation, and the corporation could reject the city's offer were the terms not right. The council did not see fit to call Potter's bluff, if indeed it was one.

The second issue concerns the impact of policy. In a narrow sense, the Central Industrial Park project was, at best, a marginal success. Virtually all of future tax revenues were pledged to repay the costs of the project. In a broader sense, the city of Detroit had succeeded in the nation's first large-scale urban industrial-renewal project, had put unproductive industrial land back to work, and had projected a national image of a coldly competent, businesslike black-run city. In the process, of course, it had destroyed a neighborhood. These costs and benefits are difficult to calculate, but they were nevertheless real.

The third issue is that of jurisdictional justice. Should one unit of local government make decisions that affect the property-tax base of other units that share that tax base? The issue of jurisdictional justice simultaneously raises the issue of governmental fragmentation: if the agreement of all units of government that share a common tax base were required in order to modify tax policies, the probability for immobilization would be heightened. Given the criticism that tax abatements and other manipulations of tax policies that are aimed at attracting industry have received, this might not be unwelcome. We only emphasize here that the issues of territorial justice and metropolitan fragmentation are "hidden" aspects of tax policies aimed at promoting economic development. Moreover, they became issues in the case at hand because of the manner in which state enabling legislation was written. By giving sole decisional authority to the municipality in decisions regarding tax increments and abatements the state had left other jurisdictions at the mercy of the city.

10

Street Theater: Organized Opposition to the Poletown Redevelopment Project

At first glance, the cause of the Poletown Neighborhood Council (PNC) would seem to have been hopeless. Arrayed against the neighborhood group was General Motors, the world's largest corporation; the city of Detroit and its aggressive, determined mayor, Coleman Young; the state of Michigan; the Democratic administration in Washington; the Detroit economic establishment; the Catholic Diocese of Detroit; and any number of highly competent lawyers, bureaucrats, and economic-development specialists. Small wonder that the PNC not only lost the war but also lost every single skirmish that it fought.

Surprisingly, however, the David that was fighting the industrial-redevelopment Goliath possessed considerable resources, and it deployed those resources well, despite several tactical and strategic errors. Moreover, the PNC deliberately defined the goals that it was seeking as non-zero-sum. This allowed considerable room for compromise, a feature of the "battle for the neighborhood" that was not reported in the lavish press coverage at all. The PNC first demanded that the project be canceled and that the neighborhood be spared. Then it demanded that the project plans be altered so that the entire 465 acres would not be used, thus preserving at least part of the neighborhood. Then it insisted that the city and GM commit resources to the revitalization of the remaining Poletown neighborhood that would be located outside of the project area. (The district of Detroit known as Poletown extended from the boarder of Hamtramck and the Dodge Main plant on the north to Mack Avenue on the south. Only about one-third of the neighborhood lay in the project area.) Finally, in a last-ditch desperation effort, the PNC tried to save Immaculate Conception Church, the major Catholic church in the area, by staging a dramatic sit-in.

Every objective was lost. The project plans were not altered. The mayor refused to commit city funds to Poletown South. And Immaculate Conception was destroyed, despite GM's offer to move the church at a cost of approximately $6 million.

Assets of the PNC included almost universally favorable press coverage.[1] They included a sophisticated organizational strategy and considerable political experience, technical skill, and personal abilities on the part of its leaders. They included the ability to draw on resources external to the area—in particular Ralph Nader's group of consumer activists. Most importantly, they included a sophisticated understanding of the most important resource: that because of GM's stringent timetables, delay would mean victory.

We have, then, a paradox. Why did the PNC fail to achieve even a minor, symbolic victory? American politics, it is said, is about compromise and conciliation, yet both were notably absent from the city's response to the PNC's "defense of the neighborhood." Though the PNC was willing to compromise, the city was not. Nor, in the end, was the PNC able to force concessions, even minor concessions, from the city. Why not?

THE NEIGHBORHOOD

Poletown was, at the outset, a misnomer. The neighborhood was multiethnic, being divided almost equally between blacks and whites (see table 10.1). While most whites in the project area were of Polish origin, the neighborhood contained significant concentrations of Albanians and Arabs, most of whom were first-generation immigrants.[2]

Black residents tended to concentrate on the southwest side of the Central Industrial Park project area, while whites lived primarily on the east side of the area, south of the Dodge Main plant (see figs. 10.1 and 10.2). Albanians were located in the far southeast corner of the project area. There was significant integration throughout the neighborhood, but it was more pronounced in the blocks that had a white majority.

The neighborhood was poor but not destitute. Although most residents had low incomes, fully 25 percent of families and individuals earned more than $15,000 per year (see table 10.1). The housing stock consisted almost entirely of detached single-family and two-family dwellings, with a smattering of apartments and three-family flats.[3]

The black community was divided between young and middle-aged families with children, most of whom were recent residents, and older couples and single individuals who had lived in the area for ten to twenty years. On the other hand, members of the Polish community were uniformly older, many nearing retirement age. Most had lived in the community for

TABLE 10.1
THE DISTRIBUTION OF INCOME BY RACE (FAMILIES AND
INDIVIDUALS), CENTRAL INDUSTRIAL PARK PROJECT AREA

INCOME	RACE					
	Black		White		Oriental and Other	
	No.	%	No.	%	No.	%
$ 0–4,999	349	50.9	193	29.4	1	5.3
5,000–9,999	206	30.0	221	33.6	4	21.1
10,000–14,999	62	9.0	105	16.0	5	26.3
15,000–24,999	55	8.0	99	15.1	7	36.8
25,000 and over	14	2.0	39	5.9	2	10.5
Total	686	99.9	657	100.0	19	100.0

SOURCE: Relocation Survey, reported in *Project Plan: Central Industrial Park* (Detroit: Economic Development Corporation of the City of Detroit, 30 Sept. 1980), p. 16.

twenty to fifty years and had developed a deep sense of belonging to the neighborhood.[4]

In both the black and the Polish communities, the church was a major focal point in the community. Eleven of the sixteen churches in the area had predominantly black congregations. Three Roman Catholic parishes accounted for almost all of the religious affiliation of Polish-Americans in the community, with Immaculate Conception and St. John's each ministering to about 40 percent of the Polish residents, and St. Stanislaus (which was outside of the project area) to the remaining 20 percent.[5] Numerous grocery stores and bars served the neighborhood, but just as many abandoned storefronts testified to the changing income characteristics and shopping patterns of the residents. No fewer than twenty-eight manufacturing concerns were located in the project area, testifying to the district's once-vital industrial base.[6]

ORGANIZATIONS IN POLETOWN

Opposition to the Central Industrial Park project came predominantly from long-term Polish homeowners who had a strong sense of neighborhood. Several neighborhood-based organizations existed before the city had intervened in the neighborhood; these served as the organizational backbone for the opposition's effort. The most important were the

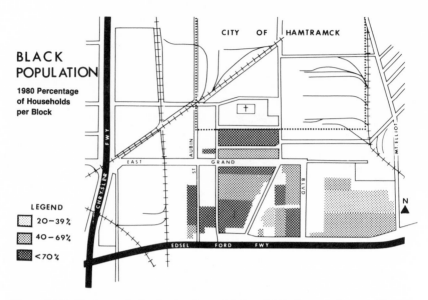

Figure 10.1. Black population in the Central Industrial Park area. Source: City of Detroit Community and Economic Development Department.

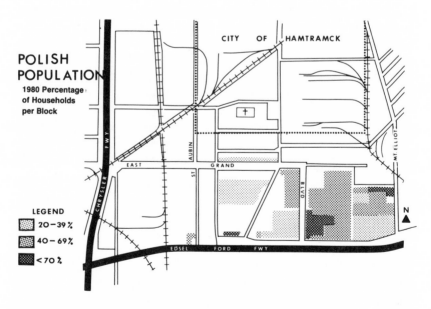

Figure 10.2. Polish-American population in the Central Industrial Park area. Source: City of Detroit Community and Economic Development Department.

churches, the Polish Interparish Council, and the Poletown Area Revitalization Task Force (PARTF). Formed in 1977, the Polish Interparish Council was an informal confederation of six Roman Catholic churches that had sizable numbers of Polish parishioners. Immaculate Conception was a member of the Interparish Council, but St. John's, the only other Catholic Church in the project area, was not.

PARTF was also organized in 1977. Thomas Olechowski, a resident of Poletown and an administrative aide to a state senator from Detroit, had contacted the Detroit Economic Growth Corporation and Detroit Renaissance (organizations of businessmen who were interested in the redevelopment of Detroit) in an effort to stimulate redevelopment in Poletown. PARTF and the Chene Area Business Development Corporation were formed as a result of these discussions. Richard Hodas, a local businessman and community activist, became involved in both organizations soon after they were founded.

Olechowski and Hodas envisioned a massive revitalization effort in Poletown, including commercial, residential, and recreational projects. They had secured grants from the Economic Growth Corporation and from neighborhood businesses and had received the approval for a grant of $100,000 from the city of Detroit's Neighborhood Opportunity Fund, a program that steered Community Development Block Grant funds to community organizations.[7]

According to Olechowski, the redevelopment was just "getting off the ground" when it was sabotaged by the announcement of the Central Industrial Park project. PARTF immediately ceased to function, and the Poletown Neighborhood Council (PNC) was formed. Olechowski and Hodas claimed that the two organizations were entirely separate; however, Olechowski became president and Hodas became vice-president of the PNC. Many participants in PARTF also participated in PNC. Immaculate Conception became the headquarters for PNC, and many parishioners were attracted to PNC's cause.

THE LOGIC OF NEIGHBORHOOD MOBILIZATION

Strictly rational humans do not normally practice in collective endeavors unless they expect substantial individual rewards. Accomplishment of a collective end is, according to this analysis, not enough to motivate individual participation because of the "free rider" problem—individuals can enjoy the collective good (e.g., the preservation of Poletown) whether or not they participate.[8] Yet the weight of custom and the habit of loyalty can cause people to join and participate in community action, and such acts of participation are often not preceded by an economically rational analysis of the relationship between individual effort and the achievement of the group's goals.[9] Richard Rich, however, has persuasively argued that the limited incentives for inducing participation in voluntary neighborhood associations put them at a significant disadvantage in comparison to organizations that possess coercive resources.[10]

One of the most important determinants of a neighborhood's mobilization in the face of an external threat is the preexisting network of social organizations. Individuals who are active in the network are likely to feel a psychological attachment to the community, and neighborhood-based interest groups can use these organizations as a base for recruiting members.[11] Jeffrey Henig, after studying six redevelopment proposals in Chicago and Minneapolis, reported significant variation in the speed and effectiveness of neighborhood mobilization in response to the perceived threat. While it was clear to him that the socioeconomic status of a neighborhood influenced its mobilization, so, too, did other factors—particularly the preexisting set of community organizations.[12]

Clearly the quality of leadership is critical to the success of any collective effort, but as Richard Rich has indicated, leadership will be supplied to an organization according to the costs and benefits that are associated with the role.[13] Hence the most effective neighborhood leadership is likely to emerge in cases where leaders possess a strong sense of neighborhood identification and where there will be considerable individual benefits to leaders if the goals of the organization are accomplished.

The PNC faced considerable obstacles to its objective of mobilizing the neighborhood. The neighborhood was not cohesive; rather, it was divided along racial, ethnic, religious, and life-cycle lines. It was not a well-to-do area, and it possessed few of the political resources that are common in middle-class neighborhoods. Most importantly, the city had moved aggressively to thwart neighborhood opposition by providing to each resident a generous relocation payment—an individual, concrete, immediate benefit that was counterpoised to the collective benefit of saving the neighborhood, which was offered by the PNC.

Yet a number of factors favored neighborhood mobilization, including a sense of community and a well-articulated set of preexisting social organizations. Moreover, the PNC's leadership, particularly Olechowski and Hodas, as residents, activists, and businessmen in the Poletown that was south of the project area, stood to benefit individually even if they failed to save the neighborhood.

The PNC achieved what might best be termed partial mobilization. It was able to attract a surprising number of concerned, committed activists to its banner and to hold them through a protracted struggle that lasted from the end of June 1980 until the late spring of 1982, when the last bitter resident of the project area was evicted from his home. Yet many—probably a majority—of the residents of the project area neither aided in the cause nor supported the goals and tactics of the PNC. While the PNC effectively organized the opponents of the project, most residents of the project area were not opposed to the Central Industrial Park project.

INITIAL DEMANDS

On 18 July 1980 the PNC sent a mailgram to Coleman Young, mayor of Detroit; Erma Henderson, president of the City Council; Thomas Murphy, chairman of the board of General Motors; and Elliott Estes, president of GM. The mailgram, which was composed by Thomas Olechowski, laid the foundation for many of the legal and moral arguments that the PNC used in future legal and political conflicts. In particular, the document argued that the demands for private profit must not dominate the good of the community. The mailgram, which echoed the ideas of PARTF, stated that the new organization (PNC) had emerged out of those organizations that had previously engaged in revitalizing the Poletown area and that the PNC had resolved to exercise its right to plan, develop, and implement revitalization strategies to rebuild its community. In addition to a host of entitlements and preconditions, the PNC wanted the city to recognize its self-proclaimed right to participate in the process of planning and implementing the Central Industrial Park project. Moreover, the PNC wanted the city to treat Poletown as a single entity, namely, the area extending south of the Hamtramck border to highway I-94, the Ford Freeway (the project area), as well as the area south of I-94 to Mack Avenue (the remaining Poletown area).

The mailgram listed specific revitalization projects for the Poletown area south of I-94. It suggested that Chene Street be rehabilitated along ethnic themes; that sidewalks, curbs, streets, and alleys be repaired; and that landscaping, street lights, and other amenities be "placed generously throughout Poletown."[14] It also asked for increased city services—police, fire, emergency medical service (EMS), recreational, senior-citizen programs, housing-rehabilitation projects, and so forth—in the Poletown area south of I-94.

Finally, the PNC insisted that there be full disclosure of all facts, plans, minutes, procedures, meetings, and so forth, pertaining to the project and that GM and the city demonstrate the necessity for executing plans that would cause irreparable damage to the community. The PNC also asked GM and the city of Detroit to become involved in the revitalization of the remaining part of Poletown south of I-94. In exchange, the PNC suggested that it would be willing to cooperate with the implementation of the project.

The mailgram and the demands that it contained were the result of a severe internal conflict that haunted the PNC and contributed to its final defeat. At the initial PNC meetings during the first two weeks of July 1980, some PNC members wanted to resist the project at all costs. That position, according to Olechowski, would have meant political suicide. He said, "We would be written off as nuts standing in the way of progress . . . our position should be against imposition without democratic input from the community."[15]

Most of those members who wanted to resist the project "at all costs" were not really opposed to the project. They never wanted to "stand in the way of progress." They felt that alternatives that would spare their neighborhood and still allow the plant to be built were not seriously being considered. In particular, they suggested that the enormous amount of land that GM was demanding was not necessary and was excessive. Several of these PNC members viewed Olechowski (who lived outside of the project area) with suspicion. Some resented his position as delineated in the mailgram, which they perceived as surrendering the project area. However, the intense arguments over the two positions became academic when neither the city of Detroit nor GM responded to the demands of the PNC. These differences remained submerged until a year later, in July and August 1981, after Immaculate Conception Church had been demolished, when they became the basis of a critical if not fatal fissure within the organization.

A PUBLIC SHOW OF FORCE

Even before the mailgram was written, the PNC had launched its attack on the project at public meetings. On 9 July 1980, more than four hundred angry residents and PNC members, jeering at public officials, crowded into a public meeting that was held in the gymnasium of a public school in the project area. One by one, residents expressed strong opposition to the project.[16] At another public meeting on 4 August 1980, residents again expressed their hostility, uncertainty, and fear in regard to the project. Richard Hodas exhumed the issue of the revitalization project that was in progress for the neighborhood.[17]

The Citizen's District Council (CDC), which was established specifically as the community agency for the project, was another target of the PNC and the angry residents. The CDC, whose members were picked by the Community and Economic Development Department (CEDD) and approved by the City Council, held regular public meetings. Although a few PNC members were appointed to the CDC, the CDC was staunchly supportive of the project. Consequently, PNC members and discontented residents often appeared at the open CDC meetings, jeering and heckling the representatives of the CDC.

On 31 October 1980, at a City Council meeting, forty PNC members attended, wearing black armbands, heckling the council members, and shouting "Sellout!" when the council officially voted in favor of the project.[18] PNC members immediately filed for an injunction to keep the city from making offers for homes and businesses in the project area, thus transferring its battle to the judicial arena.

THE LEGAL LABYRINTH

The PNC used the courts extensively, yet, as we noted in chapter 8, the organization gained no worthwhile victories. Judge Victor Baum of the Wayne County Circuit Court refused to issue an immediate temporary injunction on the grounds that the case should be decided in a full hearing. Poletown's legal counsel, Ronald Reosti, raised important legal and constitutional issues, but on 9 December 1980, Judge George Martin issued a judgment in which he dismissed all of the plaintiff's complaints (see chap. 8). Attorneys for the PNC filed a claim of appeal with the Court of Appeals, and on December 15 they filed an application for by-pass of the Court of Appeals to the Michigan Supreme Court.

On 3 March 1981 the Michigan Supreme Court began to hear arguments on the case. As planned a month in advance, more than seventy PNC members and residents of the project area traveled to Lansing, the state capital, to demonstrate their support for PNC's position. The mood of the participants was feisty; one demonstrator commented: "The church we belong to, the bingo, my friends, everything we know is in that neighborhood. . . . I own that home free and clear, and they come along and tell you you've got to get out. I'm here to fight!"[19]

On 15 March the PNC suffered a devastating defeat when the Michigan Supreme Court ruled against the PNC on every issue that had been brought before the court. The decision jolted the morale of the PNC and shattered its base of support. Nevertheless, the PNC counterattacked in federal court and developed new arguments for suits in lower state courts. On 17 March the PNC brought suit in federal court, challenging HUD's role in financing the project.

On 17 April, as federal Judge John Feikens heard closing arguments on this case, attorneys for the PNC filed another case in federal court, contending that the city had violated the Federal Clean Air and National Historic Preservation acts. The Federal Advisory Council on Historic Preservation had sympathized with the PNC and had demanded that the city stop demolition in the Poletown area because the city had violated an earlier agreement that it had made with the Advisory Council. However, the Advisory Council had no power to enforce the agreement, and the federal court ruled against all issues that the PNC raised in both federal cases.

On 27 March 1981, PNC's vice-president, Richard Hodas, filed an objection to the city's taking his property. Hodas claimed that the city, although required by law to inform residents about the proper procedures to be used in raising objections, had misinformed residents on how to file objections. Circuit court Judge George Martin, in whose court the motions were filed, ruled in favor of the city. Hodas immediately appealed the case, and because time was critical, the Michigan Supreme Court allowed the case to by-pass the appellate court. On 7 May the supreme court ruled in favor of Hodas, and the case was sent back to the lower court, but Judge David Vokes of the Wayne County Circuit Court ruled in favor of the city.

Although the PNC had not achieved any worthwhile victories in the courts and had not even been able to delay the project significantly, it nevertheless continued its legal challenges. As time progressed, opposition to the project increasingly focused on Immaculate Conception Church. After the church had been sold by the Archdiocese of Detroit to the city, the archdiocese signed an agreement to waive the legally required ninety-day notice to vacate the premises. A PNC court challenge in May provided the neighborhood organization with its only court victory when Wayne County Circuit Court voided the waiver.

In June, Hodas had decided to appeal his case to the United States Supreme Court, but the process would have taken several years, and the area in which he resided was scheduled for demolition within a year's time. Attorneys for the PNC decided against appealing the Michigan Supreme Court's decision to the United States Supreme Court primarily because they had neglected to include proper grounds for such an appeal in their arguments before the Michigan Supreme Court. This was a costly error. Nevertheless, with the exception of this error, the PNC utilized the judicial arena in a sophisticated manner, but to little avail.

MEDIA EXPOSURE

Attracting media exposure and raising the saliency of issues and demands are critical strategies used by protest groups, and the PNC was no exception.[20] The organization issued press releases, called news conferences, and raised the types of issues that are most likely to attract media exposure. Officials wrote letters to local newspapers. Attracting media attention was a means of soliciting public support and of raising the public awareness of the problems and concerns of the PNC. It was also an indirect means of pressuring public officials and of maintaining the momentum of the organization.

Coverage of the Poletown issue appeared not only regularly in the local news; the issue also received national and international attention. Local news reporters wrote stories that were sympathetic to the plight of the neighborhood; but their papers supported the project editorially. The media sometimes depicted the project as representing an unfortunate trade-off between a dying neighborhood and the future survival of the city. Such a conceptualization of the project undermined sympathy toward the PNC, for it suggested that the complete destruction of the neighbrhood was necessary for the survival of the city. The newsworthiness of "David v. Goliath" did not, however, escape local news executives, and much coverage, especially on television, stressed the human dimensions of urban renewal. This sympathetic media image was projected both locally and nationally and tended to offset the drier analyses of redevelopment that were presented by both of the metropolitan daily newspapers.

The PNC also initiated petition drives as a means of publicizing its concerns and of soliciting support. Contacting supporters who signed petitions served as a means of expanding the ranks of the faithful during critical periods.

DIRECT LOBBYING

Direct lobbying, testifying at hearings, and offering the analyses of experts are not tactics that are normally associated with protest groups, but the PNC did use such tactics with some limited success. During the summer of 1980 Richard Hodas, an architect who was the vice-president of PNC, used his expertise to prepare a preliminary study of historic sites in the area. His report was instrumental in influencing officials of the Federal Advisory Council on Historic Sites (FACHS). The city's initial impact statement suggested that there was nothing of historic value in the area. FACHS, like most federal agencies, was dependent on local agencies or groups for information. It initially accepted the city's assessment, although with some skepticism, and made inquiries to verify the city's report. As a result of actions by Hodas and representatives of the Advisory Council, an entire section of the final impact statement was devoted to historic sites. Moreover, an agreement was reached between the state and federal agencies on historic preservation and the city of Detroit to develop procedures whereby the owners or tenants could move historic structures.[21] The city's violation of this agreement led FACHS to support the PNC's federal lawsuit in April 1981.

Another lobbying effort was initiated by a representative of Ralph Nader's organization, Gene Stilp. At a PNC meeting, after listening to many problems that residents of the project area had suffered, Stilp asked the residents to document the abuses they had experienced. The letters or documentations were sent to the Department of Housing and Urban Development (HUD) in Washington. Stilp claimed that HUD had forwarded the letters to Mayor Young and Emmett Moten and had required that city officials respond to the letters and to alleged abuses. However, the ability to lobby and obtain support from HUD in order to oppose the project was critically undercut by a close relationship between city and HUD officials and by the fact that HUD supported the project. Moreover, it was HUD's general policy to support local governments, and HUD had delegated a great deal of its implementation power to the city of Detroit.

The PNC also lobbied the governor and state agencies. On 3 March 1981, when seventy PNC members appeared in the Michigan Supreme Court, a small delegation of fourteen PNC members met with Governor William Milliken. The governor listened, but he insisted that Michigan needed the plant, noting that lives and jobs depended on it.

On 11 March, another PNC delegation met with William Lukens, the acting director of the Michigan Commerce Department. Olechowski presented proposals for building the GM plant without destroying the neighborhood, and he presented strong arguments that the state's Commerce Department should support the PNC. Predictably, the state's Commerce Department was strongly supportive of the project and was not receptive to the PNC's proposals. The PNC delegates were frustrated, and the meeting degenerated into a shouting match. Olechowski was quoted as saying, "They [Poletown residents] are saying, 'When they come, we're going to die on the steps of our houses.'" There were threats to fight the project physically.[22]

At the local level, PNC members attempted on a number of occasions to meet with city officials in order to negotiate, but to no avail. Members also attended City Council hearings and testified before the council in order to influence decisions—again to no avail. PNC members sent letters to Detroit's congressmen and to Michigan's United States senators. There were no positive responses. In fact, shortly after these letters had been sent, one congressman sent letters to residents of the project area urging them to support the project and to leave the area.

OUTSIDE AID

On several occasions during the late fall of 1980, Olechowski attempted to contact consumer activist Ralph Nader. Nader sent Gene Stilp to Detroit in January 1981. Stilp's first visit was a fact-finding mission,[23] but he and a team of lawyers and community activists returned in February. The Nader team organized a systematic search for allies and solicited aid from a variety of community organizations.

The PNC and the Nader team received considerable support from various organizations, and a few organizations actively lobbied in behalf of the PNC. The Association of Community Organizations for Reform Now (ACORN) offered general aid, and the National Association of Neighborhoods issued a press release opposing "not so much the construction of the plant in the neighborhood as the needless destruction of the community." A few block clubs and a tenant's union also sent letters of support to the PNC. The American Polish Century Club and the Polish National Alliance of the United States and North America wrote letters to Governor Milliken, in which they registered the "strongest protest over the cruel and unnecessary eradication" of Poletown and urged the governor to consider alternative designs. Although the UAW staunchly supported the project, a leader of a radical faction of Local 15, one of the two locals whose headquarters would be demolished by the project, appeared at a PNC meeting on 23 February 1981 and expressed strong support for and solidarity with the PNC.

DRAMA AT IMMACULATE CONCEPTION CHURCH

Public demonstrations capture media attention and also heighten feelings of group solidarity; such nonviolent protest was regularly employed by the PNC. Members and sympathizers demonstrated regularly at public meetings in the project area, at City Council meetings, and in other public places. After the defeat in court in December 1980, PNC members demonstrated in front of the General Motors Building and again in front of CEDD headquarters on Michigan Avenue. Near the end of May 1981, PNC members marched outside the annual GM shareholders' meeting. A few PNC members obtained proxies from sympathetic stockholders and expressed their displeasure over the project at the meeting.

The most dramatic series of demonstrations involved struggles to save Immaculate Conception Church. In February, without forewarning, the Archdiocese of Detroit sold Immaculate Conception Church to the city. The act so incensed the parishioners and PNC members that they launched a demonstration in front of the Chancery Building in downtown Detroit.[24] In one of the many ironies of the entire affair, GM offered to finance the moving of Immaculate Conception Church out of the project area. This belated move was clearly a public-relations gesture. GM's management knew that the archdiocese would refuse the offer. One GM official put it thus: "[We knew] they were not going to take it under any circumstances because they couldn't afford it. They couldn't even meet their heat bills from the collection.''[25] The archdiocese refused, politely but firmly. There was no need for a church where there were no people.

On 10 May 1981, just before Cardinal Dearden ordered all church ceremonies and activities to cease, the church held its last mass, an emotional show of support for the church. Father Joseph Karasiewicz, the pastor of Immaculate Conception, preached that there was something sacred about a church, and suggested that the sacrifice of the church bordered on the sacrilegious. The church was crowded, with an estimated one thousand people in attendance. Many parishioners came in native Polish dress to symbolize their ethnic solidarity.[26] In front of the church, large signs hung, saying, "GM, Mark of Destruction," "Don't Bulldoze My Church," "Cardinal Dearden Blesses Gucci [an exclusive clothing store] While Destroying Polish Shrine."

A few days later, several parishioners initiated a continuous all-night prayer vigil. This tactic was not entirely a deliberate and conscious ploy to generate sympathy, because most of the participants sincerely believed in the power of prayer.

At the PNC meeting of 16 June, city officials informed PNC members that if they remained on the church premises after the sixteenth of June, they would be trespassing and could be arrested. The notion of a sit-in was discussed. Gene Stilp, a member of the Nader team, stated that he would be in the church in the morning. On the morning of 17 June the church basement was crowded with people.

The sit-in was continuous, lasting all night and all day. Participants camped in the church basement. Parishioners who did not participate in the action came to the church during the day, cooking meals and offering support. The prayers and candles of those who conducted the prayer vigil sustained the faithful during the evening. Enthusiasm for the sit-in began to wane by the first week of July, when the city had all of the utilities except the telephone disconnected. Obtaining fresh water and maintaining adequate sanitation became critical problems. Without a constant supply of ice, it was difficult to keep food from spoiling; candles and lanterns created fire hazards.

The city, under the pressure of GM's deadlines, could not afford to wait to win this war of attrition. On 13 July, thirty police cars and vans suddenly converged on Immaculate Conception. When twelve of the twenty protesters who were in the church at the time refused to comply with Deputy Police Chief Richard Dungy's order to leave the church, they were arrested.[27]

The assault on the church attracted a large crowd. An eight-foot wire fence was quickly constructed around the church, shielding the onlookers and television cameras from the coming destruction. Detroit police and private guards, who were employed by Turner Construction Company, patrolled the area as the church was prepared for demolition. The church was demolished in record-breaking time, as construction crews worked all day and all night. The first wrecking ball hit the church after nightfall in order to spoil television coverage, but the event nevertheless attracted considerable attention from the media.[28] After the church had been demolished, PNC members staged a final "demolition demonstration" by demolishing an old GM automobile in front of GM's headquarters.

THE FINAL DAYS

Although the assault on the church marked the final defeat for the PNC, decline had set in after the supreme court had announced its decision. The complete rejection by the high court demoralized both leadership and followers, and increasingly, residents began to negotiate with the city for the tempting relocation benefits. As the neighborhood became depopulated after March, vandalism, arson, environmental problems, and declines in city services made it increasingly difficult to remain in the area. Although the core of dedicated members stayed the same, the membership within the larger group of less committed members declined measurably. Attendance at the regular Tuesday meetings of the PNC at Immaculate Conception Church dropped from well over a hundred during the winter of 1981 to less than forty in April. It was primarily these committed activists who staffed the prayer vigil and who stood at the church.

Although the church was gone, PNC members continued to meet at the Hodas's residence on East Grant Boulevard to plan other strategies. Participants in the prayer vigil placed a wreath on the area where the altar of the church had once stood, and they continued to meet in that now-vacant area on Sunday afternoons for a year.

Although it suffered serious defeat, a central core of dedicated and often religiously committed members maintained an incredibly high sense of efficacy. The PNC executed practically every conceivable legitimate and legally acceptable tactic. Yet none of the target groups or individuals acceded to any of the demands or concerns of the PNC.

TACTICAL ERRORS

Although the PNC deployed its resources skillfully for the most part, it did make several tactical errors. In the case that they argued before the Michigan Supreme Court, the lawyers for the PNC failed to include grounds for an appeal to the United States Supreme Court. Although the PNC identified specific targets—such as Coleman Young, Roger Smith, and

Cardinal Dearden—the organization had difficulties in sustaining pressure on a single fixed target.[29] Because the project involved many different agencies, bureaucrats, and public officials, it was easy for each agency or official to divert pressure to another agency.

The organization also suffered from a lack of clear goals and an inability to mobilize the black members of the community. The group's leaders initially attempted to procure a broad base of support by depicting the neighborhood as an ethnically diverse working-class community. When the broad base of support in the community failed to materialize, Olechowski began to characterize the neighborhood as a Polish community, which, like Poland, was struggling against a major occupying foreign power.

Olechowski was not entirely aboveboard about the goals of his organization. While "Save the Neighborhood" was his slogan, it was clear that he was very interested in continuing the redevelopment of Poletown south of the project area and that he believed that the project might offer some leverage with the city and the corporate community. When it became clear, after the loss of the court battles, that the neighborhood could not be saved, Olechowski, partly leading and partly being led, adopted the "Save the Church" rhetoric, which also failed.

Olechowski clearly had a problem in balancing the need for mobilization with his desire for negotiation. Maximum mobilization entailed an appeal to symbols and a conscious simplifying of choices; negotiation entailed the realization that saving the neighborhood was impossible and the acceptance of far less than half a loaf. By the time of the "assault on the church," however, most participants in PNC were deeply committed to the symbolic goals of the organization, thus limiting Olechowski's room to maneuver. What is striking about this situation, however, is how free from tactical errors and how little constrained by the lack of full mobilization of the neighborhood were the actions of the PNC. The PNC's leadership succeeded in raising the visibility of the issues, activating residents of the project area, sustaining intense commitment on the part of a sizable number of activists over a long period of time, generating substantial support outside of the project area, and deploying sophisticated lobbying and legal strategies. Yet the PNC acheived nothing—not even a symbolic recognition of the legitimacy of its concerns—from the city, the state, the courts, GM, or the archdiocese.

LEADERSHIP

In comparison to the majority of neighborhood organizations that are active in America today, the Poletown Neighborhood Council was able to generate a wealth of political resources. It had a strong and committed ethnic base which was cemented by community institutions, particularly Immaculate Conception Church. The PNC possessed committed and able leadership. Olechowski was a knowledgeable legislative aide who had an insider's knowledge of government in Detroit and Lansing. Hodas was an architect and businessman. Immaculate Conception's Father Joseph Karasiewicz, a respected priest, added a sense of moral righteousness to the cause. The group raised enough money to mount a protracted and multifaceted legal challenge; it still had several thousand dollars in its bank account after the church had been demolished. Ralph Nader's team of lawyers and community activists aided in both the community and organizational efforts and in the legal challenges, although the team joined the effort too late to prevent the disastrous error of failing to include grounds for a federal appeal in *Poletown Neigborhood Council* v. *City of Detroit*. Many parishioners transferred their church activities to the PNC, providing a stable staff throughout the lifetime of the organization.

In particular, Olechowski's leadership was impressive. Although PNC members were free to raise issues, Olechowski controlled the agenda of each meeting. He was able to articulate goals, to moderate internal conflict (which was frequently severe), and to maintain channels of communication.[30] At a PNC meeting during the "Save the Church" phase of the organization, a serious verbal conflict erupted between a parishioner, who was a participant in the sit-in but was not a resident of the area, and a resident of the project area, who was not a parishioner. The parishioner strongly felt that the purpose of the organization was to save the church. In contrast, the resident felt that the organization had lost sight of the problems in the neighborhood and was no longer concerned with the lives of the residents who were suffering in the project area. Olechowski reassured the two members that the PNC was concerned with saving both the church and the neighborhood. He quickly generated a renewed sense of direction, purpose, and hope by authoritatively presenting a positive program of action, which consisted of (1) calling a press conference, (2) petitioning the Wayne County Grand Jury to investigate arson, (3) calling on old parishioners and supporters to join the struggle to save the church, (4) demanding that the city provide the services necessary to make the area livable, and (5) petitioning a federal grand jury to investigate why the city had failed to take action to save the church.

It is doubtful that the lack of resources of the PNC can explain its complete failure. Certainly the resources of the PNC were insignificant when compared with the resources of its opponents—the city, GM, and the Archdiocese of Detroit. However, other neighborhood organizations have achieved more success with less. Moreover, the PNC had one very important advantage on its side—delay would have been tantamount to victory.

GROUP DEMANDS

The leaders of the PNC were anything but obstructionists. Olechowski in particular recognized the cost of being inflexible, and his demands were tailored to the existing realities. During the long course of opposition politics, the PNC articulated the following demands:

1. Save the neighborhood.
2. Modify the project to save part of the neighborhood.
3. Allow the PNC to participate in implementing the project plans.
4. Revitalize the Poletown area south of the project.
5. Save the church.

All of these demands except the first were non-zero-sum. Nevertheless, the city refused to accede even partially to any of the demands. GM refused to allow any modification of the project. Participation of the PNC in implementation of the project plans had the potential for legitimizing the group and could result in delays in the project. Bargaining with the PNC on revitalization would be perceived as a "smoke-filled-room" deal and would not necessarily defuse community opposition. Saving the church was an objective that was simply not worth the trouble; by then the city had turned back all legal challenges, and the PNC was a dying organization. Moreover, the Archdiocese of Detroit realized that the incident provided a painless way in which to rid itself of one architecturally nondescript, underattended church, and the archdiocese was not about to re-create the problem by allowing the church to be moved. Although the parishioners felt strongly about their church, it had an uncertain future in a neighborhood of aging Polish Catholics and younger black Protestants.

While there were reasons for the denial of each of the PNC's demands, these reasons did not relate to the nature of the demands. The PNC's demands were flexible and reasonable to such an extent that they caused intraorganizational strain. The nature of the demands did not imply that they would be rejected; rejection was the choice of the city.

THE FORGOTTEN CITIZEN OF POLETOWN

Why, then, did the city so thoroughly reject the wishes of the PNC? The obvious answer is that city officials felt that they could win without having to compromise. Yet the PNC dragged the mayor and his director of economic development into court, fanned the media flames, and provoked the mayor into more than one hostile outburst. The organization was not without power.

The organization possessed two critical weaknesses, and the mayor knew this. In the first place, the Polish community in the Detroit area was not united behind the PNC, for the primary reason that the predominantly Polish city of Hamtramck stood as a major beneficiary of the Central Industrial Park project. Appeals to Polish ethnic solidarity were contrary to the needs of Hamtramck citizens for jobs. Hence, ethnic solidarity was immediately splintered by the very forces that caused Detroit and Hamtramck to collaborate.

The second weakness was even more fatal. The PNC was never able to bridge the racial gap in the neighborhood. Indeed, the appeal to ethnic solidarity emerged only after a multiracial strategy had failed. Blacks in the project area tended either to be supportive of Mayor Young or to be apathetic. Moreover, many had moved into the area after having been displaced by earlier renewal projects. They pointed out that they had received no support from Polish residents of other neighborhoods. Some Poletown blacks were victims of Hamtramcks' deliberate black-removal policies, which had made that community less black in 1970 than it had been in 1960. Finally, many blacks had had previous experience with urban-relocation policies, and they knew a good deal when they saw one. To the extent that blacks participated in community organizations, they tended to support the efforts made by the Citizens' District Council to extract from the city even greater benefits for individual owners and renters.

The mayor, then, could not deal with the PNC without alienating his black supporters, who, according to script, were rallying to the banner of the Citizens' District Council and were moving out. Hence, acceding to any of the PNC's demands would have raised one classic urban-renewal issue that was never raised: *Whites can get what blacks can't.*

Mayor Young, moreover, has been extremely sensitive to racial injustice. He feels that he has suffered at the hands of racist whites, particularly during the early years of his career. On more than one occasion he has expressed his opinion that racism underlies much urban conflict, once having commented that if some whites "say the only kind of black people they can deal with is some sonofabitch that they can p---- on and he'll grin, then they've got the wrong nigger in me."[31] This incident raised racial issues in subtle ways, although the racial dimension of the conflict was ignored by the media. In the mayor's mind the issue was zero-sum, part of a continuing black/white struggle.

It is easy to see why Poletown was not saved. The corporatist alliance of business, labor, government, and the church was simply too powerful for any turf-based organization to defeat. It is not so easy to see why the PNC lost so completely. The reason inheres in more prosaic urban truths—truths that involve the jostling for advantage that is carried on by racial and ethnic groups in the city. Paradoxically, by refusing to yield an inch to the "little man,'' Coleman Young kept the faith with the ''forgotten citizens'' of Poletown: the black majority of that neighborhood. And the Poletown Neighborhood Council lacked enough power to make him act differently.

PART 3

PLANTS IN THE HINTERLAND

11

Pontiac:
The Company Town and the Exurbs

General Motors, as well as the other domestic automobile manufacturers, was caught completely off guard by the rapid shift in consumer preferences for smaller, more-fuel-efficient vehicles after the Iranian crisis of 1979. Corporate officials committed the company to an enormous, expensive, and rapid capital-improvement program that had major impacts on America's industrial cities.

The inflexibility of GM's deadlines, which forced a rapid response from the city of Detroit, was replicated in the search for the replacement plant for Pontiac Assembly. In a presentation to the Orion Township Planning Commission, Barbara Spreitzer of GM's Real Estate Division noted, on 24 April 1980:

> A little more than a year ago, new cars were selling at a near-record pace and big cars were leading the way. The revolution in Iran cut off that country's oil shipments; gasoline prices went up; sales of big cars dropped off; and demand for small cars shot up so much that U.S. automakers could not satisfy it. Cars produced by foreign manufacturers began to fill the gap.
>
> Although General Motors had anticipated this shift from large to small cars, we were *not* able to foresee the crisis that sped up this shift. Suddenly, we were forced to put into immediate effect a product development program that originally had been planned for implementation over a ten-year period.[1]

This interesting admission of corporate fallibility gives some indication of both the complacency of automotive corporate management during the late 1970s and its rapid response to the deep penetration of the imports after 1979. In hindsight, the declining demand for automobiles that was caused by the major recession of the early 1980s, which resulted in delays in transferring operations to the new assembly plants, and the increases in demand for larger automobiles after the stabilization of gasoline prices make the rapid response look like panic. Nevertheless, there is no doubt that automobile executives felt themselves to be under heavy pressure as sales and profits declined after the spring of 1979. This demand for a rapid response colored the entire search for locations for the new assembly plants which were made necessary because of the front-wheel-drive strategy that GM's executives were pursuing. Two of the first plants that were slated for replacement in the modernization program were the body-making and vehicle-assembly operations in the city of Pontiac. In this chapter we examine GM's decision to locate a new facility in Orion Township, three and one-half miles north of Pontiac, and the responses of Pontiac and Orion Township to that decision.

For several reasons the Orion Township project was able to proceed more rapidly than the one in Detroit. At the time that GM announced its project, it had already completed its site-selection process. The site, on the southern border of the township, was essentially a "green field" site: much of the property was owned by Oakland County and was largely un-developed, with only a few private homes being located on it. Land acquisition involved GM in the direct purchase of property from Oakland County. Public costs for preparing the site were limited to the construction of roads, sewers, and water lines, in contrast to the over $200 million in state and federal funds that Detroit had spent on acquisition, demolition, relocation, and other costs of preparing the site.

Similarly, fewer aspects of the Orion Township project required public approval than did the one in Detroit. Project planning was done entirely by the corporation. Approval of the site plan by the Orion Township Planning Commission was required only because rezoning was needed for the project. The involvement of local public officials and citizens in the formulation of policy took place primarily in the context of the rezoning request, although the planning commission and the township board also discussed and approved a wetlands permit for the project, because a small portion of the site was protected as wetlands. Later, township action was necessary on a tax abatement for GM and for the sale of bonds to finance sewer construction for the project. Because state law requires that relocating forms which request tax abatements must obtain approval from the municipality that they are leaving, Pontiac's City Commission also voted on the tax abatement.

Although no officials from either community had been included in the planning, most of them reacted positively to the announcement and supported the project. Yet Orion Township's tax base was growing, and governmental functions were limited, so that there was no compelling need to attract the project in order to bolster the tax base. Because Orion Township's property-tax levy was so low, moreover, its total tax benefits from the plant would be much less than Detroit's. Finally, the mammoth plant unquestionably did not fit into the semirural character of the community. Pontiac, in contrast, was experiencing unemployment levels as high as, if not higher than, was Detroit; and Pontiac had been trying unsuccessfully for several years to implement a downtown-redevelopment project. The announcement of the GM relocation probably had a negative effect on this effort.

Why was there so little opposition to the plant in Orion Township? Why didn't Pontiac officials object more strenuously and try to persuade GM to build the plant in Pontiac? Why did Orion Township officials react so positively to a project that would substantially alter the highly valued (among residents) semirural character of the area? The reactions of Pontiac and Orion Township, in comparison to those of Detroit, highlight the complex relationships between governments and corporations.

GM DECIDES TO GO TO THE COUNTRY

Prior to a site-selection recommendation by GM's Real Estate Division, a set of criteria was set out by corporate management. These included:

1. If at all possible, the existing experienced work force was to be retained for staffing the new facility
2. Site location was to be as close as possible to the existing Pontiac facilities (which included facilities for parts manufacture as well as Pontiac Division Headquarters)
3. Site selection was to be confined to properties that could be ready for ground breaking in June of 1980 in anticipation of a September 1982 production start-up.[2]

In addition, the site's dimensions (450 to 500 acres), transportation, soil load-bearing capacities, and zoning classifications were specified. Finally, "the project should be acceptable to the community as demonstrated by a willingness to extend privileges under P.A. 198."[3] This refers to the tax-abatement provisions that are available under Michigan law. If a suitable site, conforming to the management's specifications, could not be found, the site-selection committee was instructed to investigate backup sites simultaneously and to secure an option on alternative property for the replacement of the plant.[4] Not surprisingly, when the document was released by the corporation, local officials viewed this statement as a thinly veiled threat to relocate if GM's demands were not met.

The site-selection task force investigated properties within the city of Pontiac and within a radius of forty miles. Within Pontiac, several possibilities were examined but were eliminated for various reasons. All of the properties were being used for other purposes and would have required extensive site preparation. "Time constraints were judged to be too demanding to consider these properties as realistic locations for the new assembly complex."[5] The task force reported that this situation was disappointing, "because of the obvious logistic advantages, as well as the potential for large tax savings associated with a City of Pontiac location."[6]

The site-selection task force quickly eliminated the area south of Pontiac because of its substantially urban character and because it lacked any large enough sites that also met the transportation requirements (particularly rail connections). Sites that were too far to the north and northwest of Pontiac were problematic because of limitations of the water and sewer systems.[7]

The task force recommended a site in Orion Township, north of the city of Pontiac, that included the Oakland-Orion Airport, which was almost entirely owned by Oakland County. This had the advantage of simplifying the negotiations but was not the primary consideration for the recommendation. A spokesperson for the company reported to Orion Township officials that this site was the only property in the forty-mile radius around Pontiac that fulfilled most of the site criteria established by GM executives.[8]

POLITICS IN EXURBIA

Located three miles outside of Pontiac, in northern Oakland County, Orion Township had a population of 22,473 in 1980. Although it had experienced steady growth in population—up from 11,844 in 1960—the township retained a semirural, primarily residential character, which its planning commission was committed to preserving. Over 70 percent of the township's tax base in 1981 consisted of residential property, and the largest development prior to GM's proposal was a K-Mart store. Several thousand acres are taken up by Bald Mountain State Park, and another several thousand acres had been recently purchased by the state from Chrysler Corporation for another park. Most township roads are unpaved. Township officials estimated that approximately fifteen hundred of its residents worked for GM in nearby Pontiac.

Prior to the coming of GM, politics in Orion Township centered on conflicts between residents of new subdivisions and the remaining farmers in the area, and between residents of new subdivisions and the developers. Although the pace of suburban development slowed with the recession that began in 1980, many residents remain committed to being "the very last persons to come into the township."[9] Urban geographers Robert Sinclair and Bryan Thompson observed that in neighboring Oakland Township "new subdivision residents want to retain the traditional rural 'natural beauty' roads, are opposed to new subdivisions, and object to the idea of any industrial or commercial enterprise in the township."[10]

In keeping with the area's residential character, government in Orion Township is truly limited. The township is administered by a full-time paid supervisor, a clerk, and a treasurer, who are elected on a partisan ballot. Together with four elected trustees, who serve part-time and are unpaid, they form the township board, the official governing body of the community. The township relies on contractual arrangements to provide the services of an attorney and a planning consultant. Its revenues for the year ending 31 March 1981 totaled $1,089,172, of which $212,791 came from property taxes and $481,345 from intergovernmental sources. Total expenditures for that year were $794,625, with the largest budget allocations going to the Building Department, the Clerk's Office, and the Police Department.

Township taxes are low—$2.4267 per $1,000 of state equalized valuation (SEV) in 1981—but property owners also paid $48.1578 per $1,000 SEV to the Lake Orion Community School District. In contrast, Detroit taxpayers, in addition to a city income tax of 3 percent, pay property taxes of $76.951 per $1,000 SEV. Both GM's tax bill for the facility and the revenues that it generates for local government are substantially lower in Orion Township than in Detroit, but its impact on local revenues is proportionally greater in Orion Township, even with the 50 percent tax abatement. The corporation initially paid nearly $225,000 in property taxes to the township, representing a 20 percent increase in revenues.

Orion Township's tax base has grown along with its population, in sharp contrast to the decline that has characterized Detroit. The SEV increased by 14.3 percent from 1980 to 1982 and more than doubled from 1976 to 1981. The estimated SEV of almost $200 million (50 percent of its actual value) for the Lake Orion assembly plant nearly doubled again the township's tax base. Because of this steady growth in its tax base, Orion Township was not as desperate as was Detroit for the new GM plant, despite the major contribution that the plant would make to its tax revenues. Jobs, more than tax revenues, seem to have been the key to support for the plant: officials feared that GM would move out of state, taking with it the jobs of hundreds of township residents. The objective of the officials was to acquire the plant and then to minimize its impact on the surrounding area so as to preserve the semirural character of the community. Opposition to the plant also centered on its impact on the environment: opponents contended that the plant and the secondary development that it would generate would irreparably damage the character of the community, and would entail more costs than tax revenues.

GENERAL MOTORS PRESSES ITS DEMANDS

On the last day of February 1980, General Motors presented a document to Orion Township officials and to Governor Milliken, which began: "The following requirements must be satisfied in order to assure suitability of the Orion Township site for development of an automobile assembly plant."

The document then listed twenty-five demands relating to the provision of utilities, the improvement of transportation networks, the granting of tax abatements, "additional financial incentives" of an unspecified nature, and the securing of the necessary environmental permits from the state and federal governments and of variances in zoning and building codes from the township. Specific requirements included the widening and improving of the roads that would serve the plant; the relocation of a portion of one road; the improvement of freeway exits and entrances; the construction of railroad overpasses; the installation of street lights; the obtaining of state approval of environmental permits by mid May 1980; the rezoning of the site for heavy industrial use (to cover power-plant operation); the extension of water and sewer services; special rates for water and sewerage service; and the construction of a fire station within one mile of the plant site (this requirement was later dropped). The document concluded thus:

> Start of production for this plant is scheduled for the 1983 model year, which begins in July of 1982, and plant construction activities will begin this May. . . . Pursuant to the timely completion of our construction schedule, responses outlining steps wherein these matters will be resolved must be received by March 31, 1980 from State, county and township governmental units.[11]

GM left no doubt in the minds of public officials that the corporation was in a hurry. In addition to the accelerated plant-construction schedule previously announced, corporation officials claimed that the 1 June date was necessary in order to avoid coming under new Environmental Protection Agency guidelines, scheduled to go into effect on the second of June. GM's contention was supported by an official of the state of Michigan's Commerce Department, who noted that the new guidelines would require the installation of special air-quality monitoring equipment of the site, and that this could delay construction for up to a year. A 1 June ground breaking would allow the plant to use the currently approved monitoring systems.[12] Other GM officials indicated more flexibility. The general manager of the Pontiac Division, Robert Stempel, in a speech to the Chamber of Commerce of Lake Orion and Oxford, observed that the corporation would tolerate some delay, depending on the length of the postponement.[13] Later a corporate public-affairs official termed the deadline "a formality . . . not a critical point" and explained that the corporation had obtained a waiver of the environmental-monitoring requirement.[14]

During the early public meetings on the project, rumors circulated freely that GM would build the plant in the south or in Canada if its requirements were not fully met. GM did little to alter these perceptions and, indeed, kept the possibility of another plant location continually in front of the public and the governmental officials. GM's vice-president for public affairs, David Potter, explained the advantages of the Orion Township site as including the availability of an experienced labor force, the ease of transition from other facilities in Pontiac, and its concern for the unemployment of workers (and the unemployment compensation that the corporation would have to pay). But Potter added the ever-present threat of relocation that was included in virtually every public statement on GM operations: "If taxes, availability of natural gas and costs of utilities, roads, land and workers compensation were compared among states, we could only conclude that it is more costly to stay than it is to leave the area—and Michigan."[15]

The corporation also made sure that the public officials to whom it had presented its demands were fully cognizant of the company's potential to relocate. Documents presented to Orion Township's planning officials contained information on the search for an alternative site, including the obtaining of an option on the property. The Environmental Impact Statement, prepared for GM by a consulting firm, while noting that the Orion Township site was "the best alternative in a severely limited field," indicated that "back-up sites outside the State of Michigan were reviewed and are also being considered *on a continuing basis as part of the survey process.*"[16]

To many of the environmentalist opponents of the project, such threats of relocation, on top of the very tight deadline and negotiating inflexibility on GM's demands to public officials, amounted to cynical manipulation, the ultimate in the arrogant use of corporate power. GM officials, of course, saw things differently. Under extreme pressure from the imports, corporate officials wanted as little delay as possible in the political process, a process that was often characterized by delay, inaction, and attention to vocal minorities, the opponents of "progress." The threat of alternate location was one tool to help achieve GM's demands as quickly as possible.

PASSIVITY IN PONTIAC

In Detroit, GM officials contacted city officials concerning the location of the Cadillac assembly plant, and site review was conducted by a joint city-corporation committee. In Pontiac, site review was conducted exclusively by GM, and Pontiac officials passively accepted the corporation's decision. While many citizens were unhappy about the decision to relocate outside of Pontiac, the fact that Pontiac residents would have jobs in Orion served to temper their opposition. Nevertheless, some consideration was given to possible sites in Pontiac after GM had rejected that location, both by environmentalists in Orion who were opposed to urban sprawl and feared that the plant would have a negative impact on the quality of life in their community, and by boosters of downtown Pontiac redevelopment, who opposed the Orion site because they anticipated that GM's relocation would adversely affect the efforts to revitalize the central city.

Although Pontiac was a relatively small city, it had suffered as much as any community over the years from the classic urban problems: suburbanization, white flight, an aging stock of housing, and decay of the center city. Many of the stores on South Saginaw, the main thoroughfare, are vacant and boarded up. More than one-third of the city's housing is dilapidated. The unemployment ratio in 1981 stood at 24 percent, and 45 percent of its residents lived on Aid to Families with Dependent Children (AFDC) or on Social Security.

Since the mid 1960s, revitalization efforts had centered on the Pontiac Plan, which had been developed by C. Don Davidson, a professor of architecture at the University of Detroit, and his students.[17] Davidson became deeply committed to downtown development and to his plan, and over the years he had promoted the Pontiac Plan in every available forum. In the course of time, Davidson moved into private practice and continued to promote his plan, making only minor modifications in it and pushing city, state, and federal officials, as well as executives of private corporations, to adopt and implement it. Along the way, he acquired a paper, the *Pontiac-Waterford Times,* which he used as a forum in which to promote his plan and to castigate officials who had the temerity to suggest deviations from it. He also engineered his selection as chairman of the Pontiac Downtown Development Authority, the only official position he held during his fifteen-year crusade for the redevelopment of Pontiac.

In November 1979 the Pontiac Plan finally seemed to be on its way to realization with the ground breaking for the Phoenix Center, an office and hotel complex. The city had secured GM's commitment to locate the headquarters of its Truck and Coach Division in one of the new downtown buildings, and development officials considered this a key success in obtaining commitments from other private investors.

Two months later, when GM announced that it was moving some of its operations out of Pontiac, some officials feared that this would raise doubts in the minds of other investors. In particular, Don Davidson was highly critical of what he termed GM's "lack of faith." Davidson, in an editorial in the *Pontiac-Waterford Times*, presented a convincing case for building the proposed plant on the site of an abandoned state mental hospital, the Clinton Valley Center, which was owned by the city of Pontiac.[18] He also accused the Pontiac officials who had supported the relocation of having a conflict of interest. According to the one city commissioner who opposed the move, five members of the commission were employees of GM.

GM claimed at that time and still maintains that the Clinton Valley site was too small and provided no room for expansion, while another Pontiac site, although larger, would have required that property be purchased from multiple owners and that the property could not have been acquired soon enough.[19] Davidson's response to this explanation was "GM is lying."[20]

Another official who investigated alternative sites early in 1980 was State Representative Alice Tomboulian, who represented Orion and Oakland townships. Tomboulian spent a month conferring with citizens and public and corporate officials, only to conclude that "GM does not intend to provide for any deviation or delay whatsoever in the time schedule on which they have embarked; and GM intends to place the plant in Orion Township or else not within our Pontiac area and possibly not within Michigan or the U.S.A." Tomboulian observed that Pontiac "desperately" needed the GM investment and labeled the situation "another case where a distressed urban center loses its industrial base while a suburban area is forced to accept unsought development."[21]

Most Pontiac officials, however, were enthusiastic early supporters of the project, rather than merely accepting it as less undesirable than an out-of-state move. Pontiac's Mayor Wallace Holland told a meeting of GM and city officials in February 1980: "The Pontiac City Commission is in full support of your actions in the City of Pontiac. We want to see an assembly plant in Pontiac or so close to Pontiac we can touch it."[22]

Pontiac officials seem to have been extremely fearful of jeopardizing their relationship with GM. Pontiac came about as close as possible to being a "company town." Although some six thousand workers were employed in the Pontiac assembly and Fisher Body plants that were being relocated, Pontiac would still be the locus of tens of thousands of GM jobs. GM's Truck and Coach Headquarters was located in Pontiac, as well as other facilities. Indeed, the corporation contributed fully 60 percent of Pontiac's property taxes, and GM employees paid a large share of city-income-tax revenues.[23] A majority of the members of the City Commission were employees of the corporation. Although GM never threatened to do so, city officials were concerned lest other facilities be lost, and they voiced virtually no criticism of the move.

GM officials also assured Pontiac officials that "every effort would be made to find new manufacturing operations for the two Pontiac plants."[24]

These reassurances periodically reappeared in news reports during debate on the Orion plant and helped to silence demands for a search to locate a Pontiac site for the new plant. GM's statement to the Orion Township Planning Commission, for example, alluded to plans to "put new work into the existing Pontiac Motors and Fisher Body facilities at some time in the future." Company officials later suggested that the two plants would be converted to make parts for new-model cars after the new assembly plant had opened.[25] In September 1980, plans for manufacturing parts for new two-seater commuter cars in the two plants were announced.[26]

Once the new plant was under construction, GM was more vague about its plans for the old facilities. Spokesman Don Postma reported in March 1982 that the corporation was conducting a search among its divisions for ways to use the old plants; several months later, he confirmed rumors that the old Pontiac plant would be converted to the production of a low-volume sports car for the 1984 model year.[27] When Pontiac officials voted to support GM's tax abatement in Orion Township, however, they had not been told of any definite plans for the reuse of the old assembly plant.

The proximity of the new plant meant that it was unlikely that many workers would relocate, thus reducing the impact on income-tax revenues. Estimates of the effect on property-tax revenues, however, varied considerably. Combined city and school taxes on the Fisher Body and Pontiac assembly plants were $5.7 million annually, but how much of this revenue would have been lost depended on what was to be done with the facilities.[28] Pontiac officials chose to emphasize the positive. Finance director Jose Santiago, basing his estimate on the reuse of the plants to manufacture commuter-car parts, calculated that there might be an increase in tax revenues as a result of the relocation. He suggested that automation of the new operations would increase the property value of the plants but would reduce employment, thus resulting in increased property-tax and decreased income-tax revenues. Another positive consequence, according to Santiago, would be a heightened awareness of the need to diversify the city's economic base.[29]

The psychological effect of the move and the possibility that it might generate negative feelings that would hurt efforts to revitalize the city's central business district was, to some city officials, far more important than the specific calculations of tax loss.[30] Tom Padilla, the lone Pontiac city commissioner who voted against GM's Orion tax-abatement proposal, cited this impact as his primary reason for opposing the move. According to Padilla, GM's announcement of its plans to move to Orion Township shortly before a contract was to be signed with a developer of a new downtown hotel complex was responsible for the developer's decision to pull out of that project. Plans for a downtown shopping mall, Padilla believed, were also scrapped because of the GM relocation announcement. Land for these developments was still vacant more than two years later; it was owned by the city, with redevelopment "at a standstill."[31]

As required by Michigan law, the Pontiac City Commission approved the relocation in early June, thus clearing the way for approval of the tax abatement on the new plant by the Orion Township Board. Retention of jobs, more than tax impacts, seemed to have been the primary concern of Pontiac officials, union members, and citizens, as it was for Orion Township supporters of the project. According to a member of the Pontiac Planning Commission who had doubts about the project, "to be against it was made to appear almost un-American."[32]

In the context of its lengthy involvement with the city of Pontiac and with its more recent participation in downtown redevelopment efforts, GM might, as it did in Detroit, have offered Pontiac an opportunity to bid on a plant site. Why such an initiative was not made is, of course, a moot issue but is worthy of some speculation because it is suggestive of factors that contribute to the success of local economic-development strategies. One plausible explanation is suggested by GM's description of the site-selection process: its site-review committee simply was able to find a suitable site near the old Pontiac plants with relative ease but was not able to do so in Detroit.

GM also emphasized its commitment to maintaining Detroit's tax base, but why should it be less committed to Pontiac, where it employed thirty-six thousand people, has been located for seventy years, and contributed significantly to downtown redevelopment efforts? Perhaps the answer is simply that a large-enough site could not be found in a city the size of Pontiac. Perhaps, because of the earlier timing of the Pontiac announcement, Pontiac officials were unaware of the provisions of Michigan's "quick take" law, which would have given them the ability to assemble a site from multiple parcels of property. Despite their extensive program to revitalize the central business district, Pontiac officials lacked Young's and Moten's access to high-level federal officials, which provided Detroit with the assurance that federal funds would be available to cover public-sector costs of pursuing a project on the scale of the GM project. Because they lacked the resources to assemble land for the project, Pontiac officials abandoned efforts to pursue the plant and then accepted the nearby Orion Township site as preferable to the much-feared out-of-state move. At least this would retain jobs for Pontiac workers, although it would take property-tax revenues away from the city. Or as Davidson and Padilla have charged, the Pontiac officials may have been acting, not as public officials, but as loyal company employees, concerned with protecting their jobs and fearing the wrath of the city's major employer.

SOME MODIFICATIONS IN PLANS

Although alternate sites were apparently never seriously considered, revisions were made in the Orion site plan prior to its presentation to the Orion Township Planning Commission. GM's statement to the commission implies that these changes were made in response to citizen concerns, noting that the earlier plan, which had shown rail yards on the eastern end of the plant site, "raised concern that residents of the area, particularly those in the mobile home part (which abuts the site) could experience adverse impacts. As a result of these concerns, consulting engineers recommended a new location."[33] Others who were involved in site planning claim that the change was made in response to the Grand Trunk Railroad's preference for an off-site location for the rail yards, because of the railroad's concern that noise regulations might be violated in the initial location of the rail yards. An official of Grand Trunk explained that the location of the rail yard on the plant site would also have required extensive and expensive excavation and filling of land; he estimated the cost of grading the site at $12 million. A consultant study, he added, found the off-site location to be more economical, because it would require less excavation and filling and because its distance from residential property would mean that regulations in regard to the noise level would not be violated. Although this plan for the rail yards required that Grand Trunk purchase 188 acres of land at a cost of $1.6 million, the yards were constructed for $11.5 million, slightly less than it would have cost just for landscaping the on-site location.[34]

This revision then, differed significantly from those proposed by opponents of the Detroit project plan, in that it did not increase the cost of the project and was proposed, not by "outsiders," but by a key partner in the planning and implementation of the project. GM did not feel compelled to raise the threat of out-of-state location when it was faced with these revisions of its plan. Nevertheless, this receptivity to modifications of the initial plan suggests that the corporation was not as wed to site specifications as it had claimed to be in the case of Detroit.

OPPOSITION DEVELOPS IN ORION

Opponents of the project in Orion Township sought, not to modify GM's plans, as did the Poletown Neighborhood Council in Detroit, but to prevent the plant from being built in their community. Under the title of Area Citizens for a Rural Environment (ACRE), opponents focused their efforts on GM's request for the rezoning of the plant site, which, they charged, violated the "semirural" concept of the community, which was embodied in the township's master plan.[35] They also expressed concern about the plant's impact on taxes and on the cost of providing police, fire, and other services for it.[36] ACRE's head, Paul Barbeau, a resident of neighboring Oxford, argued that population and economic growth that would be stimulated by the plant would result in greater needs for services and in higher taxes for the township, which at that time enjoyed the second-lowest tax rate in the Wayne-Oakland-Macomb tricounty area.[37] ACRE also considered taking legal action against GM, and Barbeau claimed that 250 homeowners had contributed to a legal fund. GM's response to the proposed suit, with its potential to delay construction, was to reiterate its threat to relocate.[38]

Other sources of opposition were residents of the Village Green Mobile Home Estates, which bordered on the plant site, and HiHill subdivision, which was located along a proposed sewer line for the plant. Fear that blacks would move into the township seems to have been one reason for opposition. Residents of these areas raised the possibility of a referendum on the rezoning decision. A newspaper report of the situation suggested that if the referendum could not be held until November, GM officials "might start serious talks with officials in Arkansas or Alabama." Corporation officials, according to the report, had confirmed that "viable alternative sites" existed in Alabama, Arkansas, and Canada.[39]

The threat of relocation was a realistic fear for local officials and for GM workers, as widespread public speculation about out-of-state sites took place throughout the policy discussions. One source for such speculation was the UAW, whose support for the project was early, consistent, and intense. Union officials repeated the rumors of relocation at public hearings, predicting that seven thousand jobs would leave the area if the plant were built out-of-state.[40] These views were repeated in newspaper editorials supporting the project, which forecast "economic devastation" for the area if the project were abandoned.[41] A committee of GM workers was established so as to generate support for the project among township residents, and union members circulated petitions in the township and at GM plants in Pontiac.[42] A particular concern of UAW members was that the plant might be located in Canada, where, they said, workers would have no rights to relocate.

At least one official of Orion Township, supervisor Joann Van Tassel, claimed to have been skeptical about the threats to relocate. Van Tassel observed that the amount of time that GM officials had invested in the Orion project—attending meetings, opening an information center, explaining their plans—suggested to her that they were not seriously considering other locations. She also noted that a move to the Sun Belt would be more costly to GM than the company had suggested.[43] Opponents of the project also challenged the credibility of the threats to relocate, checking to determine if GM had initiated applications for environmental permits at any other sites.

THE PLANNING COMMISSION ACTS

Despite the threats to relocate, township officials resisted pressures to alter their standard operating procedures in order to meet GM's deadlines. The Planning Commission held to its pattern of holding three meetings before acting on the site plan. The rezoning request required approval not only by the Planning Commission but also by the township board and by the Oakland County's Planning Division; it was not approved finally until June 18. The Planning Commission scheduled two public hearings; then it held two special meetings to discuss comments that had been received at the hearings. These were followed by a study meeting and another special meeting before the rezoning request was approved—all in a period of three weeks. Three days after the Planning Commission had approved the rezoning request, another public hearing was held by the township board, which approved the request two days later, at its regular meeting on 19 May 1980.

GM's presence altered the conduct of the meetings. Planning Commission meetings and public hearings were dominated by the presence of fifteen to twenty corporate representatives, including public-relations, real-estate, engineering, and environmental experts, who would confer among themselves before answering questions. Planning Commission members, although they received advice from a planner, an engineer, and a lawyer, felt inadequately informed. The commission did not have enough time to study the project, and it was pressured to act quickly by the supporters, who repeated the threat of an out-of-state location for the plant.[44]

A REFERENDUM ON DEVELOPMENT

Opponents of the project did not give up the fight after losing before the Planning Commission. Michigan law makes it possible for citizens to challenge the actions of elected officials through the initiative, the referendum, and the recall. Opponents of the project had already laid the groundwork for challenging the rezoning approval when the township's Board of Supervisors voted on May 19.

The right of voters to approve or reject acts of legislative bodies (such as the township board) is established by the Michigan Constitution (art. 2, sec. 9). Referendum petitions must contain a number of signatures equal to or greater than 5 percent of the persons who voted for gubernatorial candidates in the last gubernatorial election. For such a question to be voted on in a state general, primary, or special election, wording for the ballot must be approved by the local or county clerk at least forty-nine days before the election. Petitions for the questions to be placed on the ballot must be filed with the county or local clerk at least fourteen days before the date by which the wording of the ballot must be certified.[45] With the state primary scheduled for 5 August 1980, this timetable meant that organizers of the petition drive had to work quickly after the township board approved the rezoning request on 19 May.

The prospect of the referendum rekindled fears of relocation and generated increased activity by groups that supported or opposed the project. Before the township board had approved the rezoning request, the *Oakland Press* speculated that scheduling the referendum in November (during the regular election) rather than in August (during the primary) might prompt GM to initiate serious discussions with officials in Alabama or Arkansas.[46] Nevertheless, opponents of the project were able to complete the task of circulating the petitions in time for the August primary.

As the August referendum date approached, interest in the rezoning issue sparked a sizable increase in voter registration. Supporters of the project rented sound trucks and billboards, distributed yard signs and handbills, and mobilized a telephone campaign. A full-page advertisement in the *Lake Orion Review*, which was paid for by the Orion with GM Committee, raised the threat of relocation: "If the referendum is not passed, GM will have to consider other alternatives." This ad pointed out that the rejection of the plant would result in the loss of "six thousand jobs to support local taxes, six thousand jobs that generate approximately $135 million in incomes."[47]

The metropolitan, as well as the local, media were supportive of the project; again the loss of jobs was the primary concern. A "TV2 Viewpoint" observed: "This plant ought to be built. It'd mean 6,000 jobs, jobs that might be lost to another state if GM is blocked from following through its original plan"; it urged Orion Township's voters to support the plant.[48]

The highly charged issue also mobilized groups that were usually nonpolitical. One strong supporter was the United Way of Pontiac/North Oakland County. As early as March 1980 a memorandum was circulated to executives of United Way agencies, requesting that they testify in support of the project. On 18 April a follow-up memo asked not only for "immediate assistance which could be crucial to the final result of present deliberations" but also specifically for information on the impacts that the plant would have on agency financing, staffing, client load, and demand for services "if General Motors is forced to move a major portion of its operation to another state (or country)."[49]

Opponents of the project, led by ACRE, had initially emphasized the negative effect that the plant would have on the township's "semirural character." Now the financial costs of the plant were stressed in fliers that they circulated prior to the referendum, which claimed that the plant would result in higher taxes and lower property values for township residents. Unlike the Poletown opposition, they presented no alternatives, implying that *any* location for the plant was preferable to that in Orion Township. An analysis prepared by one opponent of the project concluded that (1) additional tax revenues that would be generated for the Lake Orion School District by the plant would result in no net gain, because they would serve only to reduce state aid; (2) most of the financial benefits from the plant would go to the state of Michigan (in the form of a reduction in state school aid, which is tied to SEV) and to Oakland County (because its tax rate was higher than the township's); and (3) the township's share of GM tax revenues would be less than the expenditures that would be necessitated by the plant, including a new fire station, fire equipment, and additional costs of law enforcement.[50]

More than 40 percent of the township's registered voters voted in the rezoning referendum of 5 August 1980. GM and its development-oriented allies won overwhelmingly—4,311 in favor, 1,178 against, a difference of 79 percent to 21 percent. On the next day, GM obtained its building permit for the plant. Ground-breaking ceremonies took place two months later.

SEWER POLITICS

The start of construction of the plant, however, did not signal the end of public controversy over the project. Still to be resolved were the location and financing for sewer and water lines, which were surprisingly controversial.

There were several possible alternative arrangements for the plant's sewer connections. GM suggested three possible routes to Orion Township's Planning Commission and to its Board of Supervisors: connection to the Pontiac system, connection to the Clinton-Oakland interceptor to the south of the site, and connection to the Paint Creek interceptor to the northeast of the site. According to a statement filed by GM with the Michigan Department of Natural Resources, the Clinton-Oakland and Paint Creek routes, which connected to the Detroit sewage system, were preferable because of "contractual and jurisdictional constraints on the Pontiac plant."[51] The Pontiac connection would have benefited that city, whose sewer system had been built to sufficient capacity to accommodate GM, and some Pontiac officials tried to obtain the hookup. Pontiac officials were also concerned that secondary development along a new sewer route would be drawn from Pontiac.

Both political and technical factors appear to have influenced the selection of the more costly Paint Creek route. One explanation sees the choice as a consequence of pressure from Oakland County executive Daniel

Murphy, who, one township official claimed, would benefit financially from any secondary development along this route. According to this official, township board member Van Tassel, who then worked for Oakland County, had changed her position on the sewer issue and had explained this by saying, "Dan Murphy is my boss." Van Tassel, however, offered an explanation that emphasized the cost and capacity of the alternative systems. The Clinton-Oakland route, she claimed, did not have enough capacity for GM, because much of its capacity was in residential use. Using this system would have required that arrangements be made with surrounding communities to obtain more capacity, which would have been very costly, according to Van Tassel. Use of the Pontiac system would have necessitated tunneling under Interstate 75 and securing the agreement of other communities through which the sewer would have had to run. Routing the sewer northeast to the Paint Creek interceptor, she claimed, was financially most desirable and was most feasible from an engineering standpoint. That interceptor had an adequate capacity, and more connections to it were needed in order to pay off the bond issue for the construction of sewers. Connection to the GM plant would absorb 53 percent of the line's capacity and would provide the township with funds to pay for its share of the bond costs, which otherwise would have required it to levy a tax.

Selection of a sewer route, however, did not end the dispute over the sewer issue. Problems arose over payment for the sewer because GM refused to pay any sewer charges before the plant had been built, yet the sewer connection had to be constructed before the plant could open. An agreement was negotiated providing for Orion Township to sell bonds to finance the building of the sewer connection and for GM to make repayment over a thirty-year period at the same interest rate as that for the bonds. The cost to GM will total $7.2 million, including approximately $6.5 million in capital charges (which go toward paying for the interceptor capacity) and $763,000 in lateral charges (GM's share of the cost for the connection from the interceptor to the plant). The cost of the lateral line, however, was $2.1 million, so additional hookups to it will be needed in order to pay off the bonds.

The township subsequently encountered difficulty in selling the bonds; therefore it had to advance $1.5 million in township funds so that the sewer construction could begin. Although the $1.5 million would be returned when the bonds were sold, $150,000 in interest would be lost.[52] The bonds, which were marketed jointly by Oakland County and Orion Township, were first offered in June 1981 but found no buyers at a 10 percent interest rate. Another issue in December 1981, which bore a 13 percent interest rate, also found no buyers.[53] After a third unsuccessful issue in January 1982, supervisor Van Tassel raised the possibility of a tax levy to cover the cost of the township's payments of interest and principal for the sewer connection.[54] Inability to sell the bonds contributed to a controversy over GM's request in February 1982 that the partially completed plant be connected to the new sewer line. The township board initially refused the request, claiming that the connection could not be made until the bonds had been sold; so a GM attorney threatened to sue the township. After a lengthy and heated meeting, the board voted 5 to 2 to allow the connection, which involved the removal of a concrete plug in the system at a cost of less than $200.[55] The bond issue finally was successfully issued on 12 May 1982 at an effective rate of 11.5 percent.

Arrangements for water lines for the plant were completed more quickly and with less controversy. The plant was to be connected to the Detroit water system through the construction of a $3-million water line from the south. An April 1980 letter from the director of the Detroit Water and Sewer Department, Charles Beckham, to the township board indicated that money for the construction could be diverted from the city's $33-million water revenue fund.[56]

CONCLUSIONS

The passivity of Pontiac in the face of its loss of a major facility contrasted dramatically with Detroit's aggressiveness (and, as we shall see, Flint's). There is no doubt that GM's massive presence in Pontiac affected the performance of city officials. The company contributed heavily to the city's tax base; it was far and away the major employer in the city; and many of the city's part-time elected officials were employees of GM. Indeed, five of the seven members of Pontiac's City Commission were GM employees. Mayor Holland, a physical-plant employee, was granted extensive released time for his work with the city. (Holland had received a company promotion when he was selected as mayor.) Moreover, during the period of negotiations between GM and the city, Pontiac had a council-manager form of government. Hence, no public official with an independent electoral base was available to perform the roles that Coleman Young performed in Detroit: namely, rallying public support for an initiative and aggressively pursuing policy options with federal, state, and other local units of government.

Finally, the city of Pontiac was heavily dependent on the corporation for the success of its downtown-redevelopment efforts. GM had agreed to locate the headquarters of its Truck and Coach Division downtown, and city officials felt keenly the need to work with corporate officials if redevelopment were to be successful. Of the major political figures in Pontiac, only publisher C. Don Davidson, the father of the Pontiac Plan for downtown revitalization, publicly questioned the failure of city officials to pursue the option of a Pontiac location for the new assembly plant.

The abililty of General Motors to generate overwhelming support for a move *out* of town is important evidence of the ability of a corporation to influence community decision making by indirect means. Clearly, direct threats were important to the decision made by Pontiac officials to remain silent while GM left town. These threats by corporate officials played on the fears that jobs would be lost for the entire area. If Pontiac and Orion Township were not amenable to relocation, then Michigan might lose the facility entirely. Pontiac officials knew full well that workers who lived in Pontiac could easily commute to the Orion facility—indeed, this was one of the reasons that GM chose the Orion site.

Indirect influences on decision making were, however, more important. Making decisions that were contrary to the wishes of GM in Pontiac seems to have been simply out of the question. Prevailing community opinion was not favorable to an attack on the major provider of economic livelihoods in Pontiac. Many city officials were GM employees, who shared with other employees the fear of loss of jobs. The company had invested heavily in Pontiac's redevelopment. The factors provided a backdrop of community concern that operated to define attacks against the corporation as being beyond the pale. Hence real conflict never really emerged on the relocation issue.

The situation in Orion Township was very different. Environmentally concerned citizens mounted a vigorous attack on the project, and they generated substantial support in their attempt to kill the project. Township officials were concerned primarily with the threat of the loss of jobs from the area; they considered the direct additions to the property-tax base only secondarily. The battle lines were drawn between the proponents of jobs and economic growth, on the one hand, and the proponents of maintaining the quality of the living environment in the township, on the other. The conflict followed the classic growth-versus-no-growth lines of conflict in exurbia, but it was extraordinarily intense because of the economic recession in Michigan at the time. Opponents included environmentally conscious middle-class citizens and residents of subdivisions in close proximity to the proposed plant. Supporters included virtually all other community political actors: the local retailers, the UAW, area (and metropolitan) newspapers, governmental officials. The opponents of the project were able to initiate a ballot review of the township's decision to rezone the GM property, but they were soundly defeated in the ensuing election. In this controversy, the direct threat of relocation was raised again and again by GM and by other proponents of the plant, especially the UAW.

The kinds of political coalitions that were activated in Detroit and in Orion Township, then, were substantially different. The quality-of-life coalition in Orion was comprised of middle- and upper-income residents, many of whom were connected with nearby Oakland University. It contrasted starkly with the Poletown Neighborhood Council's base of elderly Polish-Americans who had modest incomes. It was, however, equally ineffective.

There were other contrasts between politics in the city and politics in exurbia. The most striking was the political disagreement in Orion over the extension of the sewer lines. Such problems were handled without incident in Detroit, but they generated a great deal of heat in Orion, which lacked Detroit's efficient public bureaucracy for dealing with such items on a more-or-less routine basis.

12

Flint:
Political Maneuvering and Buick City

Flint will always be a General Motors Town. . . . Heaven help us if
we are not.

—James Rutherford, mayor of Flint, Michigan

The relationship between the city of Flint and the General Motors Corporation is simple and direct: the latter is the raison d'être for the former. Genesee County and Flint are home to eleven major GM manufacturing facilities, including the main assembly plant for the Buick Motor Division, AC Sparkplug Assembly, Chevrolet Engine and Assembly plants, and three Fisher Body plants. In addition, the city is home to Buick World Headquarters and AC Sparkplug Headquarters, as well as several GM research and development facilities. In 1982, GM's worst year since the Great Depression, the corporation provided employment for more than fifty-five thousand residents of Genesee County, had a payroll of $1.7 billion, and added more than $4.2 billion to the local economy through the payrolls of and purchases from suppliers in the area.

In Flint, GM means jobs. When the company is selling cars and trucks, people work. When the company is experiencing difficulty in selling its products, people don't work. From 1956 to 1982 the correlation between automobile production by GM in the Flint region and the unemployment rate in the region was a robust −.80.[1]

Despite the massive GM presence in Flint, the first impression that a visitor to the city has is not industrial might but main-street America. The city is built on the gently rolling slopes of the Genesee River, and houses, stores, and winding streets at first conceal an industrial city which has a number of decaying neighborhoods and a substantial number of empty stores on Saginaw Street, Flint's central artery. The massive impact that America's industrial revolution has had on Flint is brought home, however, only when one encounters the sprawling Buick complex on the city's north end. The wooden workers' cottages and two-flats that once clustered around the factory, reminding one of the peasant huts crowding the walls of a medieval city, are now in a state of disrepair, if they are still standing. But the dominant feature of Flint's landscape is the huge headquarters and assembly complex; not the winding streets or the rushing river or the new high-rise hotel downtown. Even the decayed neighborhoods and boarded-up storefronts no longer strike one as being important. One's impression of Flint is forever changed by one glance at this industrial behemoth.

Flint, however, almost lost this huge assembly facility. The same set of corporate decisions that brought the Poletown plant to Detroit and replaced the Pontiac "home" plant with the new Assembly Division plant in Orion Township targeted Buick's "home" assembly plant in Flint for closure. Only a fortuitous combination of changing economic circumstances, bold leadership at Buick, and a "masterful stroke" of leadership by Flint's mayor kept Buick in the assembly business and, therefore, kept Buick in Flint. An appreciation of this convergence of events requires some understanding of the public economy of the birthplace of General Motors.

POLITICS AND GOVERNMENT

Flint's formal governmental structure is of the classic "unreformed" variety. The mayor is directly elected from the city as a whole, and he has full appointment and budgetary powers. The City Council is elected from nine single-member wards, and its members generally reflect the demographics of their constituents.

It was not always thus. Indeed, for most of its modern municipal history, Flint possessed a "reformed" structure: a city manager, a weak mayor, and an at-large council. In 1975, Flint reformed its "reformed" structure, introducing a strong elected mayor and a ward-based council, along with other changes in its charter.

Electoral politics in Flint has traditionally been union politics; the only issue is which union. In recent years, three have been important: the UAW, the AFL-CIO, and the AFSCME (American Federation of State, County and Municipal Employees). The UAW established itself as a force to be reckoned with in Flint when it organized the sit-down strike at Fisher Body number 1 in 1937. The AFSCME and other municipal unions came to power much later, riding the wave of the unionization of the public sector during the 1950s and 1960s.

The UAW endorsement is the single most important prize that a candidate for public office in Flint can win. As James Rutherford, the two-term mayor of the city, put it, "Anybody who says they don't want the UAW endorsement in Genesee County is foolish."[2] The endorsement brings instant voter recognition, which is especially important in council elections, and campaign aid.

In recent elections, Flint's black community has asserted itself and is currently a key factor in local politics. In November 1983 a black staff member of the state senate, James Sharp, defeated incumbent mayor James Rutherford, despite the fact that Rutherford had endorsements from all of the major unions. Sharp's razor-thin victory was accomplished through

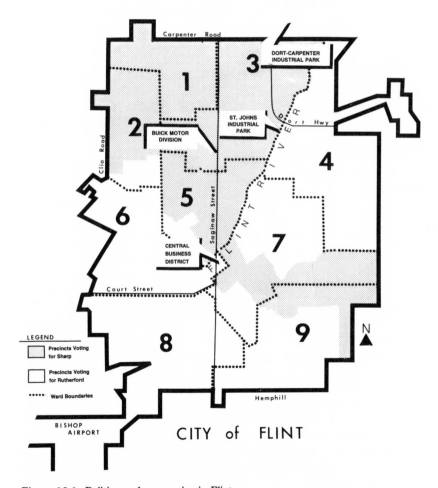

Figure 12.1. Politics and economics in Flint.

superior organization in the city's black neighborhoods. Black churches acted as the key component of the organizational network. Sharp also had substantial appeal in white neighborhoods, a phenomenon that the head of the Genesee UAW–Community Action Program has attributed to Rutherford's closeness to big business and to his endorsement by the *Flint Journal*.[3] Union endorsements continued to be important in council elections, however, with several contests simply being tests of strength among the three major unions.

Business interests are notably absent from electoral politics in Flint. The predominantly working-class electorate has not been sympathetic to business-backed candidates, even when they have been "consensus" candidates. In recent years, no candidate could afford to be perceived as being too close to "big business," which generally means General Motors.

GM, for its part, stays as far away as possible from local electoral politics. There are several reasons for this, the most important of which have to do with the lack of necessity to engage in local politics. Most issues that would require political action on the part of the corporation are dealt with at the federal or state level. Moreover, when local action has been necessary, GM has been able to count on the support of city officials regardless of their political affiliations. Everybody realizes the importance of the corporation to the local economy and is unlikely to engage in actions that would endanger the relationship.

Any political action that is initiated by the corporation could, given Flint's political culture, be counterproductive. The sheer size and importance of GM to the local community means that it is a powerful symbol, an object to attack when things go wrong. According to at least one GM executive, the company stays out of local politics as a matter of corporate policy:

> I cringe every time anybody says that "They're trying to run this community." We stay out of Flint politics; we stay out of all local politics. We are too big for them.
>
> For example, Mayor Rutherford, he is a good guy, but I'll bet we didn't give him twenty-five dollars in campaign contributions. I hope that he is not too upset; I hope he understands.[4]

Elections, then, in recent years have been the province of the unions, although increasingly the black community and its churches have provided an independent electoral base. Business interests are far less important, and the largest business interests are almost completely uninvolved in the electoral process. General Motors does not endorse candidates; it does not make campaign contributions; it does not work with other business interests to back candidates silently. Elections are not the manner in which the corporation influences community policies. Indeed, for the most part, the corporation is not interested in influencing community policies.

MOTT, GENERAL MOTORS, AND CIVIC PROJECTS

In no community do major projects of civic development spring fully completed from the dreams of politicians and city planners. This is doubly true of a declining industrial community such as Flint, where attracting private-sector investment is somewhat like getting the Genesee River to flow upstream. Only with concerted civic action can such projects be completed.

In Flint the job of "leveraging" has been somewhat eased by the existence of the Charles S. Mott Foundation, whose headquarters are in the Mott Building in the central business district. The nation's tenth-largest philanthropic organization was established by Mott, a Flint industrialist and early investor in General Motors; and it is still firmly in the hands of the Mott family today. The president of the foundation since 1971 has been William S. White, a son-in-law of Harding Mott, a former president of the foundation. Under White, the foundation has continued its commitment to social-service projects, but it has also been important in taking the lead on a number of critical civic projects. These projects include the Flint campus of the University of Michigan, the Hyatt-Regency Hotel complex, a new state office building, and Autoworld, a theme park and automotive museum. A grant from the Mott Foundation has underwritten the acquisition of properties for a downtown pedestrian shopping mall.

The foundation has contributed to civic projects by "putting up front money to do some studies, find out what is needed and what can be done. They put up the money, bring in the experts, package the deal."[5] The packaging of the deal means rounding up other investors, which always include General Motors. GM contributed $1 million to the Autoworld complex and invested $900,000 in the Hyatt complex. More importantly, however, GM's commitment to the project meant the use of it by executives, who were encouraged "to entertain in 'our hotel.' "[6]

The result is that the foundation serves as a focal point for civic action. A GM executive who had worked in both Pontiac and Flint commented:

> Pontiac really does not have that prime mover like the Mott Foundation, and we are just not able to fill that role in Pontiac. And there is really not anybody else to do it. I think they are suffering because of that. I don't know that there is any more money in this community than there is in Pontiac, if you eliminate the foundation from consideration. There is nobody there who is willing to step in and do that initial organization that needs to be done. We serve on committees that are doing some of that

work, but they just don't have the same tone to them that is available here.[7]

What has emerged is a close cooperative relationship between the Mott Foundation, city government, and the Flint Area Conference, Inc. (FACI), an association of business officials which has a paid staff whose sole purpose is economic redevelopment in Flint.[8] The activities of FACI are supported financially by the Mott Foundation. Although the city has seldom taken the lead on civic projects, it has provided the necessary public-sector support for projects, including tax incentives, changes in land use, and expertise in arranging the ever-necessary state and federal grants.

General Motors rarely takes the lead in civic projects in Flint. It can be persuaded to invest in such projects, but the company generally has concentrated on the automobile business. GM is not an organization that aids in mobilizing community resources to achieve community ends, and its officers generally do not participate in such activities. In Flint, it has been the Mott Foundation that has taken the lead in civic mobilization, with GM as a passive investment partner.

A "MASTERFUL STROKE"

Corporations influence communities far more by their business decisions than by their political ones. Like Dupont, which, according to Raymond Bauer, Ithiel Pool, and Anthony Dexter, engaged in few attempts to exert its influence in Delaware, GM did not need to "dance among the chickens" in Flint.[9] But it would be a mistake to conclude that GM's influence in the community was also low. Public policy in Flint is influenced, and not so subtly, by the business decisions that are made by the corporate giant that provides livelihoods to most of Flint's residents.

In the spring of 1980, Mayor James Rutherford faced the most severe crisis of his political career. GM announced publicly that it planned to replace Buick's "home" assembly plant with an Assembly Division (GMAD) plant and that it was investigating several possible sites. The new plant would produce the company's new front-wheel-drive line, and Buick Division would lose control over the assembly operations. The move was part of GM's capital-improvement program, and it reflected the standardization of production that the company had adopted as policy. Not only was the plant to be prototypical, but it was also to produce a standardized "world car," which might end up being labeled Buick or Oldsmobile or Chevrolet. Because the new factories used a "unitized" body design, Flint would also lose the Fisher Body facilities that supplied Buick's home assembly plant. While the specifics were far from clear, it was evident that the city of Flint was facing an economic disaster of the first magnitude.

Rutherford recalled the situation thus: "We knew that they—somebody—was buying up property in Vienna Township, getting options. But the first we knew that they had planned that was when they made the public announcement that they were going to build a Poletown type of plant out there."[10]

Rutherford immediately contacted Argonaut Realty, the real-estate arm of GM, and objected to the decision. He was informed that the company had already considered sites in Flint and that no possible sites existed; the city simply lacked the square mile of territory that was necessary for the construction of a modern assembly plant.

As a courtesy to the city of Flint, GM's President Thomas Murphy offered to delay the site-selection process for a month to give the city an opportunity to study the feasibility of a site in Flint. It was Rutherford's belief that "they were convinced that there was no way that we could find the square mile that was acceptable to them and that it could be cleared. They didn't want another Poletown. They hadn't really gotten into the nitty-gritty of Poletown, but they knew that they didn't want to be involved in the problems of relocating thousands of households."

The director of Flint's Downtown Development Authority (DDA) expressed the belief that this offer came about because of the company's public relations efforts on the Detroit Poletown plant:

> You know General Motors—they don't give a damn about the city. They are bottom-line oriented. The statements by Murphy in Detroit boxed the company. Murphy was saying what a great city Detroit was, what a good place it was to do business, and how the company would not desert the city. The company felt it had to at least ask if Flint could produce a site, but they gave the city thirty days.[11]

Rutherford and his economic-development officials, however, never considered the possibility of obtaining and clearing a site inside the city limits. Instead, they immediately began to examine the possibility of annexing land in the surrounding unincorporated townships. This was a risky strategy at best: suburban/city relationships were not good, and there were significant legal problems with the annexation option. Nevertheless, this was the only avenue that was even partially open to city officials.

The first site that the city examined was a combination of city-owned land at an airport in Flint Township. The company quickly rejected this site, claiming that it was not large enough. Then the city negotiated with Mundy Township to "square off" the airport site and came to agreement in principle with both townships on annexation.

While GM never actually rejected the site, it did raise a number of concerns. This led city officials to begin the search again. The city owned seventy-five acres of land just east of Genesee Township's Dort-Carpenter

Industrial Park, northeast of the city of Flint. City officials approached Genesee Township, and again an agreement was reached. The city's land could serve as a starting point for the square mile of territory that would be needed for the plant, and land was available in the industrial park. From the standpoints of the governments involved, the site was ideal.

In a meeting at corporate headquarters in Detroit in July, both the Mundy and Genesee Township sites were presented to corporate officials. Although neither site was rejected, it was clear that neither site made the corporation happy. "They seemed commited to the Vienna Township site, but they were never direct about their intentions," Rutherford noted.

On 26 September, city officials met with GM officials in Rutherford's office. Again, the company representatives were not encouraging about either site. Then the economic-development coordinator, Patrick Martin, proposed that several hundred acres north of the Genesee Township site be obtained. Martin recalled: "The GM engineers loved it. It was the right size, close to the railroad, near the freeway."[12]

Argonaut Realty, however, was not enthusiastic about the new site. A not inconsiderable amount of professional pride was involved in this, as Argonaut's real-estate specialists had not considered the Genesee Township site. George Fox, the head of Argonaut's site-selection team, expressed reservations about the city's ability to assemble the necessary options in a timely manner. Rutherford felt that these objections were rooted in concerns of personal status rather than in real problems with the site:

> They hadn't given us the opportunity of being on a par with them. Yet we had our options signed almost as quickly as they finalized their's. That's professional problems. Professional ego. They paid more for their property than we paid for ours—after everybody knew what we were doing. They had already announced what they were doing, and it became a newspaper thing where everybody knew pretty well what must be happening. We paid a pretty stiff price for it, but we were going to end up with another two hundred acres of economic development area for suppliers.[13]

Flint had offered Genesee Township the opportunity to split the tax proceeds from the GM plant at Flint's higher tax rate on a fifty-fifty basis in return for the township's agreement to the annexation plan. The city and township then worked together to obtain the necessary property options, which was simpler because of the small number of owners in the area. As each owner signed the option, he or she also signed a petition for annexation. Genesee Township hired the Michigan Township Association's leading antiannexation attorney to represent its interests before the state's boundary commission. The attorney expressed considerable surprise at being retained to argue in favor of an annexation.

The legal agreements took almost three weeks to complete; they were not finished until hours before they were approved by the township board and the City Council. The entire plan was greeted with skepticism by state and local officials who were familiar with annexation law. As Flint's city attorney recalled, "Everyone—including the attorney general's office, GM, the township's attorney—told us we couldn't do it." Yet the state's new Charter Township Act, which was designed to protect townships from being annexed by cities, included provisions that allowed annexation if the township boards approved.[14]

Jack Litzenberg, the city's director of economic development, immediately applied to the United States Department of Housing and Urban Development for a $17.8-million Urban Development Action Grant (UDAG) in order to buy and prepare the site. Flint's application was approved, and with the approval of the annexation arrangement by the state, the package was complete. City officials had been able to put together the package at less cost than had the Argonaut Realty specialists, even though by that time all owners knew why the city was buying land.

General Motors now faced making a choice between the Vienna Township site, assembled by its own realty division, and the Genesee Township site, assembled by the city. Although the company would pay up to $1 million more in property taxes at the Flint site, water and sewer service would be substantially more expensive at the Vienna site. Flint also levies a 1 percent corporate income tax, based on the share of a company's new income that is attributable to a plant.[15] Nevertheless, Flint had the good word of the president of the company that a Flint site would be considered seriously, and Flint officials believed that GM now had little choice but to move ahead with the site that they had offered. Rutherford claimed: "We had them locked. They could have never proceeded with Vienna Township. They would have had so much egg on their face. We lived up to every condition they had."[16] According to the DDA's Director William Whitney, it was "a masterful stroke" of leadership.

"ALL OF OUR WORK FOR NAUGHT"

It is commonplace for urbanists to observe that city policies are influenced by forces external to the city. Not only do other levels of government affect local decision making, but city officials must also deal with corporations that increasingly are being organized on an international scale. What is less commonly noted, however, is that those same international corporations often affect local affairs as a consequence of attempting to adjust to forces that they do not themselves control. Hence, cities can experience strong second-order effects. As corporations adjust to changes in the international economy, they make decisions that affect localities.

In 1981, Roger Smith assumed the position of chairman of the board of General Motors. The company faced the worst economic situation since the Great Depression. Automotive sales were plummeting, and profits were dropping to record postwar lows. It was clear that the company's optimistic capital-improvement plans would have to be scaled back. The retrenchment in the construction of assembly plants began, with the company canceling construction plans in Baltimore, in Kansas City, and in Flint. "We walked into a meeting with General Motors, told them we had the UDAG grant, and they began backing off," reported Jack Litzenberg, Flint's director of economic development.[17] "All of our very expeditious work went for naught," lamented the mayor.

THE ENTREPRENEUR IN THE GREY SUIT

Lloyd Reuss, head of GM's Buick Division, had not been pleased at the prospect of losing control of assembly operations. When it became clear that the new assembly plant that was planned for the Flint area would very likely be an Assembly Division plant, Reuss assembled a team of twenty to twenty-five corporate decision makers and planners in order to examine the possibilities of restructuring Buick operations within the existing facilities in Flint. The "Buick City" team, headed by Reuss's aide Herb Stone, was particularly intrigued with the "kan ban," or just-in-time, inventory system that was being used in Japanese automotive manufacture, and the team made trips to Japan to study the method. The result was a presentation to the company's corporate board, where the proposal was greeted with considerable skepticism. Economic turbulence, however, aided Reuss's cause. Because of the severity of the economic recession, even GM was relatively short of capital, and the Buick City program would require a considerably smaller capital investment than would a new Assembly Division plant. Reuss won the day and was given the go-ahead for his Buick City concept. Reuss commented: "The awarding of this massive project to Buick by General Motors means that Buick will remain in the assembly business for years to come. Without it, Buick would cease to be an assembler."[18]

The openness of the corporation, which had long been regarded as a bastion of conservative management practices, to the new approach is itself interesting. The corporation has long been of two minds on the issue of decentralization, on the one hand claiming wide latitude on the part of division managers, and, on the other hand, increasingly centralizing the making of decisions at corporate headquarters in Detroit. As development, engineering, and finally, assembly operations were set up separately from the traditional divisions and as much of design became standardized, many observers questioned the autonomy of the division structure. The company, however, has a policy of competition among divisions for work that has to be done for all divisions, and the divisions must bid on projects that have been authorized by central management. One consequence for cities is that if a division loses a project, the area will lose jobs, and plants will be vacated. An imaginative manager may be able to attract another project to the idle space, but that is not guaranteed.

A consequence of this system is that city economies are very dependent on the abilities of division managers to deal competitively with other parts of the corporation. One GM executive commented: "Hell, there is more competitiveness within than without. Our managers in every city are looking for ways to save their business and add jobs. They all have to win, and they have to keep on winning. Nothing is guaranteed. That has been one of our greatest strengths."[19]

This can lead to some instability in local employment patterns, even during flush economic times. During the late 1970s, Oldsmobile Division in Lansing underbid Buick for conventional rear axles, manufactured by Buick for most GM divisions. That left vacant productive space in Flint. Later Buick filled the space by winning a contract for torque converters. This internal competitiveness leaves city economies more at the mercy of changes in internal policies at GM than if a more stable internal pattern of contract placement were followed. It also makes city policies more sensitive to GM's internal decisions. As the economic-development administrator of Flint admitted, "We try to keep local plants in as competitive a position as they can be, so when they have to bid on a project they can hopefully bid lower than other plants, and keep the jobs here."[20]

The system of internal corporate competition allowed Buick's management to argue a proposal that ran counter to corporate management's plans to build new Assembly Division facilties to assemble automobiles. While this worked in favor of Flint, the system of internal competition also adds additional instability to local economies that are dependent on GM. It also offers local plant managers an additional opportunity to extract benefits from local governments under the threat that the local facility will not be competitive with other GM operations. From the point of view of city officials, it is certainly a mixed blessing.

A CORPORATE COMPACT

The new "Buick City" complex, which was to rise, phoenixlike, from the Flint Buick Assembly plant and the surrounding decaying neighborhoods, was aimed directly at the corporate bottom line. It was not designed to save Flint; it was designed to save Buick. While the corporation was commited to investing $235 million in Buick's modernization project, it would also close Flint Fisher and merge the body-building plant with the assembly operation in the new "unitized body" design to be used for the company's X cars. Buick was building bodies for its rear-wheel-drive cars at Fisher, and then was transporting them by truck to Buick Assembly; this was enormously inefficient. (It also led to charges made by some local observers that the interstate highway through the city followed its course because of this system.) The merger would, even if successful, cost the city some 3,600 jobs. Of the 8,600 workers normally employed at the two facilities, only 5,000 would be retained at Buick City.

Buick City has spawned a whole new set of relationships between management, workers, the government, and corporate suppliers. Buick is committed to a less adversarial relationship with workers, but the real commitment from the corporation that is not known for its forward-looking labor relations has yet to be tested. The Buick City team had union representation from the outset, and periodic reviews of the project have included UAW leadership. Union representatives have also served on project-implementation teams, and input from union representatives has been taken seriously, a clear break from past practices.

SUPPLIERS

Under the Buick City plan, relationships between the company and its suppliers are changing dramatically. In the past, contracts with suppliers were of short duration, and jobs were bid regularly. The economic-development administrator of Flint has noted:

> The relationship they have with their suppliers is like night and day. Before, GM was in an adversarial relationship with its suppliers. They were constantly badgering them to get their prices down, and if they didn't get their prices down, you gave the contract to somebody else. As a supplier you had a one-year contract with no guarantee of extension. You produced at the lowest possible expense you could. You got by with old equipment and methods.
>
> Now they have made it worthwhile for the supplier firm to make investments to put up a state-of-the-art production facility, because they are going to have a long-term relationship that will allow them to pay off that capitalized expense.[21]

If Buick was giving much to its suppliers, it was because it expected much. The kan-ban inventory system meant that the supplier would have to deliver small lots of parts in a timely manner and that the quality of the parts would have to be much higher than had previously been demanded, both because of the company's drive to improve the quality of its products and because of the lack of an inventory to supply replacement parts. (GM's Orion Township assembly facility experienced several delays in its start-up date and has been closed for extended periods because of parts from suppliers that did not meet the stringent new quality standards.)

Buick also made it clear that it expected supplier firms that were granted the long-term arrangements to locate in the Flint–Southeast Michigan region. In announcing Buick City, Lloyd Reuss claimed that "right now, we know we can source 99 percent of the parts within a 300 mile radius, 93 percent within 200 miles, and 83 percent within 100 miles." Three hundred miles is about a day's transit distance. "In the years ahead, we will encourage our suppliers to locate closer to Flint. . . . Ideally, we would envision a ring of nearby suppliers delivering parts directly to the assembly line, with no inventory floats at all."[22]

GOVERNMENT

From the first major automotive assembly plant to the present, government has been involved. Public improvements have always been necessary when a major industrial facility has been built. More recently, local governments have been willing to grant tax abatements and to help to finance facilities, train workers, and request grants and loans from other levels of government. But the level of cooperation between government and industry reached a new plateau with the Buick City concept. While much of this interaction between government and corporation was of a "traditional" variety, Buick City also represented a subtle shift to a new form of cooperation between industry and government. Until that project, companies routinely requested aid by using the implied or actual threat of relocation as a resource in the bargaining process. Buick City involved something new: the company and the city cooperated to attract supplier firms to Flint.

This new cooperation was based on a tradition of better relations between the city and Buick than between the city and other Flint-based GM divisions. Buick management has been viewed more favorably by city officials than have the officers of other GM operations in the city. Mayor Rutherford claimed: "With Buick City and Lloyd Reuss it is much more intimate than with the other General Motors plants and divisions. All of the managers of Buick have been more intimate with me than the Chevrolet people. They have tended to give us more reading on what was happening. They considered themselves more of a Flint factory than Chevrolet did."[23]

The closer relationship between Flint city officials, the local business elite, and Buick management is explained by GM officials in organizational terms. "It is the difference between being your own boss as division head and having to run to somebody every time you have to make a decision."[24] (Chevrolet plant managers report to division headquarters in the Detroit area, while Buick and AC headquarters are in Flint.) Flint officials ranked AC second to Buick in being "Flint oriented."

Even where decisions about plant closures have been made, divisions have handled community relations with differing abilities. Flint's director of economic development echoed the prevailing sentiment about Chevrolet:

> There is a vast world of difference among the GM divisions. In my opinion, Chevrolet handled their outting here lousy. Fisher Body did a much better job. They came to us early in the game, accepting proposals from us as to how to come up with a solution to the problem. They have tried a couple of things that have failed, unfortunately, but the door is open and you have a communications link. Chevrolet just treated this city shoddily. They just said, Bam, we're done.[25]

Buick City brought with it a new level of intimacy between the city and the company. Flint's economic-development administrator has described just how close this relationship is:

> Buick City management decides the various supplier firms they want to ask to locate in this Buick City complex, and then they set up a meeting. The Buick people present their material on Buick City, and then they call us over, and we do a presentation on the various economic incentives, training programs, and land sale terms that we can work for them. . . . We have advance knowledge about the operating costs of that particular industry, usually about that particular business. We try to tailor a package that will allow them to operate at least as efficiently here as they did at their other locations. . . . GM helps us in providing us with the basic information, then we work out the proposal.[26]

Buick, which is committed to a new system of production, is not only using corporate persuasion to attract suppliers to the Flint region but is also working directly with local government to do so. By supplying information on the financial and operating status of suppliers, the corporation is handing the city a major bargaining chip in its dealings with suppliers. This has the effect of disadvantaging other localities that are interested in attracting suppliers.

It is not only the city that is involved in the act; county government is also deeply committed to the Buick City project. The Genesee County Economic Development Department also works directly with Buick City administrators, jointly finding sites for supplier firms that are interested in becoming suppliers to Buick City's assembly operations. The county operates four different economic-development corporations that are used to raise capital to help finance plants for such supplier firms. The county general fund provides staff, and city or county budgets "fill in the gaps when we put together a development package for a company and it does not come to closure."[27]

TRADITION

While Buick City involves a new kind of cooperation with local government, the new links are superimposed on traditional relationships. Cities have been involved in urban-renewal activities at least since the Federal Housing Act of 1949. Since 1954 the federal government has permitted cities to use federal grants to underwrite nonresidential building. Many cities have moved aggressively in acquiring land for redevelopment and in some cases have moved more rapidly than either the grants or the demand for land could support. In the late 1960s, Flint had declared that the land to the west of the Buick complex was to be an urban-renewal project area but had failed to complete the project because of a lack of demand for the land. In the classic pattern of "blight by announcement," owners refused to invest in properties because of the uncertainty of city plans, and the area had slowly decayed and lost population; not surprisingly, the area was suffering a high rate of vacancy and abandonment.

The city owned land, and the corporation now had need for land for expansion. According to Flint's director of economic development:

We had let the facilities manager over at Buick know for some time that we were interested in taking some land to the west of the plant and using it for Buick expansion. It was an old urban renewal area, and the housing was rather poor, and the residents wanted us to complete the project. When they decided to go ahead with the investment, they sent emissaries over here, and we sat down and came up with a funding scheme at that verymoment. The primary sources were an Urban Development Action Grant and the Michigan Department of Transportation.[28]

The city also owned available land to the east of Buick Assembly. It had developed the St. John's Industrial Park there earlier, with money provided by the federal Economic Development Administration (EDA). It seemed natural to unify the St. John's park with the emerging Buick City concept, especially given the lack of success in attracting other industry, and EDA officials agreed to this modification in the concept of the industrial park. This meant that land was immediately available for supplier firms in the shadow of Buick City.

The city encountered none of the political problems of neighborhood removal that Detroit experienced in Poletown. In fact, the city had been the subject of a lawsuit, filed by the residents of the area, demanding that the urban-renewal process be completed. The residents had negotiated an out-of-court settlement that was favorable to them, in which the city had agreed to use Community Development Block Grant funds to complete the relocation phase of the project. As a consequence, Flint paid no premiums to the residents to gain their compliance: "We gave them only the benefits required by federal law."[29]

COORDINATION

As was the case for Detroit's Poletown plant, the city and the corporation established a planning team to monitor the progress of the project. City officials have been generally pleased with the working relationship, but they note that differences in the standard operating procedures between the public and private sectors not infrequently cause frustrations on both sides. Decisions in the public sector are linked in a way that they are not in the private sector. Approval for one decision must be obtained before moving to the next. One city official who was intimately involved in the project has described the misunderstandings arising from the linked nature of public-sector decision making in these terms:

> When GM delays in giving us answers to our questions, it is irksome to us because we can't move. They are cooperative; they just don't have it. But when they are ready to move, they just move. We have to go through a process of bidding, getting city council approval, maybe holding public hearings; you never know. So the situation is that they can move faster, and we can't keep up with their schedule, and they can't give us the information we need when we want to move.[30]

ECONOMIC-DEVELOPMENT TOOLS

The Buick City package contains plans for a tax-increment district, to be used as a backup financial arrangement for the project. Property-tax abatements have been granted. Federal grants are a part of the package. Although GM does not, as a matter of policy, utilize direct governmental loan arrangements for construction, supplier firms do. These are the standard community economic-development tools.

Of all development tools, community officials dislike tax abatements most intensely. Abatements represent a drain on the local treasury that goes directly to corporate coffers, whereas other incentives leave more discretion in the hands of local officials to negotiate use of them with companies. For example, tax-increment districts can be used to finance public improvements in the project area that would have to be completed in any case.

Litzenberg described his distaste for the tax abatement:

> It is unfortunate that everyone has used that vehicle. From a city perspective you are almost forced to use it. You are forced, from a negative angle, to use it. . . . We have companies that come in, say, "We have this offer. What can you do?" They do that all the time. Oftentimes we can talk them out of tax abatement. We try to get them into increment financing where we are doing something for the city at the same time we are doing something for the plant. . . . The plant pays its taxes, only those taxes go to pay for an infrastructure improvement that we need and they need.[31]

Flint has tried to limit the use of tax abatements through a policy that ties the granting of the abatement to the estimated employment that will be generated. City officials would like for the generated income tax to offset the abatement, and they try to adjust the granted abatement to the income tax that will be generated (up to the statutory limit of the abatement). This "hold harmless" formula is used "unless it is an industry that we need to move our entire economic development program ahead. If GM Robotics had wanted to come, we would have done anything, because we are trying to change our image as a blue collar town."[32]

There is a second exception to limits on the "hold harmless" rule: "When GM gets involved, they are going to get their abatement. They are going to get both abatement and increment."[33] Were city officials to try to take a tougher negotiating stance, pressure from the City Council would mount: "When you have a labor-oriented city, you are not going to get them screwing around too much. You would think it would be the opposite. There is always a lot of talk; no, no, we shouldn't; but that is all rhetoric. The city council wants someone else to make the decision."[34] Here politics plays a curious dual role: elected officials want to attack the symbol of the greedy corporation, but they are also fearful that the denial of public benefits will result in a loss of jobs. It is easier to engage in furious rhetoric and then allow administrators to make the difficult decision. Detroit's City Council has played a similar role in tax-abatement approvals.

CONCLUSIONS

In negotiating anything with General Motors, Flint city officials are at an overwhelming disadvantage. They know that the economic livelihoods of the citizens of their community are uniquely linked to the company. Civic projects are always dependent on support from General Motors, even when they are spearheaded by the Mott Foundation. Maneuverability is further circumscribed by union leadership, which dominates the City Council. Labor-backed politicians want to be able to decry the insensitivity of the corporation to the community, but they are extremely fearful of doing anything that the corporation might view too negatively.

Flint is so thoroughly dominated by General Motors that even the standard dream of economic diversification takes on a new coloration in the community. The city's director of economic development envisions a future that is all GM: "I'd like to see us work with GM to diversify within the GM structure. I think the single real hope is to diversify with General Motors. If we could get that type of dialog going with General Motors, I think we can do some things. If we can do that, without fanfare; that's what I hope."[35]

Yet even in this milieu, Mayor Rutherford was able to put the giant corporation into a situation that would have made it almost certain that corporate plans would have to be changed. His only leverage was the company's sensitivities to public opinion and its impulse to try to mold that opinion by, in the words of one GM official, offering the citizens "a hat full of rainchecks knowing they were not going to take it under any circumstances."[36] Hemmed in by the local political culture, the overwhelming power of the company, and the circumstances of decision, Rutherford creatively expanded the potential choices in a manner that the corporation did not expect. By creating a new situation in regard to its choices, the mayor put the company on the defensive. The result was delay. This delay may well have allowed the coming economic disaster to swamp the plans for construction; without the delay, it is possible that GM would have continued with the Flint plant. In turn, the delay that was caused by the economic disaster allowed the aggressive management of the Buick Division to press corporate headquarters in Detroit for the authority to proceed with Buick City, thereby ending the possibility of an Assembly Division plant in the Flint area. Buick may well have stayed in Flint because of a fortunate union between the creative response of Rutherford and the imaginative leadership of Reuss. Internal corporate politics and external local politics became intertwined in an unpredictable manner to yield changes that were favorable to Flint. Both men had made an impact on the course of local events.

Not infrequently, political outcomes hinge upon an interaction between decisions made by politicians, decisions made by businessmen, and changes in the broader public economy. Actors are always constrained by circumstances that are far beyond their controls, but they are almost never slaves to them. Even when the situation is as bleak as the one faced by Mayor Rutherford, *creative bounded choice* may be possible.

PART 4

URBAN REGIMES AND SOLUTION-SETS

13

Automobile Politics: A View
from the 1990s

The activities of cities and corporations that we depicted in the earlier chapters of this book were all initiated in the severe economic contraction of the early 1980s. The automotive industry was just beginning a massive restructuring; obsolete assembly plants were being closed, and tens of thousands of workers were being laid off, with no realistic prospect of ever returning to their jobs. Automobile manufacturing was undergoing a spasmodic transformation from a labor-intensive industry to one far less reliant on human capital. Cities, accustomed to the inflationary revenue growth of the 1970s, scrambled to add to their property tax bases to cope with the high levels of demand for services exacerbated by the manufacturing dislocations.

Were the patterns we have studied in the early 1980s time bound? Given the subsequent solid performance of the midwestern economy, led by the automotive manufacturers, one might expect that they were. On the other hand, most of the social conditions making the Midwest's auto cities desperate for investment are still in place. Moreover, the existence of long-run informal relationships between city governments and the business community in many cities suggests that the patterns of influence established earlier would continue to hold, barring major disruption.

In this chapter and the chapter following, we examine the changes in the automobile economy and polity. We show that, far from adapting to changing circumstances, the auto-city regimes have tended to continue with automobile companies the same relationships that were forged in the early 1980s. What was once innovative and imaginative, even if controversial and risky, has become a preprogrammed solution that is no longer appropriate for changing circumstances. In the economic-development sphere, the regime's solution-set has ossified.

URBAN REGIMES AND THE AUTOMOTIVE ECONOMY

Clarence Stone has defined an urban regime as "the informal arrangements by which public bodies and private interests function together in order to be able to make and carry out governing decisions."[1] Earlier we noted that the governing regimes of Detroit and the other Michigan auto cities were characterized by strong sectors with different primary interests – government, business, and labor – brought together through peak bargaining in both formal and informal arenas. We termed this distribution of urban power "sectarchy."

In the community power structure debate that characterized the study of urban politics in the past, it was assumed that someone ran the city. Stone argues, however, that governing is hard work, because public leaders must bring together disparate elements of the community with different primary interests to accomplish collective ends. Hence "running things" is by no means automatic. The strong informal links that Coleman Young in Detroit and James Rutherford and his successors in Flint were able to forge with the multinational automobile companies whose facilities were located in their cities was a defining characteristic of the auto-city regime during the 1980s. The decision-making styles and public policies that developed from these arrangements were also present, to some degree, in other cities throughout the nation as they struggled to cope with increased capital mobility. But the pervasiveness of the linkages between city officials and the heads of multinational manufacturing industries was unique to Michigan's automobile cities. It is clear from the above case studies that achieving the cooperation of the heads of these corporations was extremely difficult and was dependent on policies that cost cities a great deal of money and effort.

Urban regimes are forged on informal understandings. But they are codified into standard modes of interaction and access that give the regime a character – that is, allow it to be characterized as "pluralist" or "entrepreneurial" or "sectarchial" or in other terms. Stephen Elkin claims that the development of standard modes of access leads to systemic bias in the way in which problems reach the public agenda. "Much political activity is, in fact not directed at making decisions at all (i.e., at allocating goods and services and issuing regulations) but at maintaining existing patterns of access and excluding formulations of the public's business that will impede policies."[2] That is, the informal linkages reinforce understandings of what problems the city faces and what solutions are appropriate.

City bureaucracies are often constructed or expanded to implement the decisions that are forged through bargaining among peak leaders (or other forms of informal interaction among members of the urban regime). These agencies, with their bureaucratic decision rules and standard ways of approaching problems, are the organizational solutions to the city's problems as they are defined during elite bargaining. What happens, then, is that urban regimes develop *characteristic solution-sets* to problems. These patterns of solutions dominate decision making in specific situations both because they reflect the understandings of the causal connections between problems and solutions by governing elites and because these understandings are codified in the bureaucratic structure of city government. When new problems emerge, there is a distinct tendency to apply the old solutions to new problems. Sometimes this works; sometimes it doesn't.

Certainly, as Stone argues, urban regimes "have to do with managing conflict and making adaptive responses to social change."[3] On the other hand, what was adaptive in an earlier period can be quite outmoded today. Because of the forging of standard processes of interaction among urban elites and because of the construction of public agencies to implement these interactions, the urban regime itself can become maladaptive – or at least produce policies that are ill-adapted to new challenges.

One can view this behavior in two perspectives. The first emphasizes the distribution of advantage and systemic bias. Businessmen may have access to city officials with their favored programs that neighborhood groups do not. This characterization really does not fit the politics of auto cities, simply because politicians must lure businessmen into participating in city projects. Nevertheless the need to attract mobile capital to cities does lead to a structure of solutions that is biased toward industry inducements and increasing the tax base.

The second perspective, which has been termed "social learning" or "social intelligence," stresses the capacity of governments to solve problems.[4] If decision making is biased toward certain solutions advocated by limited sectors of the urban political economy, such as the business community, then "problem-solving is also likely to be ineffective, simply because some desirable alternatives will go unexplored."[5] Not only do alternatives go unexplored, but the lack of continuous search is often justified in terms of the adequacy of the existing organizational arrangements. Any other approach would threaten jobs and livelihoods, as well as general understandings of social causation. This is another way of saying that regimes develop characteristic patterns of solutions, and that the exclusion of alternatives during subsequent searches for appropriate solutions to emerging problems limits the adaptability of regimes. It is this aspect of regime politics that we emphasize in what follows.

In the earlier chapters of this book, we observed how city leaders struggled with new problems and initiated creative solutions, at least in Flint and Detroit. Now we will explore how those solutions became part of the core of the solution-set defining the urban auto-city regime, how they succeeded and failed, and how they were applied as the restructuring in the automotive industry affected other plants.

CONDITIONS IN THE AUTOMOBILE INDUSTRY, 1980–1991

At the time of the case studies that we have presented, American automobile companies were facing a severe and sustained challenge for the domestic automobile market from Japanese manufacturers, who were benefited by changes in American consumer demand in the wake of the rise in gasoline prices in 1979 and by the reputation that they had for craftsmanship. Their compact cars appealed to millions of Americans who were deeply troubled by the gasoline inefficiency of American cars and the decline in quality of the American product. All American auto makers were losing money in the early 1980s, and they were desperately trying to cut costs, increase quality, and meet the burgeoning consumer demand for smaller cars.

By the middle 1980s, all that had changed. "Voluntary" quotas on the importation of Japanese automobiles had been negotiated by the Reagan administration in 1981. These quotas were lifted in 1985, as much as anything a reaction to the return of good times to the domestic automobile industry. Consumer anxiety had eased as gasoline prices had stabilized, then had fallen, and the demand for large rear-wheel-drive cars had increased. This put the domestic industry in a better competitive position than they had enjoyed a few years previously. Cost-cutting measures, including renegotiations of labor contracts with the UAW, meant that the manufacturers could make a profit on a far smaller number of automobiles than had been possible five years earlier. In 1982, GM and Chrysler made small profits, and 1983 ushered in a period of record profits for all the domestic automobile makers, with 1984 being the peak, at almost $10 billion. After dropping to below 7 million cars and trucks in 1982, domestic manufacturers produced more than 10.5 million units in each year for the rest of the decade. Production peaked in 1985 at 11.6 million, slightly above the pre-recession peak of 11.5 million in 1979. In 1984, for the first time since 1979, imports amounted to less than 25 percent of total sales (see Figure 13.1).[6]

Decision making among manufacturers began to reflect the new prosperity. GM, which had cut back its capital-improvement program in 1981, renewed its program of modernization. The company began to import cars manufactured in Japan by Isuzu and Suzuki, in which it acquired a 33 percent interest. After winning the approval of the Federal Trade Commission, the company established a joint venture with Toyota Motors in California. The most dramatic initiative, however, was the initiation of a new division for the production of small cars, the first since the addition of Chevrolet in 1916.

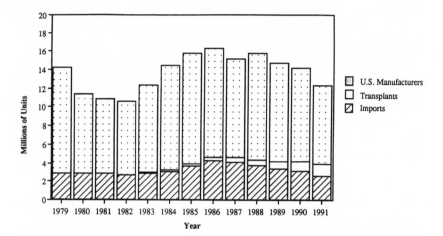

Figure 13.1. Motor vehicle sales in the United States. *Source:* Motor Vehicle Manu-facturers Association, *MVMA Facts and Figures 1990* (Detroit: Motor Vehicle Manu-facturers Association, 1990), p. 7; 1990 figures from *MVMA Facts and Figures 1991*, p. 7; 1991 figures from *Ward's Automotive Reports*, January 13, 1992. All are retail sales except for 1991, which are dealer sales.

The new division was christened Saturn, and it built an assembly plant in Tennesee after spirited competition among several states.

The end of the decade, however, brought another cyclical downturn in the industry. Both imports and Japanese "transplant" plants have steadily increased their share of U.S. auto sales since the middle 1980s. Motor vehicle and equipment manufacturers experienced a pretax loss of $1.4 billion in 1989, their first since 1982. Even so, the domestic auto companies had been so successful that they had accumulated $4.5 billion in cash, the largest amount in history.[7] The recession which began in the fall of 1990 and the incomplete recovery in 1991 caused major losses in both years for domestic auto manufacturers. Even with their cash accumulations, GM and Ford had to enter the capital markets to improve their balance sheets, and Chrysler sustained severe financial problems. Car and light truck sales for 1991 fell to their lowest level since 1983, with sales of domestic manufacturers down 13.2 percent and Japanese imports down 5 percent.[8]

Boom or bust, the automobile economy, in the words of Richard Bingham, "is a sector of the economy which is in constant turmoil."[9] Even during the boom years of the 1980s, automakers continued to restructure, relying less and less on domestic production for profits, and more and more on part ownership of foreign manufacturing concerns and on subsidiaries.[10] During the 1980s, seventeen U.S. assembly plants, including eleven GM plants, were closed. Of the seventeen new assembly plants which opened in that ten-year period, eight were GM plants, and seven were Japanese transplants.[11]

Imports and transplants increased their market share in the 1980s: in 1975–1979, import sales of 9.5 million comprised 18.3 percent of total sales of 51.8 million; ten years later, import sales had increased to 15.2 million, representing 28.5 percent of total sales of 53.3 million in 1985–1989.[12]

Michigan in the late 1980s remained heavily dependent on the automotive economy and continued to be the number one auto-producing state, with 32.6 percent of U.S. car assemblies for model year 1989 (2,321,666 – including 228,756 at a Mazda plant in Flat Rock). In 1987, 235,717 workers in Michigan were employed by motor-vehicle and parts manufacturers, 24.1 percent of manufacturing employees in the state, and 31.8 percent of total U.S. motor-vehicle and equipment manufacturing employment.[13] Detroit's share of this employment, however, declined in the 1980s; the closing of Chrysler's original Jefferson Avenue assembly plant in February 1990 left GM's Poletown plant as the only assembly plant in the city.[14]

FLINT AND ORION TOWNSHIP

The similar assembly plants at Poletown and Orion Township became mainstays of GM's production process. Production levels at both plants, and sales of models produced there, remained steady throughout the late 1980s. Detroit's Poletown plant produced about 80,000 luxury models for the period, while Orion Township produced about 250,000 units. Production and sales of Buick City's models fluctuated more than those made at the Poletown and Lake Orion plants, but also remained strong by the end of the decade, at about 150,000 vehicles. By late 1991, the fate of the Orion plant became less certain, as GM announced that Orion's second shift, which produced Cadillac DeVilles and Fleetwoods, would be moved to the Poletown plant, transferring two thousand jobs from the suburbs to the city. The Orion plant was among twenty-one targeted for possible closing by 1995.[15]

The city of Flint remained in the early 1990s solidly a GM town. The total state equalized value for all GM property (real and personal) in Flint in 1988 was $713,245,300, 41.4 percent of the city's tax base. Nevertheless, Flint did well for itself in the financing arrangements for the Buick City complex, which was built on the site of Buick's Flint assembly plant and surrounding neighborhoods. Buick City contributes a substantial sum in property taxes to the city of Flint, because its tax abatements for both personal and real property (equipment, land, and buildings, respectively) were smaller than those granted GM for the Poletown facility.[16] At the city's tax rate of $65.70 per $1,000 in state equalized value, the plant generated in 1990 $14,445,590 from the ad valorem tax roll, and $4,387,608 in industrial facilities tax. Because one-half of the latter tax was abated, the abatement cost nearly $4.4 million – assuming, of course, that the facility would have been built in Flint without the abatement. Because Flint also collects a 1 percent "administrative fee," GM's total tax bill for Buick City was $19,021,608.[17]

General Motors employment in Flint in 1991 was 49,000, 6,000 less than during the 1982 recession, but still a substantial portion of the area's work force. Jobs lost through plant closings, including those of Fisher body and Buick assembly facilities which Buick City replaced, were only partially regained with the new assembly plant and the relocation of 2,000 GM engineering employees to a new engineering and development center built on the site of the Fisher number one plant, site of a famous sit-down strike by early UAW organizers.

Few Buick City suppliers have located in the Flint area, despite a highly publicized cooperative effort by government and GM officials to attract them. As Detroit also discovered, the just-in-time inventory system used at the new plants required only that suppliers be within two hundred miles of the assembly facility. Buick City produces its own engines, and paint and seats are manufactured "locally," according to a GM spokesperson, who reported that the effort to attract suppliers was "not as successful as we would have liked" because it was sidetracked by reorganization at GM and because suppliers were reluctant to relocate in the unionized and expensive Flint labor market.

GM's taxes in Orion Township are much lower, because township tax rates are lower, and because its abatement comprises a larger share of the value of the plant. Only $6,289,400 in real property and $11,342,600 in personal property at the plant are taxed at the full rate of $56.521 per $1,000 of SEV; the 50 percent abatement ($28.26 per $1,000) applies to $83,260,600 in real property and $49,379,700 in personal property. GM's taxes for 1990 were $4,744,993.[18] Nevertheless, by late 1991, the Orion plant had been selected for production reductions and possible closure—emphasizing once again the limited influence that local public policies have on corporate decisions.

CONDITIONS IN DETROIT

After being scheduled to open in mid-1983, GM's Detroit-Hamtramck ("Poletown") plant began in fall 1985 to produce Cadillac Sevilles and Eldorados, Buick Rivieras, and Oldsmobile Toronados. These models have been made there continuously since that time, with the Cadillac Allante added in 1987. The boom years of the mid-1980s brought full use of Detroit's automotive capacity, with operation of two shifts at both the Clark Avenue Cadillac plant and the new Poletown plant for the 1987 model year. The planned reduction in capacity resumed in the late 1980s with the closing of the Clark Avenue plant.[19]

Neither the automotive boom nor Detroit's economic development strategies have reversed the economic and social malaise of the city. The population of the city continued to decline in the 1980s, and the remaining citizenry is poorer than ever. Between 1980 and 1990, Detroit's white population decreased by 46 percent, to 222,316, while its black population increased by 2.5 percent, to 777,916, or 76 percent of the total.[20] Detroit is not the most economically deprived municipality in the metropolitan area, but its relative position has continued to decline. Better-off whites and blacks have continued to migrate to the suburbs, leaving behind a poorer and blacker population than ever before. Unlike many other American cities, movement of wealthy whites back into the city has not occurred, nor has the infusion of new immigrant groups diversified the center city. Detroit remains America's premier black, industrial city, while the predominantly white suburbs continue to display considerable social and economic diversity, a clear pattern of "uneven development."[21]

Social change did not translate immediately into budget difficulties, however. Good times in the automotive industry and better budgeting practices in the city led to five years of surpluses during the mid-1980s. But the continued economic and social decline and the economic downturn of the early 1990s led to budget deficits in FY 1990 and FY 1991. Neither was as severe as those of the early 1980s: $33 million in 1990 and a projected $50 million in 1991, compared with $80.8 million in 1980 and $115.7 million in 1981. Factors contributing to the 1991 deficit included: 1) income tax collections $7 million below their budgeted level, a result of layoffs, and a declining economy; 2) utility tax collections $16 million lower than projected, owing to an unusually mild winter and lower heating bills; 3) a 9.2 percent cut in state spending, which reduced state aid to Detroit by $4.1 million; 4) a population decline from 1.2 million in the 1980s to 1.027 million in the 1990 census, resulting in a reduction of $19 million in population-based state revenue sharing.[22] What was missing this time was the speculative budgeting that had occurred in the late 1970s. Nevertheless, by the fall of 1992, Moody's Investors Source had dropped its rating of the City of Detroit's general obligation bonds to below investment grade. Analysts cited a chronic imbalance between revenues and expenditures, although the major problems were cosocioeconomic ones, not budgetary gimmicks.[23]

THE CONTINUING STRUGGLE OVER
THE CENTRAL INDUSTRIAL PARK PROJECT

Our analysis of the probable costs and benefits of the Poletown project, presented in the earlier chapters of this book, has proved correct. The project, rather than generating new revenues for the financially strapped city, has instead obligated it to pay substantial expenses, to repay loans and to settle court cases related to land acquisition for the plant. As a consequence of tax abatements and tax increment financing arrangements, all property tax and income revenues from the General Motors plant are being used to repay loans and other debts incurred for land acquisition and site preparation, and, with a balloon payment of $48 million due in 1996, further refinancing and extension of debts is likely. The ongoing costs of the project present serious obstacles to solving the city's fiscal difficulties in the 1990s.

Two factors have complicated the implementation of the Central Industrial Park project (CIP). In the first place, land acquisition costs have proved to be considerably more than the city estimated in its analyses. Court settlements in condemnation cases pushed the costs of acquiring the property for the Central Industrial Park project at least $46 million above initial estimates.[24] Moreover, Michigan P.A. 87 – the "quick take" law – entitles owners who receive court awards that are higher than the city's final offer to receive up to one-third of the difference between these two amounts for attorney's fees. One member of the city council estimated this cost at more than $3.5 million.[25] In 1989, land acquisition costs of "more than $130 million" were reported.[26] A year later, costs were reported to be "about $200 million, according to court records, attorneys, and city officials."[27] As of this writing, a settlement has not yet been reached on the price for one major property, St. Joseph Hospital, but it is rumored that this will add $50 million to $150 million to land acquisition costs.[28]

In the second place, the complex and speculative financial plans that undergirded the project have proved difficult to complete. As they have been revised, additional loans have been required, extending the time period for repayment. Detroit used a $35-million Section 108 loan and a $65-million letter of credit from the U.S. Department of Housing and Urban Development to pay for land acquisition and other site preparation expenses. Repayment is being covered by Community Development Block Grant funds and General Obligation bond sales. Through fiscal year 1988, block grant funds were used for both principal and interest payments because the city's precarious financial situation precluded it from issuing bonds. Since that time, bond sale proceeds have been used to repay principal and block grant funds to repay interest. As table 13.1 indicates, nearly $60 million in block grant funds and $14 million in bond sales had been used for repayments by 1992. The bonds must be repaid, with interest, either from future project revenues or from the general fund budget. This has the effect of extending the costs of the project beyond the September 1995 date of the last annual payment on the initial HUD loans. Payments of approximately $6 million per year must be made through 1995, with a final balloon payment of $48 million due on 1 September 1996. Additional refinancing will be required for the balloon payment, probably through the sale of tax increment bonds, with property and income taxes from the tax increment district being used to repay the project debt until it is retired.[29]

TABLE 13.1

REPAYMENT SCHEDULE FOR LOANS FROM THE FEDERAL GOVERNMENT
FOR THE CENTRAL INDUSTRIAL PARK PROJECT

YEAR	CDBG FUNDS	BOND SALE
1978–1979 to		
1982–1983	$ 6,005,000	
1983–1984	8,800,000	
1984–1985	5,000,000	
1985–1986	9,425,000	
1986–1987	7,126,000	
1987–1988	6,200,000	
1988–1989	3,000,000	$ 6,200,000 (Nov. 1988)
1989–1990	4,300,000	4,700,000 (Dec. 1989)
1990–1991	4,576,000	1,425,000 (Oct. 1990)
1991–1992	4,406,000	1,950,000 (to be issued)
Totals	$58,838,000	$14,275,000

SOURCES: For 1978–1979 through 1990–1991, CDBG Status Report, Detroit City
Planning Commission, 22 April 1991; for 1991–1992, interview with Marcus Loper,
Detroit City Planning Commission, 23 July 1991.

Financing the increased costs of the project also involved the issuance
of $54.2 million in tax increment bonds by the Economic Development Cor-
poration – which serves as the CIP Tax Increment Financing Authority – in
1984, creating another long-term debt obligation. Unfortunately, the tax increment financing arrangements have not yielded enough revenue to retire
these bonds.[30]

Because of this shortfall, base property tax revenues (which were small
because the assessment was made after the destruction of the buildings in the
project area) and income tax revenues, as well as incremental property taxes,
have all been made part of the Central Industrial Park project's revenue pool.
The income tax revenues are collections from employees at the plant.

Thus taxes from all of these sources are allocated to repayment of project
costs; none of these revenues contributes to the general fund, nor do any
funds go to the future improvement of the area. This appears to be contrary
to the provisions of P.A. 450, which prohibits the use of more than 80 percent
of tax-increment revenues for the purpose of repaying the bonds. In any
case, it is certainly far afield from the earlier notions of the use of tax increment financing, which were to generate collective improvements for a city
district. For FY 1988–1989, debt service obligations for the bonds totaled
$8,610,637; this was paid through a combination of CIP property taxes, cash,
investment earnings, and *part* of CIP income tax collections. This was the
first time the CIP had generated more than enough in total tax revenue to
meet debt obligations.[31]

As of August 1989, the city of Detroit had a total of $220 million in out-standing limited tax obligations. Nearly half of this – $38.5 million in TIFA bonds and $58 million in Section 108 loans – was attributable to the Poletown project, while most of the remainder was related to the Jefferson Avenue assembly plant, discussed later.

Although General Motors continued to modernize its new assembly plant by installing new equipment, the tax revenues generated by the improvements were significantly reduced by tax abatements. In 1988, the Detroit City Council approved a $2.8 million abatement over twelve years on $20.9 million in equipment for the Poletown plant, after earlier rejecting the same request.[32] Two years later, GM requested another tax abatement on the installation of new equipment to upgrade the paint and body shops (including robots) and for new assembly equipment to produce longer-wheelbase Cadillacs for 1992. The projected abatement would save the corporation a total of $9 million in taxes. Although the improvements will generate a total of nearly $12 million in new taxes for the project area Tax Increment Financing Authority, they would have produced twice that amount without the abatements. As we noted earlier, the plant itself also received a twelve-year, 50 percent abatement.

THE VALUE OF POLETOWN

A memorandum from City Council fiscal analyst John Marco, dated 21 September 1988, projected that "no property tax and very little income tax from Poletown would be available to the General Fund for approximately 20 more years." In effect, the city of Detroit had pledged all revenues that were generated from the project in the form of captured tax increments, base property taxes, and income taxes toward the repayment of debts incurred in completing the project. Moreover, the city has already used almost $60 million of its Community Development Block Grant funds to repay federal loans, even as that program has been dramatically scaled back by the federal government. Finally, the city has relied on General Obligation bonds ($14 million so far) to replace reliance on community development funds. This has the effect of moving expenses from the current operating budget to the long-term capital budget.

In a word, the project has not paid for itself. One might treat the taxes captured through the tax increment plan as new city revenues. (This estimate would be more reasonable if the project area had been assessed prior to demolition.) GM plant modernizations, even with abatements, would also go on the "plus" side of the project ledger, since they increase taxes going to the CIP Tax Increment Financing Authority (the EDC). These revenues, however, have been insufficient to cover public expenditures on the project.

The CDBG funds and general obligation bonds issued by the city of Detroit for the project totaled approximately $75 million by early 1992; future expenditures in principal and interest payments through 1996 are estimated at $24 million, with a balloon payment of $48 million due that year. By 1996, then, the city of Detroit will have paid $100 million in excess of revenues generated by the project and will still owe $48 million. This is in addition to direct subsidies by the state and federal governments.

We wrote in the epilogue to the first edition of this book that "continued prosperity in the automobile industry and the successful operation of the Poletown assembly plant are essential to the generation of enough revenues to repay the debts that the city of Detroit has incurred because of the project. Excess revenues . . . were never a real possibility. Shortfalls in tax-increment funds could result in the pledging of general-fund revenues for the purpose of repaying the bonds." Even in the boom years of the mid to late 1980s in the automobile industry, the city of Detroit was forced to rely on general fund revenues.

We contended that the project "was initiated, not in order to generate positive revenues, but for symbolic reasons. At best, it is an investment in the present economic image of the city and in the city's economic vitality." It was, moreover, initiated by a mayor who enjoyed both conflict and taking large-scale risks, as Young biographer Wilbur Rich has pointed out.[33] With the Central Industrial Park project, he got both.

It can be rational for political leaders to pursue what might be called a "loss leader" strategy. Even if an economic development project is a net drain on public resources, it may yield long-run benefits for a city. In the case of the Central Industrial Park project, substantial symbolic rewards accrued to the mayor, his economic development bureaucracies, and the black citizens of Detroit. Poletown gave birth to a new way of thinking about economic revival. Rather than focus solely on downtown development, cities might also consider large-scale public-private partnerships directed at *industrial* urban renewal. Moreover, there was the potential for the project to serve as a stimulus to the industrial revitalization of the city. Even if it did not "pay for itself" in tax revenues, it would save jobs (even if not necessarily for city residents). It might also stimulate business activity, particularly by attracting suppliers. Finally, it could serve as a beacon to other industries that Detroit was a city that welcomed heavy industry.

As creative as the Detroit model of industrial urban renewal was, it must be considered at best a questionable approach. The Central Industrial Park project is not even paying for itself, let alone serving to bolster the tax base. Suppliers have not flocked to Detroit, and jobs have continued to decline. A key question is the reaction of the Young administration and its coalition partners. Had industrial urban renewal become part of a regime solution-set, or would the regime flexibly search for new solutions to its continuing problems?

14

The Chrysler Jefferson Project:
Poletown Revisited?

Detroit's Poletown and Flint's Buick City projects were immense in scale. They were creative responses to the pressures of the restructuring of a recession-ravaged automobile industry whose troubles were affecting city taxes and threatening the livelihoods of citizens. These urban industrial renewal projects were pathbreaking in their size and in the extent of public-private cooperation necessary to complete them. They were the first to apply strategies developed to encourage commercial development in downtown business districts to the renewal of manufacturing facilities. Both were implemented with ruthless efficiency and without apparent corruption. On the other hand, the projects were controversial and disruptive. They consumed vast amounts of time and resources in the two cities, diverting attention from other problems. And the Poletown project has proved to be far more costly to city coffers than estimated at the time.

Creative solutions generated by organizations under stress often become institutionalized. The necessity to be creative sometimes results in the forging of new relationships between city officials and businessmen. Over time, however, these interactions often become regular and repetitive, through both informal channels and formal organizations, such as economic development commissions. Such interactions and organizations are the social technology that comprises a solution-set for an urban regime. They involve both regularized ways of doing things and consensual definitions of the problems facing cities. When new problems arise, the creative solutions developed under stress, now routinized, are often brought forward as appropriate for the new situation.

In this chapter we will see how the city of Detroit used the economic development tools developed in the Poletown project in a public-private development of a new assembly plant for Chrysler Motor Company. It was not, however, only the development financing arrangements that were imported into the new situation. The entire social technology – from the interactions among participants, to the operation of organizations, to the very definition of the problem – that had emerged from the Poletown project was applied to the Chrysler project.

Unfortunately, three things had changed. First, the problem was different. Automobile companies were in the midst of unprecedented prosperity. Furthermore, because of the industry's restructuring, assembly plants generated far fewer jobs than even half a decade previously. Second, social learning had altered the relationship between the tools of development and the targets of action. In particular, businessmen had learned how to manipulate the relocation program, resulting in cost overruns. Finally, the financing of the Poletown project had not developed as anticipated, as we have shown in the previous chapter. The situation had changed enough that the application of the old social technology resulted in serious problems for the city.

CHRYSLER MODERNIZES

Shortly after production began at GM's Poletown plant, city officials began discussions about a new assembly plant project with Chrysler Corporation. Chrysler continued to operate Detroit's oldest assembly plant, Jefferson Avenue, which was built in 1907. The company was in the midst of a vigorous rebound following its brush with bankruptcy in 1979–1980, and was rebuilding its aging capital stock. It was natural for the company to look at its old multistory Jefferson Avenue assembly plant for replacement. The Chrysler project, billed by the Young administration as the cornerstone to rehabilitation of its surrounding eastside neighborhood, paralleled Poletown in several significant respects, most notably in its major cost overruns for site preparation and its complex, uncertain financing arrangements.

Because the state of Michigan had contributed to the bailout of Chrysler corporation in 1979–1980, the company had agreed to keep the Jefferson plant open. By 1985, Chrysler was demanding major incentives from both labor and government to do so. In addition, following the example set by Mazda in early discussions of construction of its U.S. assembly plant in nearby Flat Rock two years earlier, Chrysler required a "new, streamlined local labor agreement" with the UAW prior to renovation or construction of a new assembly facility at Jefferson Avenue.[1] Company officials repeatedly hammered home the need for union concessions and assistance from the state and city governments.[2]

Commitments were forthcoming from union members and city officials within weeks after Chrysler requested them. In late January 1986, members of the UAW local representing the plan voted unanimously to allow the union to renegotiate the local contract terms (including job classification and work rules). Simultaneously, top Detroit development officials pledged more than $200 million in direct and indirect state, federal, and city financial assistance to Chrysler and potential suppliers locating in the area. Among the city's incentives were 500 acres of land at a "reasonable price."[3] The threat of plant closing and an out-of-state location for the replacement facility hung over the discussions. Chrysler reportedly had "no plans" for the Jefferson Avenue plant after phasing out K-car production in 1987, and UAW Vice-President Marc Stepp reported that Illinois and Indiana were "competing for the project."[4]

When Chrysler officially announced plans for the new plant several months later, company officials called again for a satisfactory union contract and financial assistance from the city and state. Gerald Greenwald, chairman of Chrysler's automotive operating group, observed, "It's going to take doing the impossible to make financial sense out of the Jefferson plant. . . . We think we've come close to doing the impossible. We think we have a concept, we think we have an idea, but it's going to take a very modern labor agreement. It's going to take help from the city. It's going to take help from the state to make sense of it."[5]

COPYING POLETOWN

Detroit development officials revealed the details of the necessary public assistance in July 1986. The plan was a virtual carbon copy of the Poletown arrangements. It included a $106 million HUD guaranteed loan to the city of Detroit, to be repaid with block grant or other city funds, which would be used for land purchases, demolition clearance, relocation, and site preparation and utility work; $35 million from the federal, state, and city departments of transportation and Conrail, which would go for transportation, roads and rail lines; $35 million from the state, which would fund employee training programs; and $20 million from a HUD Urban Development Action Grant, which was needed for land costs.[6] In comparison to Poletown, only the job training component was new. Chrysler appears to have again drawn from Mazda's example, for state assistance with job training costs was a key element of the incentive package for its Flat Rock assembly plant.[7] The state agreed to provide a total of $150 million for job training and road and rail-line improvements at Jefferson Avenue and at Chrysler's new technology center in suburban Auburn Hills; the bulk of the funds, $93 million, was reported to be for highway construction in Auburn Hills.[8]

Detroit Finance Director Bella Marshall and Community and Economic Development Department director Emmett Moten, in asking city council approval for a $35 million HUD loan application for land acquisition and clearance, pledged, "We learned our lesson," from Poletown cost overruns, and claimed that this wouldn't happen with the Jefferson project.[9] The loan request was approved by HUD later in September, along with a $15-million Urban Development Action Grant (UDAG) for land acquisition.[10] The Detroit Economic Development Corporation (a key actor in the Poletown project) approved a financing plan and agreement for transferring 400 acres of land for the project; 230 of the 850 parcels needed were owned by the city, while the remainder would be acquired through condemnation proceedings. The Economic Development Corporation, after obtaining the land from the city, would sell it to Chrysler for about $5 million, less than half of what General Motors paid for a slightly larger site. The financing plan, approved also by the City Council, committed the city to providing $155.3 million for the project, most of which was to come from the state and federal governments in loans and grants.[11] Despite the absence of an official Chrysler announcement, the council also approved spending $2.8 million in city money for property appraisals, survey studies, and drafting of an environmental impact statement; $2.3 million of this cost was to be paid with anticipated CDBG funds.[12] Chrysler Chairman Lee Iaccoca formally announced the new $1.2-billion assembly plant project in October 1986 at a ceremony in which he and Detroit Mayor Coleman Young praised Michigan Governor James Blanchard, then in the closing days of his reelection campaign, for providing state help for the project and for sponsoring the 1979 federal bailout of Chrysler from the brink of bankruptcy.[13]

Increased public sector costs for the project were already evident six months later when the City Council unanimously approved plans for the project, which included $200 million in city, state, and federal funds for land acquisition and clearance, and a twelve-year city tax abatement for Chrysler. Like the Poletown project plan, this one included some "sweeteners" for residents of the project area: $15,000 to help residents buy new houses, a $1,000 bonus per household, $1,500 for those whose property taxes increased as a result of relocation, and an additional $500 for senior citizens.[14]

When market factors look unfavorable, automobile companies first delay adding new capacity. When complex public-private partnerships are involved, such delay can cause both political and financial problems for the governmental partner. Slightly more than a year after Chrysler's official announcement, the corporation announced a one-year delay in construction for the project. Among the reasons mentioned for the delay were Chrysler's purchase of AMC, the New York stock market crash of 19 October 1987, and Chrysler's decision not to build a full-size pickup truck at the plant as an interim project. Market conditions were also mentioned by Chrysler

Motors Chairman Gerald Greenwald as a critical factor in Chrysler's plans to keep the existing plant open during construction of the new facility; the promise was repeated by another Chrysler official in January 1988.[15] In less than two years, changing market conditions would result in a reversal of this commitment, and an announcement of imminent plant closing.

THE APPRAISAL SCANDAL

The city of Detroit has historically been relatively free of scandal. Reform has meant something in the city and yielded a professional, efficient bureaucratic structure. The Poletown project, as controversial as it was, never generated any charges of misfeasance or mismanagement. This was not to be the case for the Jefferson Avenue project. The charges against Jefferson Avenue involved escalation of land acquisition costs. The issue surfaced early in 1988 and remained a focus of media attention throughout the year.

Initial reports on court settlements with 12 of the 118 businesses located in the project area indicated that $48 million, $8 million more than had been budgeted for *all* land acquisition, had been spent.[16] In February 1988, Finance Director Bella Marshall and CEDD director Emmett Moten requested approval of an additional $40 million for land acquisition, which in turn necessitated transfer of $3.3 million from the city's general fund to the Chrysler development fund and obtaining $40 million from Chemical Bank through an extended credit line. Repayment of the loan, according to Moten, would be made with tax revenues generated by the plant.[17]

Later in 1988, the *Detroit News* initiated a full-scale investigation of the land acquisition process, culminating in a lawsuit to acquire city documents. These documents formed the basis of several lengthy, front-page articles alleging incompetence on the part of various city officials. The city's resistance to providing the information also led to the brief jailing of Law Director Donald Pailen for contempt of court, while the local judge's order was appealed to the Michigan Supreme Court on the grounds that the requested materials should not be released because they were the subject of a grand jury investigation. The appeal was denied, and Pailen agreed to release the documents.[18]

The city blamed the company for the escalated costs, saying that the expensive settlements and lack of careful scrutiny were due to the deadlines for land acquisition imposed by Chrysler, under threat of losing the project. Chrysler later revised its construction schedule so that the parcels which were the subject of the investigation were not needed by the stated deadline.[19] The investigation also revealed action by the City Council in legally proscribed closed sessions, failure of administrators to provide the council with complete information, and an agreement on the purchase of industrial inventories, which amounted to signing a blank check. Both the council and the administration were berated by the *News* in an editorial that termed the deal "a monumental case of bad management on the part of the Young administration and lack of proper oversight by the City Council."[20]

Subsequent articles alleged that businessmen in the project area had manipulated the property acquisition process by inventory padding – moving equipment into warehouses immediately prior to appraisal of the properties. Businessmen stalled the city's appraisers by refusing to cooperate in allowing access to properties. Appraisers had not been allowed on site when the agreement to pay for inventory was signed on 10 December 1986. They were not permitted on the site until 10 January 1987, the deadline set by Chrysler for acquisition of the property.[21]

The city also had problems in disposing of the equipment it had acquired in the condemnation proceedings. An auction of equipment for which the city had paid $35.8 million yielded $1.7 million, a return of less than 5 cents on the dollar.[22] Nearly all of the auctioned equipment was bought back by its original owners at a fraction of what they had received from the city for it.[23]

While the revelations generated little immediate response from the Young administration, they were certainly having an effect. Emmett Moten, the financial wizard of industrial urban renewal, left city government in the summer of 1988. Mayor Young implied in an interview the following year that Moten's departure from city government was related to the cost overruns for land acquisition. After attributing the costs to a "mistake in judgment" by administrators, Young was asked whether "heads were going to roll as a result." The mayor responded, "Some of the heads have already rolled. If you can't figure that one out, I won't help you."[24]

THE POLITICS OF TAX ABATEMENT

Like GM, Chrysler requested a tax abatement for the new plant. However, because its request coincided with the initial revelations of cost overruns, the City Council's initial reaction was negative. The twelve-year, 50 percent abatement would apply to $615 million in new machinery and facilities, according to Chrysler, and was estimated to reduce the corporation's property taxes by $8.6 million annually, or a total of $103 million. Chrysler's taxes on the old plant were $3.2 million annually; even with the abatement, Detroit would receive $5.4 million more per year in taxes from Chrysler than if the plant had not been built.[25] If one assumes (as many officials did at the time) that the old plant would have closed imminently in the absence of firm plans for the new one, the city's gain could be calculated as $8.6 million per year. The council, however, was more concerned about the costs of the land deal and the failure of the administration to provide it with sufficient information on that issue and rejected the initial tax abatement request on 19 September 1988 by a 4-to-2 vote.[26]

Predictably, Chrysler responded with a threat not to build the plant, and Mayor Young voiced his concurrence: "We'll be faced with a big vacant field out there, a barren desert" if the abatement were denied. According to Chrysler's director of governmental affairs, Michael M. Glusac: "It would have been a heck of a lot easier to build this plant in a farm field. We chose not to do that because we felt an obligation to the very people who supported us over the years." Chrysler's position was that the city had an obligation "to fulfill its side of the bargain" by granting the abatement. In preparation for a new council vote on the abatement a month later, city officials revised their estimate of the total cost of abatement to $67 million, instead of $103 million, over twelve years. The earlier estimate, they explained, did not include depreciation and other accounting rules that would decrease Chrysler's tax burden.[27]

In response to council demands that Chrysler guarantee the plant would stay open and employ at least 2,500 workers as a condition for receiving the abatement, the company countered that it had "given all it could by agreeing to invest $1 billion in the plant and by promising to pay off $53 million in bonds to finance the project, even if the plant were to close." Furthermore, according to company officials, continued production and employment at the plant were dependent on the unpredictable future demand for cars made there.[28] As it had done earlier that year with a GM request for a tax abatement on equipment at Poletown, the council reversed itself and voted 5 to 3 for the tax break on 19 October 1988.[29]

ENVIRONMENTAL CONCERNS

Yet another threat to plant construction emerged in December 1988, with reports of leaking underground storage tanks on the site; eighty-two tanks, the largest number of underground tanks ever discovered in Michigan, were found to be contaminating the soil with petroleum by-products. Clearly the cleanup would add considerably to site preparation costs. Moreover, Chrysler's contract with the city permitted the company to abandon the project if major environmental problems made construction impossible.[30]

Requirements for cleanup gave rise to a debate between the state Department of Natural Resources and city officials, with the city's attorneys claiming that standards imposed by the state would cost a prohibitive $50 million.[31] The dispute continued for several months, delaying the start of plant construction from its scheduled date of April 1989 to late May. During that time, contractors hauled 52,000 cubic yards of contaminated soil to sanitary disposal facilities and shipped 80,000 gallons of chemical wastes for processing and subsequent burial.[32] The Department of National Resources granted approval on 26 April 1989, contingent on installation of a drainage system to collect rainwater and provision of clay covering for areas that would not be occupied by buildings or parking lots. Permitting reuse of a contaminated site was reported to be a first for the state agency, and it required both deed restrictions and financial assurances from Chrysler that it would maintain the runoff collection system.[33]

THE IMPACT SHIFT

By the time groundbreaking occurred for the plant on 31 May 1989, public expenditures totaled approximately $160 million, not including likely additional costs for toxic waste removal. One benefit of the sizable investment of public funds in the project was said to be that it provided an additional "political incentive" for Chrysler to keep the plant open, should demand for vehicles produced there be less than anticipated. The long-awaited new vehicle to be produced at Jefferson Avenue turned out to be a Jeep, a four-door, four-wheel-drive, updated, streamlined version of the Jeep Cherokee produced in Toledo, Ohio.

With a capacity at the new plant for 200,000 vehicles per year, and annual Jeep sales for 1988 of 254,454, Chrysler would either have to nearly double its Jeep sales, add another product at Jefferson Avenue, or close one of its older Jeep plants in Toledo or Canada. The anticipated efficiency of the new plant, combined with the size of public and Chrysler investment in it, suggested that the corporation would find a way to keep it open, increasing the vulnerability of its older plants in other cities.[34]

Detroit's success in getting the Chrysler facility meant that it had moved its vulnerability to the loss of jobs due to plant closing from greatest (the old Jefferson plant was the worst of Chrysler's plants) to least. But this had implications for other cities, whose plants were now at risk. This is simply a real-world example of the economist's point that governmental locational incentives do not affect overall investment (because such incentives are a small part of the cost of doing business). They do, however, reallocate the economic pain.

Early in 1989, Chrysler also initiated a series of production shifts which again recalled the problems of communities relying on the automobile industry for sustenance. These changes would ultimately result in the company's failure to honor the commitment to keep the old Jefferson plant open until production began at the new one. In December 1988 Chrysler ceased production of its K-cars at Jefferson Avenue and closed its Kenosha, Wisconsin, plant. Production of Omni and Horizon subcompacts was shifted from

Kenosha to the old Jefferson Avenue plant in March 1989. A first shift of 1,200 workers was recalled in early March, with a second shift scheduled to return in early May, and production of these models was to continue until late 1991.[35] Low Omni and Horizon sales, however, forced cancellation of the second shift recall; 1,600 workers laid off in December 1988 when K-car production ended would remain on indefinite layoff, possibly until completion of construction of the new plant.[36]

In November 1989, Chrysler announced that production at the old Jefferson Avenue plant would stop on 2 February 1990. A drop in sales of the Omni and Horizon models produced at the plant and the corporation's need to reduce its operating costs by $1 billion were responsible for the shutdown. Jefferson Avenue was not the only victim of corporate restructuring: the second shift at Chrysler's St. Louis plant was also scheduled to be dropped in early 1990, laying off 1,900 workers. According to analysts, Chrysler's expenses had increased as a result of the Kenosha closing and shift of Omni-Horizon production to Jefferson Avenue: $250 million was spent on training, separation pay, and benefits for laid-off Kenosha workers, and an estimated $150 million went into setting up Omni-Horizon assembly in Detroit.[37]

Auto-industry analysts viewed the plant closing as necessary to the long-term well-being of the corporation, noting that Chrysler never made much profit on Omni-Horizon and that sales suffered because of competition and changing consumer preferences. U.S. sales of subcompacts dropped 9 percent in 1989, while Omni-Horizon sales dropped 32 percent from the previous year.[38] The impact of market forces was stated succinctly by Anthony St. John, Chrysler's vice-president of labor relations, the day the plant closed after more than eighty years of operation: "Chrysler and the other car companies are in business to make automobiles. If those cars could have been sold, we would have sold them, but where they're not selling, we can't continue to make them."[39]

Expert prognosis for the new plant was not much more optimistic, as the industry and the national economy appeared on the verge of a recession: "Auto industry analysts have suggested the plant is a financial fiasco, with little hope of ever paying off for Chrysler because of the tough times the auto industry is expected to face."[40] If payoffs for Chrysler were uncertain, the implications for project financing and the fiscal stability of the city of Detroit could be even more ominous.

ESTIMATING THE COSTS: LEGISLATIVE-EXECUTIVE SPARRING

There are two sources of financial problems in economic development projects. The first is the problem of cost overruns. These are costs of the project itself that are greater than what had been estimated in the original financing plan. These cost overruns make it necessary to alter the financial plan. The second source of difficulty lies in the operation of the financing arrangements. Cities are forecasting complex behaviors in their economic development plans. Because officials tend to be very optimistic in estimating future economic growth, it is probable that some facets of the financial plan will go awry. Indeed, the very complexity of financial arrangements is a warning sign that paying the bills for the project is not going to be easy. Both sources can affect estimates of total project costs and projected revenues, which often become the source of debate.

By July 1989, cost overruns for site preparation for the Chrysler project totaled $100 million, and public sector expenses were reported to be more than $264 million, including the following: land acquisition, $114 million; relocation of businesses, $13 million; demolition, $87 million; contamination cleanup, $8.3 million; planning, engineering, legal, and administration, $22 million. The City Council was asked to approve $30.4 million in additional city money: $25.2 million for environmental cleanup, $3.2 million to buy five remaining parcels of land, and $2 million for a backup electrical system.

The $30.4 million would be raised by long-term bond sales, generating additional long-term repayment obligations from project revenues. In addition, Finance Director Bella Marshall proposed to convert $100 million in five-year bonds already sold by the city to raise funds for the project to fifteen-year term bonds, so that the city would have ten more years to pay off the debt and reduce its annual payments. City officials estimated the cost of the refinancing plan at $12.5 million a year in interest for the first two years, and $18 million a year in payment of principal, beginning in 1991 and continuing through 2004. Because the bonds were to be repaid from the general fund treasury, and not through raising taxes, no voter approval was required.[41]

Marshall's proposal was accompanied by a report that estimated Detroit's share of project costs at $170.9 million, or $48,825 in site preparation expenses for each of a projected 3,500 jobs.[42] City Council fiscal analyst John Marco released his own report, which estimated total costs of $436 million and a per-job cost of $124,571, based on a projected 3,000 jobs. Marco's figures included an estimated $136.7 million in interest on bonds (because taxpayers will have to pay increased taxes or give up city services to pay for interest); he also included $16.8 million for relocation of public lighting lines, $12.5 million to move water and sewer lines, $39.5 million for the tax abatement, and $59.5 million in tax-increment revenue, not included in Marshall's figures.[43] Marco observed that while tax-increment financing and tax abatement "might well be a necessary development tool," they represent costs in the form of "foregone taxes to the taxing jurisdictions."[44]

Marshall challenged Marco's inclusion of tax abatement and interest as costs: "If there were no new Chrysler facility, there would be no tax revenue. Therefore, there would be no abated taxes." Implicit in her position is the assumption that construction of the plant in Detroit was contingent on the abatement, while Marco assumed that the plant would be built without an abatement, generating twice as much in tax revenues. Marco, in responding to Marshall, countered inclusion of interest and abatement costs was standard government accounting practice.[45] Marshall also disputed Marco's estimates for tax-abatement and tax-increment revenues, noting that the correct figures for the city's share of tax-abatement and tax-increment revenues were $30.1 million and $25.5 million, respectively.[46] Marco subsequently conceded that inclusion of tax-abatement and tax-increment revenue as costs of a project was "arguable," but defended his inclusion of interest expenses.[47] Clearly he is right here, because the interest payments are foregone opportunities to fund other programs in the future.

The Marco-Marshall debate is an indicator of the adversarial political relationship between the legislative and executive branches of government in Detroit. While the City Council generally goes along with the mayor's proposals, some of its members view it as serving as a check on executive authority. The council's staff therefore frequently presents it with recommendations contrary to those of executive departments, and council members use the information in these reports to challenge the mayor. In recent years, as the number of mayoral supporters on the council has decreased, challenges to administrators have become more frequent and resistance by those administrators to council requests has increased. In this environment, more heat than light can be generated.

One of the strategies of the Young administration in gaining council acquiescence in economic development plans has been to present the plans in exquisite detail, derailing opposition through arcane financial presentations. Marshall's extended explanation of the complex financial arrangements for the project followed this pattern. Some council members contend that the administration does not want them to *understand* its proposals, only to *approve* them.

On the other hand, the arrangements were legitimately complex. As outlined in materials presented by the Finance Department and the Economic Development Corporation to the City Council, the major components of project financing included the following: tax revenues generated by the plant and committed to a Local Development Finance Authority (created for the project under State of Michigan Public Act 281 of 1986), estimated at $171.3 million from 1990 through 2018; interim financing from the Detroit Economic Development Corporation, requested in July 1989 in the form of $52.5 million in notes, with payments on the notes to be made from tax increment funds and payments by Chrysler under a lease-purchase agreement; at the end of three years, the LDFA would issue its own bonds to pay off the interim note obligations and begin making payments on these bonds from tax increment collections.[48]

Financial arrangements became even more complex in June 1991, when the Finance Department requested support from the City Council for a "limited tax pledge" from the city to support a portion of the $53.5 million LDFA bond issue. "Current economic conditions affecting the Chrysler Corporation," according to Finance Director Marshall, had made the LDFA bonds unmarketable; as a consequence, Chrysler had agreed to purchase $42 million of the bonds, with the remainder to be supported by the city. The resolution termed the city's obligations as "tertiary," with tax-increment revenues to be the primary source of repayment and the secondary source a corporate guarantee or letter of credit from Chrysler. However, it also included a statement that the LDFA bonds "shall be secured by the full faith, credit and resources of the City which may be payable from taxes levied within constitutional, statutory and charter limitations and the City pledges to pay the principal of, premium, if any, and interest on the LDFA bonds from any funds legally available therefor as a first budget obligation of the City, and if necessary to levy sufficient taxes on all taxable property of the City for the payment thereof within applicable constitutional, statutory and charter limitations."[49]

In guardedly recommending approval of the resolution, council fiscal analyst Marco articulated a "we are in too deep now to back out" argument, expressing concern that failure to sell the bonds could mean the "shutting down" of the project due to a cash shortage. He noted that the city would only be responsible for the bonds in the event of "failure of the Chrysler Plant to come on line and operate" *and* the bankruptcy of Chrysler Corporation. With the steep downturn of the early 1990s in the automotive sector, this was not out of the realm of possibility at the time.

JEFFERSON AVENUE AND POLETOWN: A COMPARISON

The city of Detroit's relationship with Chrysler has paralleled that with GM in several ways. The corporation, with its mobile capital, was able to extract commitments from city officials which imposed long-term costs on a city government that could ill afford them. Chrysler, like GM, threatened to build its new, state-of-the-art assembly plant elsewhere and close the old, obsolete Jefferson Avenue plant, leaving Detroit with only one assembly plant, $3 million less in property taxes, and 3,000 fewer jobs.

The Chrysler project was designed by the same actors who formulated plans for Poletown, Mayor Coleman Young and CEDD director Emmett Moten, both strong supporters of large-scale, visible development projects.

The same attorneys who assisted businesses in the Poletown area in obtaining larger settlements from the city were able to negotiate even more generous payments, aided by Chrysler "deadlines" for property acquisition, which were later extended indefinitely. While Moten eventually paid with his job for the inflated land-acquisition costs, others were left with the task of finding the additional funds. Cost overruns escalated with the discovery of contaminated soil on the site and the state of Michigan's requirement that the city resolve this problem before transferring the property to Chrysler. As costs increased, so did the riskiness of project financing, with the city committing itself to repayment of more than $100 million in bonds and loans through increased tax revenues from the project, at a time when a similar debt and complex refinancing scheme existed for the Poletown project.

There are, however, some significant differences between the two projects. First, there was no neighborhood opposition to the Chrysler project, primarily because the city already owned a large proportion of property in the area. There were, as a consequence, no legal challenges and no opportunities to contest the earlier court rulings. In the absence of protest demonstrations, media attention instead focused on the costs of the project and the irresponsibility of city officials in permitting such excesses.

Perhaps the most significant difference is that Chrysler was able to extract such costly commitments from public officials at a time of prosperity for the auto industry. In 1985 production and sales were at their highest point since the pre-recession year of 1979, and motor-vehicle and equipment manufacturers' profits, while down slightly from a record $9.9 billion in 1984, were still higher than any other year since 1978. Even though the automotive industry had gone through vast changes during the early and middle 1980s, with a huge restructuring program, and though it was awash with profits, the interaction between the city and the corporation in the late 1980s replicated earlier patterns.

OSSIFICATION AND REGIME POLITICS

The decision on the Poletown assembly plant, as we have shown, had more to do with symbolic aspects of politics than with a concern over matching explicit revenue flows to project expenditures. It was the biggest industrial renewal project in history, and it was achieved efficiently and with no allegations of corruption. It raised the image of "David versus Goliath" as the neighborhood was destroyed by the city to make way for the corporation, but Mayor Young's constant public discussion of jobs and racial solidarity defused the opposition. The budget surpluses of the mid-1980s indicated that the city could handle repayment within its means.

In contrast, the Jefferson Avenue project was both revenue disaster and symbolic fiasco.[50] Revenue projections were no better, and possibly considerably worse, than those for Poletown. Even worse, the Young administration lost its stature as an efficient and professional organization because of the large cost overruns and the appraisal scandal. Cost overruns were always possible on the Poletown project, but they were less visible because of the particulars of the "quick take" law (which put the issue of cost into court, later) and because media attention focused on the drama of the destruction of the neighborhood. In the case of the Jefferson Avenue project, however, cost overruns and corruption became the dominant counterimage to the efficient city producing jobs and tax revenues for its citizens. This was far more costly to Young than the battle for the neighborhood and led to the loss of Emmett Moten, the financial wizard of industrial urban renewal.

The city of Detroit had, in effect, developed a solution-set for industrial development. When it was approached by Chrysler, it already had a model. There needed to be none of the scrambling to understand the problem, to comprehend just how to put together relocation incentives, to build a complex and contingent financing plan. Industrial urban renewal had become both a priority and a solution; by raising the specter of leaving the city, Chrysler could call forth the now-programmed solution. The first use of the solution, at Poletown, was bold, entrepreneurial, exciting, and pathbreaking. The second use was, if not exactly routine, at least familiar. As a consequence, it carried with it unrecognized risks.

Moreover, the city of Detroit had developed over the years policies that were quite complementary to its approach in industrial renewal. Most important, the Young administration's approach to downtown development emphasized very large, highly visible projects that relied on tax incentives and intergovernmental approval and financing. Though all are not identical, such projects as the Renaissance Center (a very large and insulated hotel/office complex), the expansion of Cobo Hall, the downtown people mover, and other schemes were all large in scale and designed to attract further investment downtown. Like industrial urban renewal, these projects met with mixed success at best. Hence the entire approach to urban development in Detroit hinged on massive public investment from multiple levels of government in complex financing arrangements for large and visible projects. The approach to industrial development, then, was embedded in a broader solution-set toward how the city goes about defining and solving its problems.

A major defining characteristic of urban regimes is the development of such solution-sets. New regimes come into being when new solutions are created to deal with social change. Not infrequently, regime changes are associated with the election of a new mayor and are defined clearly when the new mayor faces a serious challenge. But regimes ossify, applying the newly developed technology to problems in an increasingly routine fashion. One is able to induce an underlying philosophy of the regime through observation of the application of the regime's solution-set.

With the problems of the Jefferson Avenue project, it is hard to see much of a future for the Detroit model of industrial urban renewal. Clearly there are problems with public financing of such projects, given the opportunity-cost problem of other needs. Nevertheless, the coalition partners often cling to the old solution-set, offering continuing advantage to the manufacturing corporations. On the eve of the opening of the new Jefferson Avenue plant, the president of the UAW local commented that "It's a great deal for the city of Detroit. . . . Our future depends on more plants like this being built in the inner city."[51] With private companies more interested in extracting benefits than in building cities, public costs will almost invariably be high relative to the benefit of the plant. As we noted earlier, the asymmetry of information that characterizes bargaining over plant locations favors corporate officials. Only they know exactly what it will take to cause them to locate in a particular city.

The major problem is the unreliability of coalition partners for mayors contemplating industrial urban renewal. The existing literature on urban politics continues to push the myth that businessmen want to run the city or that they have some interest in common with politicians in land inflation.[52] Stephen Elkin writes that "in their efforts to encourage growth by offering a variety of inducements to city businessmen, officials are, to a large extent, preaching to the converted. [The behavior of businessmen] is best understood as an effort to enhance the value of their fixed assets by attracting mobile capital to the city."[53] Although this may be true of certain business concerns – local banks and department stores, for example – it is most assuredly not the case for manufacturing corporations. They are quite uninterested in inflating the value of land in the city and, indeed, would have to pay higher taxes in such circumstances.

There is, then, no simple collectivity of interest between city officials and industrialists. As a consequence, industrialists prove to be particularly poor coalition partners in an urban regime. Mayors of industrial cities must either bribe or embarrass the officials of industrial concerns into cooperating on city projects – at least when those city projects involve the location of the corporation's facilities. Moreover, the automotive manufacturers also used urban industrial renewal as an opportunity to demand plant-specific concessions from organized labor. The companies not only exploited the city to the fullest, they also exploited organized labor, the third partner in the auto city's governing coalition. Because the three primary actors in the sectachy characterizing the auto city have such different primary interests, interactions among them involve both shared understandings and hard bargaining. All major participants agreed that, for the city, jobs and the tax base were of paramount importance. They agreed, then, on the definition of the problem. All agreed that industrial urban renewal was a major solution. Those very shared understandings of the causal connection between problem and solution yielded major advantages to the auto manufacturers, who took full advantage of the situation. Coalition building is a difficult process when interests diverge, even when the supposed unitary interest of growth is involved.

Manufacturing corporations focus on the market for their products and lay off workers and shut factories without regard to the influence of their activities on the value of urban land or the character of the city within which their plants are located. The volatile automotive manufacturing economy makes the corporate sustaining hand a fickle provider, far from generous in good times and undependable in bad ones.

15

Urban Power,
Political Decision Making,
and the Automobile Industry

In this book we have traced the connections between the urban industrial economy and decision making in the political systems that were established to govern the cities that grew as a direct result of that economy. We have examined the relationships between politics and economics under a special set of circumstances – namely, the establishment of new automotive assembly plants in three industrial cities: Detroit, Flint, and Pontiac, Michigan. In doing so, we have focused on three central yet interrelated issues: (1) the relationship between the local industrial economy and the local political system; (2) the structure of urban political regimes; and (3) the independence of political decision making in urban affairs.

CAPITAL AND THE LOCAL STATE

The relationship between the production of the automobile and Michigan's auto cities is both extremely simple and extraordinarily complex. On one hand, the only real reason for the explosive growth of the cities of southeast Michigan was to support automobile production. To this day, the livelihoods of the citizens of Detroit, Pontiac, and Flint are uniquely tied to the manufacture of the automobile.

On the other hand, the growth of government is not directly related to the productivity of automotive manufacturers. State and local government in Michigan grew gradually and inexorably from the mid-1950s until 1980, regardless of trends in automotive manufacture. Only with the extreme recession of the early 1980s did government shrink. Even then the shrinkage of the public sector was tiny in comparison to the shrinkage of the private economy. The recession radically altered the state of Michigan's spending priorities, however, causing increases in expenditures for welfare and abrupt reductions in spending for education.

Most public-sector expenditures are not directly related to manufacturing productivity, so that it may not be surprising that the latter does not determine the former in a straightforward fashion. For expenditures that are directly relevant for manufacturing productivity, however, the situation is different. Roger Friedland, in his cross-city study of municipal expenditures, found "two worlds of expenditures: one oriented to providing services and public employment for the city's residents, the other to constructing the infrastructure necessary to profitable private investment." The politics of consumption was dominated by classic electoral politics, but the politics of production "appeared rational and efficient, a politically neutered self-financing building program."[1]

While there is certainly nothing "politically neutered" about the politics of economic development in an auto city, clearly the politics of production is different qualitatively from the politics of consumption. Political leaders view the attracting of private investment as essential to the well-being of the cities that they govern. Coleman Young has repeatedly characterized the redevelopment project in Poletown as "beyond a doubt the most important single program that has been undertaken since I became mayor." Similarly, Flint's Mayor James Rutherford pointed to his economic-development efforts as his most important accomplishment. His black successor singled out for specific praise Rutherford's work in attracting private investment. In a different era, these same mayors might have been relatively more concerned with social order or racial justice and relatively less concerned with economic development; but in the atmosphere of fiscal scarcity of the 1980s, attracting investment was the primary item on the agenda.

It would be a mistake, however, to characterize economic-development policies as being solely "rational and efficient." While there certainly exists an element of rational analysis in this policy arena, there is also a considerable amount of political conflict, of negotiating among interests, of symbolic appeal, of incomplete information, and of snap decisions.

BUSINESSMEN AND POLITICIANS

A basic reason for the problems listed above is that capitalists and politicians in large cities that have heavy concentrations of minorities and working-class populations have fundamentally different interests that they pursue. This limits the potential for rational decision making because the major participants in the process do not agree on the basic goals. As a general rule, both politicians and business officials are committed to the organizations that they head. There are, of course, exceptions, but generally the mechanisms of accountability nudge, and nudge not so subtly, both political and business leaders toward the maintenance and enhancement of the organizations that they lead. Because organizational purpose and mechanisms of accountability are different, the interests of leaders are often different.

It would be a mistake to conclude from this observation that politicians and businessmen represent different class interests. In pursuing organizational interests, politicians may well not adopt the interests of their working- or lower-class constituents.[2] There are no logical reasons why the organizational interests of the city (as perceived by the politician) should be the same as the interests of particular groups or classes dwelling within the city. In the case of Flint, the perceived organizational interest of city officials – the development of Buick City complex – coincided with the interests of the poor residents around the old Buick plant: they would be able to move from a decaying neighborhood that held no intrinsic value to them. In Detroit, the situation was more complex. Most residents wanted to move; but an ardent minority felt otherwise, and they lost their battle completely.

The result is a somewhat ironic situation. Elections may well serve to present politicians with strong incentives to act contrary to the wishes of the economic elite, even though they may not possess the resources to do so. Elections do not, however, serve to force politicians to act in accordance with the wishes of the masses. Indeed, in many situations, such as the policy specifics of economic development, no mass sentiment exists except when political leaders act to mobilize symbolic appeals to the creation of jobs. Nor are mass wishes and neighborhood interests to be equated. If a mayor acts contrary to neighborhood interests, it does not necessarily follow that he is acting contrary to community interests, nor does it follow that he is necessarily a pawn of business interests.

The proposition that businessmen collectively pursue a common class interest in their interactions with government is itself questionable. Those who hold high positions in business organizations have strong incentives to represent those organizational interests first and foremost.[3] They are capable of making rational decisions that may do great harm to other elements of the capitalist class if such decisions are perceived as aiding their organizations. This goes much further than the simple idea that a good businessman competes with those who are in the same line of work. In working with contractors, suppliers of products, or suppliers of labor, the businessman may act to enhance his or her organization, to the direct detriment of the other organizations and in complete disregard of the long- or short-run interests of the capitalist class, the local community, and the other members of the industry.

It is common practice for an industry to organize a peak association for purposes of pursuing collective interests. In the automotive industry, this peak association is the Motor Vehicle Manufacturers' Association (MVMA). Yet its ability to present a common front to government has often been undercut by the differing interests of the manufacturers. According to a former chairman of the Manufacturing Committee of the association, who was a member of the corporate board of American Motors, differences in competitive strategies of the major firms cause continual problems in representing industry positions to government. That has kept the association weak and has meant that the corporations themselves, rather than the MVMA, have become the major lobbying instruments.[4] One difference emerged on the issue of automotive import quotas, with Chrysler being strongly in favor and General Motors, which negotiated a joint venture with Toyota based in California, being very much against such quotas. But other differences have emerged, even on regulatory issues. Chrysler, which moved aggressively into the small-car market with its K-car venture, had few objections to the regulation of fuel economy, while Ford and General Motors were forced to pay penalties because their fleets' mileages were too high. There is a continual undercutting of industry positions on public-policy issues as the firms that constitute the industry see ways to gain comparative advantage over the other firms in the industry as a consequence of governmental action. In the automotive industry, and quite possibly in other industries, peak associations are weaker instruments for influencing public policy than one might expect.

It is little wonder, then, that businessmen take full advantage of the economic-development incentives that are offered by the public sector, whether or not they are required to affect a locational decision. A GM official commented to us that he thought tax abatements were definitely wrong, but "the rule is written into the game, and we are going to play the game the best damn way we know how. We are not doing right by the shareholders if we don't."[5]

It is important to remember that the leaders of business do not always act simply and directly as heads of the corporations they run. While we have emphasized this aspect of business-government interactions, it is also true that corporate heads can spearhead civic and investment initiatives even though it is not in the direct interest of their businesses to do so. During the 1970s, Henry Ford II took a lead role in riverfront development, and GM initiated a major residential redevelopment program around its corporate headquarters. Brewer Peter Stroh and his family have invested in River Place even after they closed the Stroh Brewery in downtown Detroit. In contrast, the presumably more land-based Hudson's Department Store lost interest in Detroit as a development site after merging with Dayton's and later Marshall Fields. So while land-based companies may be able to profit financially from urban development, and manufacturers usually don't, this does not mean that they will rush to support any particular redevelopment project. The fact remains, however, that auto companies have had little, if any, corporate interest in urban development except when major incentives were provided by government. Because these and other export-oriented firms have scant financial incentives to initiate and support redevelopment schemes, they are generally less likely to do so than firms more directly tied to the economic vitality of the city.

PUBLIC-SECTOR AUTONOMY

Our evidence about the independent actions of auto-city politicians in very constrained circumstances speaks to the issue of the autonomy of the public sector in American cities. It is clear that American city governments are open to influence by private interests. What is more interesting is whether city governments can mobilize resources without reliance on upper-status individuals and institutions. Clarence Stone has argued that "Regime leadership [based on informal networks of private and civic actors] is important because formal public authority is weak. . . . A governing coalition can be created only by putting together an informal structure that joins private resources and institutions."[6] Clearly our auto-city politicians relied on business groups for support, but probably no more than on other elements—especially allies at other levels of government. The industrial urban renewal projects of Detroit, and, to a lesser extent, Flint and Orion Township, would not have been possible without the active collaboration of the state and federal governments. The generic "business community" and its informal networks were also important as part of the supporting cast, but did not play a leading role in the projects. They were no more or less important than labor leaders, religious groups, state and national politicians, and the city electorate in providing the "booster" spirit surrounding the project. The automotive companies were, of course, crucial, but their participation in the projects was entirely contingent on a very expensive package of public-sector subsidies.

This does not mean that business support is not important in the politics of urban regimes. Far from it. Rather, we want to emphasize that the support of other groups, especially labor and political figures at other levels of government, were as important as the business community in mobilizing support for the projects. Most critical of all were the local political leaders that spearheaded the effort. Robert Dahl's "executive centered coalition" seems an adequate description.[7] What Dahl and the earlier pluralists missed, however, is the dependency of city political leaders on capital, a dependency that is heightened with the potential of capital mobility. This very mobility and lack of dependency by mobile corporations makes it more likely that politicians will initiate linkages with businessmen.

We conclude that in Detroit and Flint, at least, formal public authority was powerful enough to govern. This is not to argue that auto-city politicians acted alone; quite the contrary. They courted support from many sources – the electorate, state and national politicians, labor leaders, business groups, and (to a lesser extent) religious associations. Without the support of these groups, the projects would not have been possible. But it is very difficult to see any special reliance on the informal business community in these cases, even though in the specific incidences the automobile manufacturers possessed great leverage.

FRAGMENTATION AND COMPETITION

The reality of mobile capital and stationary cities means that business-men hold a major bargaining chip in dealing with economic-development issues. This situation also means that the allocation of municipal resources is different from what it would be if local politics alone was to dictate spending priorities. Michael Kennedy's careful analysis of city fiscal strain caused by a recession fails to support James O'Connor's theory that fiscal stress is caused by an imbalance in economically productive expenses (social investment) and economically unproductive expenses (social expense or, to use an older term, social control). Social-investment expenses are most associated with fiscal strain, indicating that there is no trade-off between the two types of expenditure. The most likely explanation of this finding is that financially pressed cities are competing for capital in a governmentally fragmented system.[8] These cities are not willing to sacrifice social-investment expenditures in order to increase social-control spending. In Detroit, police were laid off at the same time that massive public subsidies were provided for the Poletown plant and other economic development projects. Like Detroit, other financially pressed cities were forced into this choice by the ability of productive enterprises to relocate.

Moreover, there exists an unavoidable asymmetry of information in deal-ings over the granting of tax abatements and certain other economic develop-ment incentives. The businessman knows just what incentives will be necessary in order to affect a decision in regard to location, but the city official does not. This allows the business to extract a corporate surplus, an amount over what would be strictly necessary to affect the decision about location.[9] Governmental fragmentation and capital mobility cause cities to spend more on social investment than would occur if local politics was determinative of urban outcomes; they also allow corporations to extract more than would be strictly necessary in a world of perfect information.

THE POLITICS OF LARGE SCALE

Certain social and economic trends have made the "peak bargaining" between political and economic leaders increasingly important. We believe that Robert Dahl was wrong when he claimed that industrial society dispersed political resources. At least in a city that experienced such a violent industrial transformation as Detroit did, industrialization concentrated economic and political power into a limited number of large organizations. The city still continued to act as a balancer of interests, but it also came to represent a very important interest in its own right. The conception of a city interest was fostered by a generation of municipal reformers—reformers who achieved spectacular success in Detroit and other cities—swept away the structural bases of ethnic politics, and put into place a strong, central chief executive who was capable of dealing on a par with powerful corporate executives.

The result has been a system of sectarchy characterized by bargaining among sectors on many issues of community interest. Each of the major sectors—primarily business, labor, and government—has different interests; but they are occasionally brought together in a single forum to debate major issues. In Detroit, this approach is termed "coalition building," although it scarcely resembles the classic political process. Because the peak association of the multinational automobile corporations is weak relative to the component corporations, peak bargaining in Detroit consists of interactions between political leaders and the leaders of the individual corporations. Corporate leaders, not the executive officers of peak associations, have the power to mobilize corporate resources for community projects. This variant of peak bargaining occurred in early discussions about the location of the Poletown plant. GM's chairman, Thomas Murphy, could make his bargain with Mayor Young, knowing full well that it was in his power to complete his side of it. He would not be undercut, in the normal course of events, by the corporation's constituent units.

Sectarchy implies that peak leaders are able to dominate elements within their sectors on issues where peak bargaining is activated. This is never a foregone conclusion because organizations within a sector have an incentive to reject policy settlements at the peak when their interests are threatened. Hence peak leaders may find themselves bargaining both with other peak leaders and with leaders within their organized sector. This is most true of the political sector.

Critical to the ability of political executives to maintain internal order is the structure of the government within which they operate. It would, of course, be a mistake to attribute the quiescence of Detroit's City Council about the Poletown plant solely to governmental structure. Mayor Young's strong city-wide electoral appeal and his advocacy of a valence issue — jobs — contributed mightily to the council's lack of action. The council and other policy-making bodies that had the power to delay or alter any executive action were incapable or unwilling to do either. This was the mayor's ball game, and he generally did an effective job of making sure that his players were not unruly. Young was determined not to lose the opportunity for the new assembly plant, so he took it upon himself to ensure that no actions within the political system would endanger it. Nevertheless, his position in the governmental structure gave him an important resource in dominating the council.

One type of governmental reform that may not be advantageous in dealing with large-scale business enterprises is the city-manager system. Detroit and Flint, both of which had strong-mayor systems, dealt more effectively with GM than did Pontiac, which was then governed by a council-manager system. Mayors who have city-wide constituencies are not as vulnerable to being undercut by a hostile council. Paul Schumaker, in a study of economic-development issues in Lawrence, Kansas, suggests that city managers and nonelected mayors may not be able to assemble the political resources to assemble progrowth coalitions to the degree that elected mayors can. Even in this reformed city, the mayor's policy position was more influential in the outcome of economic-development projects than was the city manager's.[10] In general, any reform that weakens the political executive's ability to impose order within the political sector also weakens his or her ability to negotiate with the leaders of other sectors.

Moreover, there is significant advantage to large size in dealing with organizations external to the city. It is interesting that the entire debate concerning the proper size of local government has almost entirely been approached as a problem in efficiency and control, rather than as one of marshaling resources to deal with external organizations.[11] Although those who criticize large-scale metropolitan organization are quick to point out the problems of efficiency and accountability in large, bureaucratic governments (we think they are absolutely right on this point), they are not so quick to point out the advantages that generally flow from large size when it comes to negotiating with external organizations.

Students of efficiency in urban service systems have shown that, for many services, there are few advantages to large-scale organization. Yet in the area of infrastructure provision, size is probably a distinct advantage. Large bureaucracies are more likely to have more professional staffs and more access to expertise; they are also more likely to have the capacity to absorb short-term losses so as to achieve long-run benefits. Certainly the dealings that GM had with the small-scale government of Orion Township was not as satisfactory as its dealings with the large, professionally organized bureaucracies of Detroit.

URBAN POWER

The existence of bargaining among organized sectors does not necessarily imply an equality of power among sectors. On issues that are negotiated among sector elites, however, a hierarchical arrangement usually forms among subunits within the sector. On issues that do not stimulate peak bargaining, sector elites may be more open to influence from groups and coalitions within the sector. While it is difficult to specify the kinds of issues that stimulate peak bargaining, it is probable that the larger the perceived stakes in the community, the more likely it is that peak bargaining will emerge. Economic development is a prime candidate for peak bargaining, but only when major projects are contemplated. (Much of policy making in the economic-development sphere is as routinized as it is in other areas of policy.)

Business and government are usually not on an equal footing in the negotiating process, although it is not irrelevant that bargaining occurs at all. The presence of bargaining indicates that each participant is able to command resources that the other participants respect. For a variety of reasons, however, *governmental* officials are frequently the junior partners in peak bargaining.

In an industrial city such as Detroit, community power is structured into large-scale organizations. The major organizations are those of commerce and industry, government, the media, labor, and the church. Those who wield power hold commanding positions in these organizations. They do not act as individuals; they act as representatives of organizations. Some of these leaders are more adept than others. Some have more resources than others and are able to translate these resources into political influence more efficiently than do others. A very limited few are able to exercise power even though they do not represent any major organization. Power for most people, however, is intimately connected to positions in an organization. The power gradient drops rapidly when one leaves the organization.

Of all the organizations in the community, government is the most complex. It is organized territorially; it often has severe problems of intraorganizational control; it must deal externally both with private-sector organizations and with other governmental organizations. Governments, being organizations, have organizational interests that center on the maintenance and enhancement of the organization. But government, as the receptacle of the community's police power, can also do the bidding of other social interests. Is government, at least on issues of economic development and capital accumulation, subservient to business?

In Detroit, cooperation between the business community and the city occurs in fits and starts, sometimes spearheaded by government, sometimes by business leaders. But the collaboration is always fragile and will collapse when organizational interests are threatened. In Flint, the Mott Foundation spearheads community-development projects. In Pontiac, major development downtown has been the most important item on the civic agenda for a quarter of a century, with mixed results at best.

In each case, the community effort is directed at making water run uphill: attracting capital where it would not normally flow. Bluntly put, businessmen do not need to control city governments, because they do not need the city. In a society that needs its urban agglomerations less because of technical advances in transportation and communication, businessmen can move their enterprises more freely than in the past. This fact of modern society has vast implications for the nation's industrial cities. To accomplish an economic-development program, political leaders must persuade business leaders to commit their capital to the city, a place that is still, for the most part, not as attractive as nonurban locations. Political leaders do this by offering economic-development incentives, by appealing to civic pride, and by playing to a broader public opinion of the corporation. They act generally as political entrepreneurs in putting together "progrowth coalitions" aimed at attracting businesses to the community.[12]

Most studies of the relationship between business and government in community affairs have focused on the local commercial business establishment rather than on the industrial multinational corporation. Detroit's business community does differ considerably from more commercially oriented cities in the size and scope of the city's business enterprises. Detroit's automotive multinational corporations may have less of a stake in the community than does the local commercial elite, which exists in Detroit but is a less important component of the business community than is probably true elsewhere. Increases in the size and scale of business enterprise are a national trend, however, and this makes local commitment less important. Metropolitan Detroit's major chain of department stores is in the hands of an absentee owner, and the parent corporation, Minneapolis-based Dayton-Hudson, closed its downtown Hudson's store several years ago. (In a reversal of the usual state of affairs, Detroit's commercial flagship is absentee owned, but its industrial facilities are owned by "local" corporations.) The consequence of these changes is a national trend toward mobile capital, which has strong implications for community power.[13]

One result of this state of affairs is that political leaders are almost totally unconcerned about the economic viability of particular development projects. Progrowth coalitions are based on image as much as on hard facts. A careful look at Detroit's Poletown redevelopment project indicates that there is almost no likelihood of any meaningful direct return on the city's investment.

The return is in the symbolic perception of the city as a success story, a place in which things get done efficiently and effectively. This adds to the credibility of officials in their dealings with other corporations, and presumably it adds to the well-being of the city in the long run.

Businessmen are becoming less and less interested in exercising direct influence over city policies. Politicians are becoming increasingly interested in influencing businessmen. This asymmetry is one reason that businessmen hold what Charles Lindblom has termed a "privileged position" in the community. Businessmen provide the majority of livelihoods for the community's citizens, and businesses have the power to deny that livelihood by relocating. It would nevertheless be a very bad mistake to assume that politicians cannot influence businessmen because politicians want more from businessmen than businessmen (or at least the captains of large industrial corporations) want from politicians.

Some politicians are better able to influence businessmen than are others, and such leaders are more likely to emerge in some cities than in others. In Pontiac, political leaders did not even attempt to influence GM's decision about location. They seem to have been captives of a political culture that constrained choice and foreclosed options even more than the economic reality demanded. In Detroit, the mayor and his economic development experts moved aggressively to take advantage of an offer to build a plant. It is probable that the offer was conditioned less on corporate good will and more on a gauging of the probable impact on public opinion by a corporate management that, at least since the publication of *Unsafe at Any Speed*, has learned that generating hostile public opinion is bad business. In Flint, a cagey mayor who had a good understanding of local politics affected the course of corporate decision making to the benefit of his community. City officials may be weaker in their dealings with industry than they have been in the recent past, but they are far from helpless.

The failure to understand the real sources of dependency in the city has led to gross misunderstandings of the directionality of influence in relationships between politicians and businessmen. For example, Hill has written that "today Economic Development Corporations have become an instrument through which the private sector more or less directly allocates public revenues and wields public powers in such a fashion to redistribute public resources from neighborhood residents to private investors."[14] Detroit's EDC is far more a tool of the mayor than it is of the private sector. Since the EDC has to rely on the city's Community and Economic Development Department as a source of information, the EDC is an instrument by which public power can be used to influence private investment decisions. It may be argued that the mayor's priorities are misguided or that they are driven by a capitalist logic of uneven development, but it is silly to argue that the EDC controls the mayor.[15]

NEIGHBORHOODS

Even when city officials influence businessmen on economic-development projects, the projects may or may not work to the benefit of the poor residents of the city. The common conception that urban renewal in the modern city works to the detriment of the poor and working-class residents of affected neighborhoods may be somewhat anachronistic. Since 1970, federal law has ensured that fair prices will be paid for property and that generous relocation benefits will be granted for projects that receive federal funds.[16] The issue of the availability of housing for the poor and near-poor in cities is complex, but it is at least arguable that the current housing surplus in most industrial cities has made available considerable housing for these citizens. Such cold, hard calculations clearly underestimate the worth of such intangibles as neighborhood attachment. In some cases, however, the commitment of citizens to neighborhoods may be overestimated. This may be more true in the classic industrial cities of Michigan than it is elsewhere. Industrialization, according to the research of Oliver Zunz, swept away the neighborhood-oriented ethnic culture of Detroit, replacing it with a rigid class-stratified geographic order.[17]

In the cities that we studied, neighborhood mobilization was absent among black citizens. In Flint, the mostly black residents of the Buick City complex area were desperate to leave (although their haste to leave was affected by the city's earlier designation of the area, which had been declining for some years, as an urban-renewal area). In Detroit's Poletown, the situation was far more complex, but most of the residents, and almost all of the black residents, probably wanted to move. The neighborhood was on the verge of a very severe decline, with the closing of Dodge Main and the failure of the area to attract young residents. There is no doubt that a minority, primarily composed of Polish residents, most of whom were elderly, did suffer, and they suffered badly. But by refusing to yield even slightly to the Poletown Neighborhood Council, Mayor Young protected the symbolic interests of the black residents of the neighborhood. In any case, the common media image that the city and the giant corporation were conspiring to destroy the neighborhood was mostly myth.

LABOR

In the American city, labor can be mobilized by civic leaders to support progrowth policies (or in industrial cities, antidecline policies). This allies labor with business interests in some situations, but against them in others. Usually, labor enthusiastically supports policies to attract investment to the city, but it may be mobilized against a business if that business leaves the area. Labor members of city councils often engage in considerable posturing and anticorporate rhetoric, but they vote for procorporate policies when the time comes.

In many ways, labor is the reluctant partner in the progrowth coalition of the modern industrial city. Political leaders need the active involvement of labor leaders in marshaling support for incentive packages that are assembled to attract industrial investment. Yet the initial predilections of labor leaders, which are shaped both by their status and by their organizational affiliations, are antagonistic to such business incentives. Labor leaders are the true captives of the mobility of corporate capital.

INTERNAL ALLOCATIONS

Peak bargaining allocates costs and benefits among sectors, but it also affects the distribution of costs and benefits within sectors. Subtleties of policies can play an important role in the internal distribution of values. Major internal reallocations can stem from relatively obscure details of policy. For example, in calculating the growth in property value in Poletown, a date was used that allowed the city to capture all of the value of the new assembly plant for its tax-increment district. The tax-increment district provided a vehicle for spreading the costs of the project over several different taxing jurisdictions, all of which objected to the establishment of the district. In Flint, a thorough understanding and the use of state annexation laws made it possible for the city to respond to GM's intention to build a suburban plant. In Orion Township, the seemingly mundane issue of sewer routing became a major problem.

DECISION MAKING

Many analysts have treated political leaders as pawns of the great social forces that sweep cities. Similarly, almost all theories of decision making imply a great deal of determinism. Sometimes this search for certainty leads to very different deterministic worlds. Not so many years ago, Douglas Yates depicted city mayors as riding the tiger of ungovernable cities and being pushed around much like a steel ball in a pinball machine. The forces internal to the city were too great for the typical leader to cope with.[18] A handful of years later, Paul Peterson depicted the forces external to the city as being so overwhelming that he recommended that political scientists spend little time in analyzing the local politics of the city.[19]

The deterministic approach to social analysis may be found in two schools of thought that are otherwise remote from one another. The "new urban political economy" has been characterized by a search for "deep structures," which C. G. Pickvance has defined as "non-observable structures whose existence was believed to explain surface or empirically observable structures."[20] In Marxist analysis, the deep structures are rooted in economic relationships. Pickvance contrasts Marxist analysis with the Weberian tradition of social analysis, which is based in an attempt to understand the role of organizations and the state as being independent contributors to the social order:

> For example, a Weberian study of planning decisions might explain a council's approval of a city centre development proposal in terms of the values of city leaders, the council's authority vis-à-vis its citizens, and the interests of professionals employed by the city council. A Marxist critique on the other hand might acknowledge these factors but argue that while they had been the proximate causes it was in the nature of the role of councils in capitalist societies to support proposals which favored capital accumulation.[21]

Clearly there is little room for human intention in this sort of analysis. Decision making is driven entirely by impersonal economic forces.

Determinism may also be found, in another guise, in the analyses of the rational-decision theorists. It might be said of the rationality assumption that "he who leads best follows." The rational maximizer leads his organization by adapting to his environment. In economics, the price system ensures that the firm will continually adjust to changes in the competitive market. In politics, it is assumed that governments fulfill voter preferences for public policies by rationally maximizing votes.[22] The infamous "median voter" hypothesis has guided a substantial amount of research on city expenditures.[23] Public-sector administrators maximize the size of their budgets.[24]

Most rational theorists will, of course, readily agree that the rationality assumption does not very closely approximate the manner in which most people make decisions. These theorists argue, however, that such assumptions allow them to make statements about the broader social structure. If these empirical statements are confirmed, then the abstraction of rationality will suffice.

It is not enough, then, for the proponents of nonrational decision theories to limit their critiques of rational-decisional analysis to the descriptive correspondence between actual decision making and the rational abstraction. It is necessary to link nonrational decisional modes to outcomes at the system level. Indeed, to a large extent, this has been accomplished. Aaron Wildavsky has linked incrementalist decision rules to the actual outcomes of federal budgets during the 1960s.[25] Thomas Anton has critiqued the incrementalist approach to understanding government budgets as being too rational; he explains budget outcomes in Illinois in the mid-1960s in terms of rigid decision rules and procedures that were followed with little reference to their relationships to budget outcomes.[26] Similarly, John Crecine's models of municipal budgeting stress the simple decisional routines used in the allocation process.[27] In the process of distributing urban services, bureaucratic routines and decision rules play a preeminent role.[28] John Kingdon has used the garbage-can model of organizational choice that was developed by Michael Cohen and his associates to explain policy agendas.[29] In this model, three "process streams" – problems, policies, and politics – flow through the system, and "at critical junctures the three streams are joined" to yield major changes in policy.[30]

Each of these analyses isolates nonrational (but not irrational) organizational processes as being determinative of social outcomes. They do not speak to the role of human intention in influencing these outcomes. Several studies do suggest the independent impact of leadership, however. In a qualitative study of urban fiscal stress, Charles Levine and his colleagues suggest that leadership has a fairly substantial role in dealing with financial problems.[31] Pietro Nivola has studied short-term municipal debt in the recession year of 1975 and has found that economic hardship failed to explain debt levels at all, but that employee unionization, retirement costs, and personnel costs did. Nivola suggests an important role for political choice in the urban fiscal crisis.[32] Terry Clark and Lorna Ferguson present quantitative evidence that the ideology of city mayors has affected the level of taxing and spending in communities.[33]

All of this suggests that there are three separate issues in the analysis of urban decision making. The first concerns the extent of the constraint on independent decision making. The second concerns the degree of rationality on the part of decision makers. The third concerns the degree to which political decision makers can influence the urban social order.

We, like many political scientists, see little of the full-blown rational model of decision making in the cases that we studied. This does not mean that alternatives are not studied and that action appropriate to the problem is not taken. These things clearly happen; it is just that the limits to the exercise of rational decision making are so obvious in the policy process. Herbert Simon's concepts of bounded rationality and satisficing are far more relevant to the decision-making process as we observed it. However, it is also clear that the limits on rational decision making are both intraorganizational and extraorganizational. Even if there were no limits on rationality in human abilities or in organizational dynamics, severe problems would be posed by what Simon has termed "extremely complex boundary conditions imposed by the environment."[34]

The choices that GM presented to the mayors had the effect of severely constraining the alternatives. Nevertheless, the complexity of even this environment led to different behaviors in relatively similar situations. We use the term *creative bounded choice* to describe the abilities of some leaders to find and exploit weaknesses in an environment that seems on first examination to be thoroughly unyielding and entirely overwhelming. Mayor Rutherford refused to adjust to the environment; instead he engaged in a desperate and ultimately successful search for a way of turning a bad situation to advantage. This exemplifies the notion of creativity in a situation that was characterized by severe constraints.

Some leaders at some times have the ability to deal creatively with a threatening environment; this limits the utility of models of the policy process that are built on adjustment to the environment. A model of continuous adjustment to changing circumstances in the environment may well describe most of the policy-relevant behaviors of political systems, at least if one adds some notion of environmental change being caused by the political system itself.[35] However, the fact remains that major changes in local systems often are due to creative actions taken by political leaders. This yields a certain indeterminism of form: under similar circumstances, similar systems react differently. The French mathematician René Thom has argued that such indeterminism is the essence of science: "This *science* which, in principle, denies indeterminism is actually its ungrateful offspring, whose only purpose is to destroy its parent."[36]

What is different about the social sciences is that such indeterminism leads to the age-old debate concerning determinism and free will. If it is silly in urban politics to talk of the free will of political leaders, it seems equally silly to talk about determinism. It is particularly hard to conceive of having underlying structures cause surface behaviors in these cases. It is clear that the city of Detroit rushed to do the bidding of General Motors, but it is equally clear that GM had never needed Detroit in the first place to aid it in the process of capital accumulation. Surface phenomena, even though they may be extremely complex, are often quite enough to explain political outcomes.

A more interesting issue is the degree to which leaders, even when they seem to be acting independently and creatively, actually affect the social order.[37] In none of the cases that we studied could it be said that any major transformations of the local political economy took place because of the exertion of the will of political leaders. Indeed, Detroit and Flint were probably even more dependent on automotive manufacture than otherwise would have been the case (at the same time they were also less economically depressed, which was the relevant issue for the mayors). Yet Detroit, Flint, and Pontiac are to some degree changed places because of the actions (or inactions) of their leaders.

URBAN REGIMES AND SOLUTION-SETS

A major limitation of a smoothly functioning, fully rational decision-making system on urban economic development policies is the manner in which urban regimes operate. The formal and informal arrangements that characterize the regime encourage a particular definition of a city's problems and tend to limit search processes for solutions to those problems. Any other approach would be disruptive to the understandings that underpin the regime.

Urban regimes are most often formed by the activities of political leaders, especially mayors. Where capital is mobile, politicians need the business community more than the business community needs government. Hence mayors must reach out to businessmen, and they must provide policies that appeal to the business community. In the case of Detroit, informal arrangements between Mayor Young and the executives of automobile companies and other manufacturing corporations were the characteristic feature of the regime. The regime was codified in a strong Economic Development Department and its appendages, such as the Economic Development Corporation. Planning was diverted from the traditional role of land-use provisions toward the development and financing of large-scale economic redevelopment programs. A characteristic regime style emerged in Detroit, one which was concerned primarily with showcase industrial renewal programs.

We have termed the characteristic regime style as the regime's *solution-set*, to emphasize the connections between the solutions almost routinely proposed for a city's problems and the way in which those problems are understood. Mayor Young's dicta that "there is nothing wrong with Detroit that three or four factories can't solve" symbolizes the connectedness of solutions and problems that comprises an urban regime's solution-set. Young saw urban industrial renewal as the solution for the panoply of urban ills that he had to deal with: unemployment, poverty, a shrinking tax base. All were addressed by the renewal of mass production activity in the city.

The mayor's approach to industrial renewal was in many ways an adaptation of the commercial development policies that he (and, to a lesser extent, other Detroit mayors) had pursued. Showcase public-private industrial renewal projects paralleled showcase commercial projects. Similar policy vehicles were used; for example, tax-increment financing was developed first for use in the central business district. The entire development of urban industrial renewal was characterized by limited search and consideration of alternatives "near" the familiar commercial redevelopment model. Perhaps even more important, the process was dominated by *reasoning by analogy* – commercial and industrial projects seem similar even if they differ in one important respect: commercial projects are intimately bound up with the economic vitality of the community, whereas industrial projects, supportive as they are of export industries, are not.

Urban industrial renewal as a set of policies pursued by the Young administration did not emerge from a study of alternatives. Rather, it was forged in the high drama of Poletown and was colored by the available capacity of city agencies. These agencies were skilled at financing large-scale urban renewal projects, such as the Joe Louis Arena, through complex arrangements involving the creative leveraging of federal funds. The propensity of urban regimes to defend their institutionalized policy approaches and to engage in a process of limited search and reasoning by analogy implies the generalization of policy successes to broad solution-sets.

Once the solution-set has been established, there is a clear tendency for a regime to replicate its policy initiatives in situations that are classified as similar. This is a more important determinant of policy outputs than any rational analysis of ends and means. The replication of the Poletown approach at Chrysler Jefferson by Young's administration even in the face of the problems in bringing the Poletown financing to a successful conclusion is a powerful illustration of the tendency of urban regimes to be captives of their solution-sets.

The observation that solution-sets tend to dominate the policy process during times of stasis provides a new perspective on urban power relationships. First, it implies that no actors need to manipulate relationships "behind the scenes." Because past issue definitions and institutionalized policy solutions tend to dominate current search, the continual application of control by elites is not necessary. In this respect, our approach may be compared to Stone's work on urban regimes. Stone has criticized pluralist perspectives on urban power because they view power as a problem in social control and cost of compliance; he suggests a social production model, in which collective ends are achieved through resource mobilization.[38] "That is what urban regimes are about, and it is through civic organizations and informal networks that much of the essential cooperation, exchange, and consequent mobilization of resources occurs."[39] That is, resource mobilization occurs via elite networks, and regimes cohere by preempting positive action.

Stone's approach has much to commend it because it moves the discussion of power away from arguments about who controls or manipulates whom. He is correct in emphasizing the preemptive power of the existing informal networks, and on the incomplete control of any governing coalition. But in two respects he fails to consider the independent influence of solution-sets on governing coalitions. First, he underemphasizes the role of what we have termed policy stasis on urban governing arrangements. Once in place, solution-sets tend to dominate policy search and subsequent resource mobilization. Second, fresh policy proposals and symbolic representations of them have the capacity to attract new participants to politics, altering the existing governing arrangements. That is, any regime is not simply an arrangement for mobilizing resources through the existing business and civic networks in a city. It is also a set of past policy decisions that influence the interactions among current actors. Indeed, Orr and Stoker suggest the role of new ideas in their analysis of the potential transition from a sporadic, project-by-project business-development regime in Detroit to one more rooted in human capital development. They also suggest that relying on the traditional participants from the business community, particularly the automobile companies, will retard the development of such a regime. That is, new participants will be necessary to carry new regime ideas.[40]

SOME CONCLUDING PROPOSITIONS

In concluding, we present the following propositions that have, probably like all social-science research, both guided this inquiry and been illuminated by it.

1. At root, politicians and businessmen have different interests. Incentives encourage both of them to maintain and enhance the viability of the organizations that they lead. While these interests may coincide at times, basically they differ because they are rooted in organizations that have different purposes.

2. The new mobility of capital has caused a radical change in the relationships between cities and firms. Businessmen are, on the one hand, less interested in exerting control over local government. On the other hand, politicians are more interested in influencing businessmen. This new dependency in the city means that governmental officials will attempt to influence the decisions of businessmen, rather than the other way around. It also means that urban regimes are more likely to be formed by mayors than by business executives, because mayors and other political leaders will need to initiate activity that will involve business leaders in the community.

3. Politicians are not completely lacking in the resources that they can mobilize in dealing with multinational corporations. Moreover, certain governmental arrangements add measurably to the probability of successful negotiation with businessmen: these include the sheer size of the jurisdiction, a mayoral form of government, and a professional bureaucracy. In general, any arrangement that aids a mayor in mobilizing power among the various constituencies that make claims on government also aids in negotiating with external organizations. Moreover, the sheer size of the jurisdiction aids political officials in two ways. Size allows the building of large professional bureaucracies that are able to handle more effectively the large-scale problems of large-scale economic development. Size also enhances visibility and, hence, the negotiating resources of chief executives.

4. Miscalculation is an important element in negotiations. If mayors are capable of miscalculation, so are the heads of corporations. Finding and

exploiting such miscalculations is a key element in the relationship between city governments and corporations.

5. If the interests of mayors and those of businessmen do not coincide, neither do the interests of mayors and neighborhoods. The tension between neighborhoods and central-city government is probably higher on the issue of economic-development priorities than on any other issue. Metropolitan and national media tend to portray the plight of neighborhoods in a favorable light, but the media images may well not correspond to urban realities. Indeed, the policy-driven relocation that is caused by industrial renewal may be less costly to poor residents of urban neighborhoods than "regentrification" would be. In the former case, federal law forces the payment of relatively generous relocation benefits; moreover, the necessity to move quickly means that neighborhood residents may be able to negotiate increased benefits. While saving the neighborhood may well be impossible, extracting extra benefits may well be possible.

6. The business community is not the only avenue for the mobilizing of resources by an urban regime. In the cases described in this book, the power of particular business corporations in specific decisions affecting them was evident. The generic, informal network of business and civic organizations was not so visible, and, indeed, was probably much less important in the framing of industrial renewal policies than were linkages to other public officials at other levels of government. That is, resources may be mobilized in ways that only tangentially involve the business community. It may be that other levels of government are more important in mobilizing resources in the city than local business interests in many instances.

7. Variations in community political culture define variable options for elected officials. More closed cultures constrain the options for choice to a greater extent than do more open cultures. Political cultures in communities whose economies are limited to single industries will be more closed than those whose economies are more diverse, but this does not tell the entire story. Diversity in political culture also stems from unionization and the extent of union involvement in local politics. It can also stem from involvement of so-called third-sector organizations, such as the Mott Foundation in Flint. Indeed, any separate and distinct organizational forces in politics, even if they are not *fully* independent of the dominant economic forces, add elements of diversity to the community's political culture. This increases the likelihood of "creative bounded choice" on the part of elected leaders.

8. While much has been written about cities as vehicles for capital accumulation, many cities are nothing of the kind. For a variety of reasons, many industrial cities in the United States are no longer attractive to investors. The economic-development policies that these cities pursue are less alliances with businessmen to aid them in capital accumulation than they are arrangements to make these places more attractive again. The "uneven development

of capitalism," which allows businesses to take advantage of variability in labor, land, and other costs of doing business, explains much about the favorableness with which local governments view the attracting of capital investments. A conspiracy between business and government explains little.

9. Large businesses affect city politics more by their business decisions than by their political ones. Decisions concerning capital investment, plant location, and employment capacity have major ramifications for city officials; these decisions affect the actions of city officials more than do the direct attempts to influence that business officials make (which are, at any rate, rarer).

10. Urban regimes develop characteristic solution-sets, which link policy solutions and issue definitions. These solution-sets for economic development emerge out of interactions between politicians and businessmen, and they become important determinants of future policy solutions. Urban bureaucracies are organizational manifestations of past regime solution-sets. As bureaucracies, they influence current decision making by channeling search toward the institutionalized solution routines that they embody. Moreover, the entire network of interactions among private and public actors are also subject to the limits on problem-solving capacities imposed by solution-sets. Regime participants, in contact with one another formally and informally, tend to hold similar issue definitions and hence tend to understand solutions to city problems in similar terms.

11. In the spirit of William of Occam's razor, surface phenomena are usually more efficacious in explaining economic-development policies of cities than are "deep structures." There is no evidence of the tension between social-investment and social-consumption expenditures, as envisioned by O'Connor and others. In the face of major cutbacks in funds from federal and state sources, cities such as Detroit have aggressively slashed their social-consumption expenditures and have directed more of their resources into social-investment expenditures, such as economic-development programs. While one may argue that this merely indicates that local politicians are extremely dependent on the economic system (and we would agree), it also brings into question any deep structures that emphasize the need for the state continually to increase its expenditures on social control.

IS THERE A CONTROLLING HAND?

We began this inquiry with the working assumption that considerable slack exists in the social cables that bind the local polity and the local economy. By concentrating on local economies that are dependent in the extreme on a single oligopolistically organized industry, we have explored the degree of independent maneuvering by political leaders where slack is minimal.

That such maneuvering occasionally occurred suggests the limits to economic determinism as an explanation of politics, as well as the limited utility of views of local political leaders as being pawns of business. Paradoxically, it also indicates the primacy of the desire for economic development: even Mayor Rutherford's coup was motivated by economic survival for his city. In Charles Lindblom's term, the market is a prison.[41]

There is, then, no controlling hand in community politics. No conspiracy of business and government exists. Business interests do not invariably dominate government policy even where a single industry dominates the community. However, the giant industrial companies do provide the backdrop against which the public-policy process operates in the industrial city. They are always there, seldom intervening in specific policy matters but never far from the calculations of policy makers. Moreover, economic decline has directed the attention of city leaders more and more toward the issues of economic development. This turn of events means that city leaders are increasingly interested in influencing business; as a consequence, businessmen have relatively more negotiating leverage.

We reject Justice Ryan's analogy of the controlling hand to describe the relationship between the giant corporation and the modern industrial city. "Sustaining and guiding" does not, however, seem to be too strong a phrase.

Notes

PREFACE TO THE SECOND EDITION

1. John Harrigan, *Politics and Policy in States and Communities,* 4th ed. (New York: Harper Collins, 1991), pp. 197–99.

2. See Ronald K. Vogel, *Urban Political Economy: Broward County, Florida* (Gainesville, Fla.: University Press of Florida, 1992), for a review of these issues.

CHAPTER 1
PRIVATE POWER AND PUBLIC POLICY

1. Arthur Pound, *The Turning Wheel* (New York: Doubleday, 1934), pp. 89–90.

2. Ed Cary, *Chrome Colossus: General Motors and Its Times* (New York: McGraw-Hill, 1980), p. 42; Richard Crabb, *Birth of a Giant* (Philadelphia: Chilton, 1969), p. 143. The offer to Jackson and Bay City was "probably no more than a feint to get more money from Flint investors." Durant had used the threat of relocation before — announcing that he was moving his carriage firm to Saginaw, a ploy that also worked (see Terry B. Dunham and Lawrence R. Gustin, *The Buick: A Complete History* [Princeton, N.J.: Princeton Publishing, 1980], p. 44).

3. The notion that the special role of business in the creation of wealth in society yields political power is Lindblom's (see his *Politics and Markets* [New York: Basic Books, 1977]).

4. Letter from Thomas A. Murphy to Coleman A. Young and Howard Woods, 8 October 1980.

5. R. J. Johnston, *Political, Electoral, and Spatial Systems* (Oxford: Oxford University Press, 1979).

6. Raymond Boudon, "Individual Action and Social Change: A No-Theory of Social Change," *British Journal of Sociology* 34 (March 1983): 17.

7. Thomas J. Anton, "The Imagery of Policy Analysis: Stability, Determinism, and Reaction," in *Problems of Theory in Policy Analysis,* ed. Phillip M. Gregg (Lexington, Mass.: Lexington Books, 1976), p. 91.

8. Ibid., p. 99.

9. See Robert Eyestone, *From Social Issues to Public Policy* (New York: John Wiley, 1978). John Mollenkopf has used the concept of policy entrepreneur to explain urban-development programs in the United States (see his *The Contested City* [Princeton, N.J.: Princeton University Press, 1983]).

10. Stephen J. Gould, "Sociobiology and the Theory of Natural Selection," in *Sociobiology: Beyond Nature-Nurture?* ed. George Barlow and James Silverberg (Boulder, Colo.: Westview Press, 1980), p. 258.

11. Bryan D. Jones, "Political Decision-Making and the Distribution of Public Benefits: A Political Science Perspective," in *Public Service Provision and Urban Development,* ed. Andrew Kirby, Paul Knox, and Steven Pinch (London: Croom Helm, 1984), pp. 363–89. In a similar vein, Piven and Friedland write: "It is not that economic growth determines the margin of operation for politics. Rather, it is that the state's role in economic growth is itself the consequence of politics; but it is a politics which is obscured because it is deeply embedded in the very structure of the state" (Frances Fox Piven and Roger Friedland, "Public Choice and Private Power: A Theory of Fiscal Crisis," in *Public Service Provision and Urban Development,* p. 416).

12. The whole level of analysis issue remains, of course, controversial. We will leave to others the debate over whether human systems are some simple or complex combination of the actions of their members or whether the social structure is in some sense "emergent." Interesting approaches to the problem of the combination of individual actions may be found in Hayward R. Alker, Jr., "The Long Road to International Relations Theory: Problems of Statistical Nonadditivity," *World Politics* 18 (July 1966), and Hubert Blalock, *Theory Construction* (Englewood Cliffs, N.J.: Prentice-Hall, 1969). We also skirt the issue of the relationship between the "actual" social structure and the mental imagery of the members of the social system. The classic exploration of this issue is Peter Berger and Paul Luckman, *The Social Construction of Reality* (Garden City, N.Y.: Anchor-Doubleday, 1967).

13. Paul E. Peterson, *City Limits* (Chicago: University of Chicago Press, 1981), p. 23.

14. Clarence Stone and Heywood Sanders, eds., *The Politics of Urban Development* (Lawrence: University Press of Kansas, 1987).

15. Norman I. Fainstein and Susan S. Fainstein, "Regime Strategies, Community Resistance, and Economic Forces," in *Restructuring the City,* ed. Susan S. Fainstein et al. (New York: Longman, 1983), pp. 245–81.

16. Herbert A. Simon, "Rational Decision Making in Business Organizations," *American Economic Review* 69 (September 1979): 498.

17. Robert A. Dahl, *Who Governs?* (New Haven, Conn.: Yale University Press, 1961).

18. G. William Domhoff, *Who Rules America Now?* (Englewood Cliffs, N.J.: Prentice-Hall, 1983).

19. See ibid. for a summary and evaluation of the literature.

20. Michael Parenti, *Power and the Powerless* (New York: St. Martin's, 1978), pp. 216–17.

21. The former approach has been termed *instrumentalism;* the latter, *structuralism* (see Peter Saunders, *Urban Politics* [London: Hutchinson, 1979], pp. 136–97).

22. Clarence Stone, "Systemic Power and Community Decision-Making: A Restatement of Stratificationist Theory," *American Political Science Review* 74 (December 1980).

23. John Logan and Harvey Molotch, *Urban Fortunes* (Berkeley: University of California Press, 1987), p. 50.

24. Ibid., p. 51.

25. Stephen Elkin, *City and Regime in the American Republic* (Chicago: University of Chicago Press, 1987), p. 41.

26. Mollenkopf, *Contested City,* p. 9.

27. Bryan D. Jones and Lynn W. Bachelor, "Local Policy Discretion and the Corporate Surplus," in *Urban Economic Development,* ed. Richard Bingham and John Blair (Beverly Hills, Calif.: Sage, 1984).

28. Roger Friedland and William T. Bielby, "The Power of Business in the City," in *Urban Policy Analysis: Future Directions for Research,* ed. Terry Nichols Clark (Beverly Hills, Calif.: Sage, 1981), pp. 142 and 140. The authors are summarizing what they see as a research tradition here.

29. Mollenkopf, *Contested City,* p. 4.

30. Clarence Stone, *Regime Politics: Governing Atlanta* (Lawrence: University Press of Kansas, 1989), p. 6.

31. Elkin, *City and Regime,* p. 7.

32. Clarence Stone, personal communication, 21 April 1992.

33. Although Stone has defined regimes in terms of participants, his typology of regimes also emphasizes what we have termed *solution-sets.* He has classified urban regimes according to "the degree of difficulty of the policy agenda that they are attached to." His regime types are maintenance, developmental, middle-class progressive, and lower-class opportunity expanding (Clarence Stone, "Urban Regimes and the Capacity to Govern" [Paper presented at the American Political Science Association Meeting, Washington, D.C., September 1991]).

34. See Wallace Sayre and Herbert Kaufman, *Governing New York City* (New York: W. W. Norton, 1965), and Theodore Lowi, *At the Pleasure of the Mayor* (New York: Free Press, 1964), for divergent views on the desirability of independent policy subsystems in urban policy processes.

35. Frank Baumgartner and Bryan Jones, *Agendas and Instability in American Politics* (Chicago: University of Chicago Press, 1993).

36. John Kingdon, *Agendas and Alternatives in American Politics* (New York: Harper-Collins, 1984).

37. Deborah Stone, *Policy Paradox and Political Reason* (Glenview, Ill.: Scott, Foresman, 1988).

38. Clarence Stone, Marion Orr, and David Imbroscio, "The Reshaping of Urban Leadership in Cities: A Regime Analysis," in M. Gottdiener and Chris Pickvance, *Urban Life in Transition,* Urban Affairs Annual Review 39 (Newbury Park, Calif.: Sage, 1991).

39. Roger Friedland, *Power and Crisis in the City: Corporations, Unions, and Urban Policy* (London: Macmillan, 1982).

CHAPTER 2
THE AUTOMOTIVE PUBLIC ECONOMY

1. Carl Crow, *The City of Flint Grows Up* (New York: Harper & Brothers, 1945), p. vii.

2. Richard Child Hill, "Crisis in the Motor City," in *Restructuring the City,* ed. Susan Fainstein et al. (New York: Longman, 1983), pp. 111 and 116.

3. See, for example, David Lowery and William D. Berry, "The Growth of Government in the United States: An Empirical Assessment of Competing Explanations," *American Journal of Political Science* 27 (November 1983): 665–94. The article contains citations to much of the relevant literature.

4. Paul E. Peterson, *City Limits* (Chicago: University of Chicago Press, 1981), p. 23.

5. David I. Verway, ed., *Michigan Statistical Abstract, Seventeenth Edition, 1982–83* (Detroit: Bureau of Business Research, Wayne State University, 1983), p. 476.

6. David I. Verway, "The Automotive Economy," *Michigan Economy* 2 (February 1983): 5.

7. Estimates of automotive-related manufacturing jobs are from Verway, "Automotive Economy," p. 6; estimates of total manufacturing jobs are from *Michigan Statistical Abstract,* p. 177.

8. *Michigan Statistical Abstract,* pp. 488 and 503.

9. Arthur Pound, *Detroit: Dynamic City* (New York: Appleton-Century, 1940), pp. 290–92.

10. Crow, *City of Flint Grows Up,* pp. 24–37.

11. Thomas Lauerence Munger, *Detroit Today* (Detroit: Detroit Board of Commerce, 1920).

12. Calculated from *Michigan Statistical Abstract,* p. 310.

13. Calculated from ibid., p. 310.

14. Calculated from data reported in *Michigan Economy* (May/June 1983): 8.

15. Susan Benkelman, "State Calls Business Tax Fair," *Detroit News,* 10 January 1985.

16. Terry Nichols Clark and Lorna Crowley Ferguson, *City Money* (New York: Columbia University Press, 1983), p. 86.

17. Ibid., chap. 4.

18. Pound, *Detroit,* p. 314.

19. *Michigan Statistical Abstract,* pp. 500–502. Figures from Detroit are not meaningful because of the payroll-assignment system used by GM.

20. Calculated from *Michigan Statistical Abstract,* pp. 166 and 500. Comparable calculations cannot be performed for Pontiac, because it is part of the Detroit metropolitan labor market, or for Detroit, because GM does not report statistics for the city.

21. Chrysler's Hamtramck Assembly Plant is tabulated with Detroit; the plant was located on the border between the two cities. Data are calculated from *Michigan Statistical Abstract, Seventeenth Edition,* p. 488, and *Sixteenth Edition,* p. 577.

22. The figures in this paragraph come from *Annual Overall Economic Development Program Report and Program Projection* (Detroit: City of Detroit, 30 June 1983) and *Report of the Budget Planning and Stabilization Committee, Submitted to Mayor Coleman A. Young,* 1 April 1981.

23. See Donald Deskins, *Residential Mobility of Negroes in Detroit, 1937–1965* (Ann Arbor: Michigan Geographical Publications, 1972).

24. See Robert E. Fish, "Detroit: Suburbs and City," *Michigan Economy* 2 (September/October 1983): 1–7, and Robert Sinclair and Bryan Thompson, *Detroit: An Anatomy of Social Change* (Cambridge, Mass.: Ballinger, 1977), pp. 5–24.

25. Fish, "Detroit," p. 1.

26. Ibid., p. 2.

27. Ibid., p. 7.

28. Ibid., p. 2.

29. *Annual Overall Economic Development Program Report,* pp. 111–16.

30. David I. Verway, "Focus on Detroit," *Michigan Economy* (July/August 1984): 1–3.

31. See Charles H. Levine, Irene Rubin, and George C. Wolohojian, *The Politics of Retrenchment* (Beverly Hills, Calif.: Sage, 1981); Levine et al., "Managing Organizational Retrenchment," *Administration and Society* 14 (May 1982); Levine, ed.,

Managing Fiscal Stress (Chatham, N.J.: Chatham House, 1980); Clark and Ferguson, *City Money;* and Touche Ross and Company, *Urban Fiscal Stress* (Boston: First National Bank of Boston, 1979).

32. Although automotive manufacture fell first in the 1979 downturn, and fell further, it did not recover in 1980/81 as did the rest of the economy. It did, however, lead the country out of the recession in 1983.

33. Bryan D. Jones, "Speculative City Budgeting and Federal Grants, *Research in Urban Policy II* (Greenwich, Conn.: JAI Press, 1986), pp. 3–22. See also Robert H. Phillips, "Fiscal Stress and the City of Detroit's Response to It" (unpublished manuscript, Department of Political Science, Wayne State University, 1983).

34. Thomas J. Anton, "The Impact of Federal Grants on Detroit in 1978," Federal Aid Case Studies Series (Washington, D.C.: Brookings Institution, June 1981), p. 36.

35. *Report of the Budget Planning and Stabilization Committee,* 1 April 1981.

36. Interview with Rutherford, 9 November 1983.

37. Herbert Jacob, *The Frustration of Policy* (Boston: Little, Brown, 1984).

CHAPTER 3
DETROIT: INDUSTRIAL DEMOCRACY
OR CAPITALIST OLIGARCHY?

1. Arthur Pound, *Detroit: Dynamic City* (New York: Appleton-Century, 1940), p. 1.

2. Carl Crow, *The City of Flint Grows Up* (New York: Harper & Brothers, 1945), p. 52.

3. *Final Environmental Impact Statement, Central Industrial Park* (Detroit: City of Detroit Community and Economic Development Department, Dec. 1980), p. B-8.

4. Ibid., p. J-2.

5. Ibid., p. B-3; see also *Profile of an Urban American City: Hamtramck, Michigan* (Detroit: League of Women Voters, 1980).

6. Oliver Zunz, "The Changing Face of Inequality: An Interview with the Author," *Detroit in Perspective* 6 (Fall 1982): 9–10; see his *The Changing Face of Inequality* (Chicago: University of Chicago Press, 1982).

7. Zunz, "Changing Face," p. 11.

8. Ibid.

9. Melvin G. Holli, *Reform in Detroit: Hazen Pingree and Urban Politics* (New York: Oxford University Press, 1969), chap. 1.

10. Robert Conot, *American Odyssey* (New York: Bantam, 1975), p. 241.

11. Ibid., p. 256.

12. Joyce Shaw Peterson, "Auto Workers Confront the Depression 1929–1933," *Detroit in Perspective* 6 (Fall 1982): 49.

13. Donald Deskins, *Residential Mobility of Negroes in Detroit, 1937–1965* (Ann Arbor: Michigan Geographical Publications, 1972), p. 32.

14. August Meier and Elliott Rudwick, *Black Detroit and the Rise of the UAW* (Oxford: Oxford University Press, 1979), pp. 6–7.

15. Ibid., p. 205.

16. A detailed examination of the Cavanaugh years may be found in Conot, *American Odyssey.*

17. James Geschwender, *Class, Race, and Worker Insurgency* (Cambridge: Cambridge University Press, 1977), p. 227; see also Dan Georgakas and Marvin Surkin, *Detroit: I Do Mind Dying* (New York: St. Martin's, 1975).

18. Zunz, *Changing Face,* pp. 203–16.

19. Lynda Ann Ewen, *Corporate Power and Urban Crisis in Detroit* (Princeton, N.J.: Princeton University Press, 1978).

20. Results are summarized in Thomas J. Anton, "The Impact of Federal Grants on Detroit in 1978," Federal Aid Case Studies Series (Washington, D.C.: Brookings Institution, June 1981), pp. 14–15.

21. Ibid., p. 14.

22. *The Top Forty-Seven Who Make It Happen: A Study of Power* (Detroit: Detroit News, 1978).

23. Charles Kadushin, " 'Small World' – How Many Steps to the Top?" *Detroit News,* 17 September 1978.

24. Andrew R. McGill and Barbara Young, "One Man Shakes a City: Henry Ford Has the Power," *Detroit News,* 8 October 1978.

25. Robert A. Dahl, *Who Governs?* (New Haven, Conn.: Yale University Press, 1961), p. 85.

26. John B. Schnapp, *Corporate Strategies of the Automotive Manufacturers* (Lexington, Mass.: Lexington Books, 1979), p. 130.

27. Ibid., pp. 146–47.

28. Alfred P. Sloan, Jr., *My Years with General Motors* (Garden City, N.Y.: Anchor, 1972), pp. 457–76.

29. Robert J. Mowitz and Deil S. Wright, *Profile of a Metropolis* (Detroit: Wayne State University Press, 1962), p. 630.

30. Ibid., p. 631.

31. J. Allen Whitt, *Urban Elites and Mass Transportation* (Princeton, N.J.: Princeton University Press, 1982), pp. 8–32.

32. If unifying Latin and Greek seems awkward, try the Greek stems alone: chotomarchy.

33. Charles Lindblom, *Politics and Markets* (New York: Basic Books, 1977).

34. "Mayor Young a Decade Later," *Detroit Free Press,* 2 February 1984.

35. C. Wright Mills, *The Power Elite* (New York: Oxford University Press, 1956).

36. Andrew Hacker, "What Rules America?" *New York Review,* 1 May 1975, p. 10, quoted in G. William Domhoff, *Who Rules America Now?* (Englewood Cliffs, N.J.: Prentice-Hall, 1983), p. 217.

37. Thomas Dye, *Who's Running America?* (Englewood Cliffs, N.J.: Prentice-Hall, 1976).

38. Clarence Stone, "Systemic Power and Community Decision-Making: A Restatement of Stratificationist Theory," *American Political Science Review* 74 (December 1980): 876–990.

39. Lindblom, *Politics and Markets.*

40. Paul E. Peterson, *City Limits* (Chicago: University of Chicago Press, 1981).

CHAPTER 4
THE AMERICAN AUTOMOBILE INDUSTRY
UNDER PRESSURE

1. *Ward's Automotive Reports,* 4 June 1979.

2. *Detroit Free Press,* 8 December 1979.

3. Ibid., 7 October 1980.

4. Gerald Bloomfield, *The World Automotive Industry* (London: David & Charles, 1978), p. 47.

5. Dan Georgakas and Marvin Surkin, *Detroit: I Do Mind Dying* (New York: St. Martin's, 1975).

6. *Detroit Free Press,* 8 December 1979.

7. Automotive Panel, Committee on Technology and Trade Issues, National Academy of Engineering and the Commission on Engineering and Technical Systems, National Research Council, *The Competitive Status of the U.S. Auto Industry* (Washington, D.C.: National Academy Press, 1982), p. 66.

8. Ibid., pp. 67–68.

9. Ibid., p. 70.

10. Ibid., p. 71.

11. Ibid., p. 136.

12. *Ward's Automotive Yearbook* (Detroit: Ward's Communications, 1982), p. 9.

13. *Ward's Automotive Reports,* 15 January, 7 and 14 May 1979.

14. Ibid., 11 June 1979.

15. Ibid., 5 August 1979.

16. Ibid., 21 April 1980.

17. Ibid., 9 June 1980.

18. Ibid.

19. Ibid., 24 November 1980.

20. Ibid., 4 June 1979.

21. Ibid., 7 April 1980.

22. Ibid., 19 May 1980.

23. Ibid., 28 July 1980.

24. Ibid., 14 January, 25 February, 19 May, and 9 June 1980.

25. Profit-and-loss figures are from *Ward's Automotive Yearbook* (Detroit: Ward's Communications, 1982), p. 99.

26. Automotive Panel, *Competitive Status,* pp. 25–29; Bloomfield, *World Automotive Industry,* pp. 87–94; Alfred D. Chandler, *Giant Enterprise: Ford, General Motors, and the Automobile Industry* (New York: Harcourt, Brace, & World, 1964).

27. Robert P. Thomas, *An Analysis of the Pattern of Growth of the Automobile Industry, 1885–1929* (New York: Arno Press, 1977), p. 287; see also Harold Katz, *The Decline of Competition in the Automotive Industry* (New York: Arno Press, 1977).

28. For a discussion of mature markets and the automotive industry see Kirsh Bhaskar, *The Future of the World Motor Industry* (London: Kogan Page, 1980).

29. Automotive Panel, *Competitive Status,* p. 37.

30. Quoted in Louis T. Wells, Jr., "The International Product Life-Cycle and the United States Regulation of the Automobile Industry," in *Government, Technology, and the Future of the Automobile,* ed. Douglas H. Ginsburg and William J. Abernathy (New York: McGraw-Hill, 1980), p. 290.

31. Ibid., p. ix.

32. Robert W. Crandall, "Import Quotas and the Automobile Industry: The Costs of Protection," *Brookings Review* 2 (Summer 1984): 9–11.

33. John B. Schnapp, *Corporate Strategies of the Automotive Manufacturers* (Lexington, Mass.: Lexington Books, 1979), p. 117.

34. *Ward's Automotive Reports,* 25 February and 3 March 1980.

35. Ibid., 21 January and 4 February 1980.

36. Interview with Donald Postma, General Motors' vice-president for public relations, 17 March 1982; *Ward's Automotive Reports,* 14 April 1980.

CHAPTER 5
GENERAL MOTORS SEARCHES FOR SITES

1. John B. Schnapp, *Corporate Strategies of the Automotive Manufacturers* (Lexington, Mass.: Lexington Books, 1979), pp. 155–59.

2. Alfred P. Sloan, Jr., *My Years with General Motors* (Garden City, N.Y.: Anchor, 1972), p. 510.

3. Among the chief critics have been William Mitchell, former vice-president of design, and John Z. DeLorean, who resigned as vice-president of the car, truck, and body group (see J. Patrick Wright, *On a Clear Day You Can See General Motors* [New York: Avon, 1979]).

4. Schnapp, *Corporate Strategies,* pp. 147–49.

5. Interview with Donald Postma, vice-president for public relations, 17 March 1982; *Supplement to the Project Evaluation for the Proposed General Motors Replacement Assembly Plant, Orion Township, Michigan* (Detroit: General Motors Corp., 21 Apr. 1980).

6. Interview with Donald Postma, 17 March 1982.

7. See Roger W. Schmenner, "Industrial Location and Urban Public Management," in *The Prospective City,* ed. Arthur P. Soloman (Cambridge, Mass.: MIT Press, 1980), pp. 446–68; Roger Vaughn, "State Tax Incentives: How Effective Are They?" *Commentary,* January 1980, and *State Taxation and Economic Development* (Washington, D.C.: Council of State Planning Agencies, 1979).

8. Lewis Mandell, *Industry Location Decisions* (New York: Praeger, 1975); see also Leonard Lund, *Factors in Corporate Location Decisions* (New York: Conference Board, 1979); John Matilla and James Kurre, *Detroit Intra-Metropolitan Industrial Location Study* (Detroit: Detroit Department of Planning, 1977); Donald Stone, *Industry Location in Metropolitan Areas* (New York: Praeger, 1974).

9. Interview with Postma.

10. Andrew R. McGill, "How Complex Deals Renew City," *Detroit News,* 13 January 1985.

11. *Final Environmental Impact Statement, Central Industrial Park* (Detroit: City of Detroit Community and Economic Development Department, Dec. 1980), pp. III-4 and III-5.

12. Interview with Donald Postma, 17 March 1982.

13. *Final Environmental Impact Statement,* p. III-6.

14. Ibid., p. III-10.

15. *Scoping Document: Significant and Non-Significant Issues* (City of Detroit Community and Economic Development Dept., Aug. 1980), p. 20.

16. *Final Environmental Impact Statement,* p. III-12.

17. *Scoping Document,* p. 20.

18. *Final Environmental Impact Statement,* pp. III-10 and III-11.

19. *Poletown Neighborhood Council* v. *City of Detroit* (410 Mich. 616).

20. Terry T. Buss and F. Stevens Redburn, *Shutdown at Youngstown* (Albany: State University of New York Press, 1982).

21. *General Motors Annual Report,* 1981, pp. 18–19.

CHAPTER 6
THE BUREAUCRACY IN ACTION:
MEETING GENERAL MOTORS' TIMETABLE

1. *Final Environmental Impact Statement, Central Industrial Park* (Detroit: City of Detroit Community and Economic Development Department, Dec. 1980), pp. 1–3.

2. Ibid., pp. 1–4.

3. "Memorandum of Agreement," reproduced ibid., pp. P2–P6.

4. Ibid., pp. P4–P5.

5. Katherine Warner et al., "Detroit's Renaissance Includes Factories," *Urban Land,* June 1982, pp. 3–14; interview with Harold Bellamy, City of Detroit Community and Economic Development Department, 21 April 1982.

6. Letter from Thomas A. Murphy, chairman, General Motors Corp., to Coleman A. Young, chairman, Economic Department Corporation, city of Detroit, and Howard Woods, chairman, Economic Development Corporation, city of Hamtramck, 8 October 1980.

7. Community and Economic Development Department, city of Detroit, *Project Plan: Central Industrial Park* (1980).

8. Community and Economic Development Act, 1974.

9. Ibid., as amended in 1977.

10. Michael Rich, "Hitting the Target: The Distributional Impacts of the Urban Development Grant Program," *Urban Affairs Quarterly* 17 (March 1982).

11. The Hamtramck lawsuit and later development are described in Willie S. Coleman, "Community Organization and Effective Citizen Participation in Government Decision-Making" (Master of Public Administration essay, Wayne State University, May 1984). Black residents finally had a favorable settlement because of the threat to the GM project; the city of Hamtramck agreed to provide payments to the affected residents and to build low-income housing in the city. However, the city balked once again after the settlement, claiming that the automotive depression had so depleted the city's coffers that new projects were impossible.

12. *Project Plan,* sec. 8, par. 4, n. 2.

13. *Final Environmental Impact Statement,* p. V-61.

14. Ibid., pp. V-59 to V-67.

15. For a discussion of the way in which the Young/Carter connection affected federal grants to the city of Detroit see Thomas J. Anton, "The Impact of Federal Grants on Detroit in 1978."

CHAPTER 7
THE TRAPPINGS OF DEMOCRACY

1. The Central Industrial Park Joint Venture Agreement, 1 May 1981.

2. The Urban Cooperation Act and The Intergovernmental Transfers of Functions and Responsibilities Act, Public Acts 7 and 8 of Michigan, 1967, as amended.

3. Interlocal Agreement between the City of Detroit and the City of Hamtramck, Relative to the Central Industrial Park Project, 1 May 1981, p. 13.

4. Public Act 338, sec. 22, state of Michigan, as amended in 1978.

5. Public Act 450, state of Michigan, 1980.

6. Public Act 338.

7. Remer Tyson, "Long Struggle Led to Firm Power Base," in *Blacks in Detroit: A Reprint of Articles from the Detroit Free Press* (Detroit: Detroit Free Press, Dec. 1980), p. 41. The survey was conducted by telephone by Massoglia and Associates during October 1980. Sampling error is reported at ±5 percent, within racial categories. White support dropped to 38 percent when only white interviewers were used.

8. Andrew McGill, "Who Will be Region's Leaders of the Future?" *Detroit News,* 19 January 1985. The poll was conducted by the Institute of Social Research at the

University of Michigan and contains considerable sampling error: 71 black and 29 white Detroiters responded to the question concerning Young's popularity. The study also polled white suburbanites, who held as unfavorable an opinion of Young as did Detroit whites.

9. Gary Blonston, "Poletown: The Profits, the Loss," *Detroit,* 22 November 1981.

10. Quoted in Andrew R. McGill, "How Complex Deals Renew City," *Detroit News,* 13 January 1985.

CHAPTER 8
THE DEMOCRATIC STEAM ROLLER:
POLETOWN IN COURT

1. Under Public Act 338, sec. 21, state of Michigan, 1974, as amended in 1978.

2. Testimony of Coleman A. Young in *Poletown Neighborhood Council* v. *City of Detroit,* no. 80-039-426 CZ (Wayne County Circuit Court, 1980), p. 8.

3. Ibid., p. 22.

4. Testimony of Emmett Moten in *Poletown Neighborhood Council* v. *City of Detroit,* no. 80-039-426 CZ (Wayne County Circuit Court, 1980), p. 6.

5. Ibid., pp. 19–20.

6. Young's testimony, pp. 4–6.

7. Moten's testimony, pp. 68–69.

8. Suzanne Dolezal, "General Moten Reporting for Duty," *Detroit,* 11 July 1982, p. 9.

9. Ibid., p. 11.

10. *Poletown Neighborhood Council* v. *City of Detroit,* 410 Mich 610, 304 N.W. 2d 455 (1981). The legal issues are analyzed in Emily Lewis, "Corporate Prerogative, Public Use and a People's Plight: Poletown Neighborhood Council v. City of Detroit," *Detroit College of Law Review* (Winter 1982): 907–29.

11. J. Ryan, dissenting opinion in *Poletown Neighborhood Council* v. *City of Detroit,* 410 Mich 610, 304 N.W. 2d 455 (1981), p. 2.

12. Ibid., pp. 5–6.

13. Ibid., pp. 7, 9.

14. Ibid., p. 29. Ryan's legal arguments centered on distinguishing eminent domain from the taxing power, allowing a broad scope for the latter and a narrow scope for the former. He accused the majority of confusing the two governmental functions by applying standards that are appropriate for the taxing power to the power of eminent domain. Ryan would allow eminent domain only where the government kept control over the land that was taken.

15. "City Cleared on Choice of Plant Site," *Detroit Free Press,* 23 April 1981.

16. "G.M. Breaks Ground in Poletown, A 'Day of Triumph' Young Says," *Detroit Free Press,* 2 May 1981.

17. The term is James McGregor Burns's (see his *Deadlock of Democracy*).

18. Ryan's dissenting opinion, pp. 20–21.

CHAPTER 9
THE POLITICS OF TAX LOSS

1. Testimony of Coleman A. Young in *Poletown Neighborhood Council* v. *City of Detroit,* no. 80-039-426 CZ (Wayne County Circuit Court, 1980), p. 22.

2. The Tax Increment Financing Plan and The Development Plan for the Central Industrial Park Project Development Area, prepared by the city of Detroit's Tax Increment Finance Authority, 18 March 1982, p. 4.

3. See Bryan D. Jones and Lynn W. Bachelor, "Local Policy Discretion and the Corporate Surplus," in *Urban Economic Development,* ed. Richard Bingham and John Blair (Beverly Hills, Calif.: Sage, 1984), and Roger Vaughn, *State Taxation and Economic Development* (Washington, D.C.: Council of State Planning Agencies, 1979).

4. Public Act 198, state of Michigan, 1974.

5. *Final Environmental Impact Statement, Central Industrial Park* (Detroit: City of Detroit Community and Economic Development Department, Dec. 1980), pp. V-79, V-80.

6. Tax Increment Financing Plan, exhibit A.

7. City Planning Commission Memorandum of 1 April 1981, p. 5.

8. "Tax Break for G.M. Uncertain," *Detroit Free Press,* 2 April 1981.

9. "Tax Break for G.M. Approved," *Detroit Free Press,* 3 April 1981.

10. Ken Fireman, ". . . And the City Council Tempts the Giant with a Hefty Break on Taxes," *Detroit Free Press,* 10 April 1981.

11. Interlocal Agreement between the City of Detroit and the City of Hamtramck Relating to the Central Industrial Park Project, 1 May 1981.

12. Public Act 450, state of Michigan, 1980.

13. Downtown Development Authorities had been authorized in Public Act 197, state of Michigan, 1974, as amended.

14. P.A. 450, sec. 2.

15. Tax Increment Financing Plan, "Financial Impact Study," p. 17.

16. *Final Environmental Impact Statement,* pp. V-77 to V-81.

17. Jones and Bachelor, "Local Policy Discretion"; see also Roger Friedland, *Power and Crisis in the City: Corporations, Unions, and Urban Policy* (London: Macmillan, 1982).

CHAPTER 10
STREET THEATER: ORGANIZED OPPOSITION
TO THE POLETOWN REDEVELOPMENT PROJECT

1. This feature was acknowledged even by the press (see Blonston, "Poletown").

2. *Final Environmental Impact Statement, Central Industrial Park* (Detroit: City of Detroit Community and Economic Development Department, December 1980), app. k.

3. Community and Economic Development Department, city of Detroit, *Project Plan: Central Industrial Park* (1980), p. 4.

4. *Final Environmental Impact Statement,* pp. K-4, V-54, V-55.

5. Ibid., p. K-4.

6. Ibid., p. K-11.

7. On the Neighborhood Opportunity Fund see Lynn Bachelor and Bryan Jones, "Managed Participation: Detroit's Neighborhood Opportunity Fund," *Journal of Applied Behavioral Science* (December 1981): 518–36.

8. Mancur Olsen, *The Logic of Collective Action: Public Goods and the Theory of Groups* (Cambridge, Mass.: Harvard University Press, 1977).

9. See Norman I. Fainstein and Susan S. Fainstein, *Urban Political Movements* (Englewood Cliffs, N.J.: Prentice-Hall, 1974).

10. Richard C. Rich, "A Political Economy Approach to the Study of Neighborhood Organization," *American Journal of Political Science* (November 1980): 559–92.

11. David O'Brien, *Neighborhood Organizations and Interest Group Process* (Princeton, N.J.: Princeton University Press, 1975).

12. Jeffrey Henig, *Neighborhood Mobilization* (New Brunswick, N.J.: Rutgers University Press, 1982). For a somewhat different view see Matthew Crenson, "Social Networks and Political Processes in Urban Neighborhoods," *American Journal of Political Science* 22 (August 1978): 578–94.

13. Richard C. Rich, "The Dynamics of Leadership in Neighborhood Organizations," *Social Science Quarterly* 60 (March 1980): 570–87.

14. Mailgram from the Poletown Neighborhood Council to Erma Henderson et al., 18 July 1980, p. 6.

15. Interview with Thomas Olechowski, August 1981.

16. *Detroit News,* 10 July 1980.

17. Ibid., 5 August 1980.

18. "City Council Acts to Clear G.M. Site," *Detroit Free Press,* 1 November 1980.

19. "Court Vows Quick Ruling in G.M.–Poletown Case," *Detroit News,* 4 March 1981.

20. Michael Lipsky, *Protest in City Politics* (Chicago: Rand McNally, 1970); Clarence Stone, *Economic Growth and Discontent* (Chapel Hill: University of North Carolina Press, 1976).

21. Interview with Richard Hodas, August 1981.

22. "Poletown Rebels Vow to Defend Homes with Guns," *Detroit News,* 6 January 1981.

23. "Nader's Role Looms in Poletown," *Detroit News,* 6 January 1981.

24. "New Poletown Outcry," *Detroit News,* 24 February 1981.

25. Interview with Kenneth Cameron, regional manager of public relations, General Motors, 14 November 1983.

26. "Parish Battles to Stay Alive," *Detroit News,* 11 May 1981.

27. "Twelve Arrested in Poletown Church Sit-In," *Detroit News,* 14 July 1981.

28. "Poletown Church Demolished," *Detroit News,* 16 July 1981.

29. See Saul Alinsky, *Rules for Radicals* (New York: Vantage, 1973), pp. 130–33.

30. See James Cunningham, *Urban Leadership in the 1960's* (Cambridge, Mass.: Schenkman, 1970).

31. Andrew R. McGill, "Race: A Troublesome Road toward a New Era of Trust," *Detroit News,* 8 January 1985.

CHAPTER 11
PONTIAC:
THE COMPANY TOWN AND THE EXURBS

1. Barbara L. Spreitzer, statement by General Motors Corporation to Orion Township, Michigan, Planning Commission, 24 and 26 April 1980.

2. *Supplement to the Project Evaluation for the Proposed General Motors Corporation Replacement Assembly Plant, Orion Township, Michigan,* p. 3.

3. Ibid.

4. Ibid., p. 4.

5. Ibid.

6. Ibid.

7. Ibid.

8. Spreitzer statement, p. 4.

9. Robert Sinclair and Bryan Thompson, *Detroit: An Anatomy of Social Change* (Cambridge, Mass.: Ballinger, 1977), p. 56.

10. Ibid.

11. *Site Requirements, Orion Township, Oakland County, Michigan* (Detroit: General Motors Corp., 29 February 1980).

12. *Orion Review,* 27 February 1980.

13. "'June 1 Not a Deadline,' Says Stempel," *Oxford Leader,* 12 March 1980.

14. Interview with Donald Postma, vice-president for public relations, General Motors Corp., 11 August 1982.

15. "GM Tells Why It Decided to Build in Orion," *Detroit News,* 9 April 1980.

16. *Environmental Impact Statement, Orion Township, Michigan Assembly Plant,* pp. 6, 8 (emphasis added).

17. The saga of the Pontiac Plan is traced in Rick Holman, "A Struggle for Rebirth: The History of Downtown Pontiac" (Master of Public Administration essay, Wayne State University, 1982).

18. *Pontiac-Waterford Times,* 20 March 1980.

19. Interview with Donald Postma, 11 August 1982.

20. Interview with C. Don Davidson, 13 August 1982.

21. *Lake Orion Review,* 12 March 1980.

22. "GM Move to Orion Is OK with Holland," *Oakland Press,* 19 February 1980.

23. "Pontiac Sees Peril in GM Plant Shift," *Detroit News,* 1 February 1980.

24. *Oakland Press,* 19 February 1980.

25. "Officials Answer GM Questions," *Oxford-Orion Times,* 20 March 1980.

26. "Pontiac Foresees Blessing in GM Move," *Oakland Press,* 17 September 1980.

27. Interviews, 17 March and 11 August 1982.

28. "Pontiac Frets over Plant closings," *Detroit News,* 1 February 1980.

29. *Oakland Press,* 17 September 1980.

30. This fear generated substantial press coverage (see "GM Pullout: Pontiac Fears Tax Impact," *Detroit Free Press,* 2 February 1980).

31. Interview with Thomas Padilla, 14 June 1982.

32. Interview with Jean Milton, 10 June 1982.

33. Spreitzer statement.

34. Interview with Miles Paisley, Grand Trunk Railroad, 16 June 1982.

35. "ACRE Group Opposes GM Plant," *Orion Review,* 27 February 1980.

36. "Citizens Group Won't Stop GM Plant without Support," *Oakland Press,* 5 March 1980.

37. Paul Barbeau, "GM: Blessing or Burden," *Oxford-Orion Times,* 13 March 1980.

38. "GM Jobs, Environment on the Line in Orion Township," *Detroit Free Press,* 23 March 1980.

39. "Vocal Minority Could Scuttle GM Plant," *Oakland Press,* 6 April 1980.

40. *Oakland Press,* 5 March 1980.

41. "Don't Block GM Plant," *Oakland Press,* 8 March 1980.

42. "UAW and Lawmakers Unite for GM Plant," *Detroit Free Press,* 10 March 1980; "GM Move Gets Union Support," *Oakland Press,* 10 March 1980.

43. Interview with Joann Van Tassel, 23 April 1982.

44. Interview with Myles Platt, member of Orion Township Planning Commission, 9 April 1982.

45. *Michigan Compiled Laws Annotated,* sec. 168.646a(2).

46. *Oakland Press,* 6 April 1980.

47. *Lake Orion Review,* 23 July 1980.

48. WJBK-TX, 29 July 1980.

49. J. Thomas Laing, memo to United Way Agency executives, 18 April 1980.

50. "The GM Tax Base Pie . . . Look at Orion's Small Slice" (Mimeograph, 1980).

51. "GM Submits Statement on Proposed Orion Plant," *Oakland Press,* 6 April 1980.

52. Interview with Van Tassel, 23 April 1982.

53. "Ceiling Raised on GM Sewer Bonds," *Lake Orion Review,* 24 February 1982.

54. "Headline Misleading on Tax Issue," *Lake Orion Review,* 10 March 1982.

55. "GM Plant Granted Hookup," *Oakland Press,* 12 February 1982; "Sewer Ends GM–Orion Honeymoon," ibid., 14 February 1982.

56. "Detroit Promises Water for GM Plant in Orion," *Oakland Press,* 8 April 1980.

CHAPTER 12
FLINT:
POLITICAL MANEUVERING AND BUICK CITY

1. The data are from *Michigan Statistical Abstract.* The full regression equation is $Y = 27.5 - 0.23X$, with a t-value for the regression coefficient of -3.47 and a Durbin-Watson statistic of 2.6.

2. Joseph B. Espo, "Losses Not Seen as Costly to Unions," *Flint Journal,* 14 November 1983.

3. Ibid.

4. Interview with Kenneth Cameron, regional manager of public relations, General Motors Corp., 14 November 1983.

5. Ibid.

6. Interview with William Whitney, director, Flint Downtown Development Authority, 14 November 1983.

7. Interview with Cameron.

8. Lawrence R. Gustin, "Working Alliance May Put Downtown to Work Again," *Flint Journal,* 15 November 1981.

9. Raymond Bauer, Ithiel Pool, and Anthony Dexter, *American Business and Public Policy* (New York: Atherton, 1967).

10. Interview with Mayor James Rutherford, 9 November 1983.

11. Interview with Whitney.

12. David V. Graham, "Annexation Deal Marks Triumph for Rutherford," *Flint Journal,* 16 November 1980.

13. Interview with Rutherford.

14. Graham, "Annexation Deal Marks Triumph for Rutherford."

15. David Goodman, "GM Plant Selection Process Balances Finances, Political Factors," *Flint Journal,* 23 November 1980.

16. Interview with Rutherford.

17. Interview with Litzenberg, 14 November 1983.

18. *Buick City Project Information,* city of Flint (N.d.).

19. Interview with Cameron.

20. Interview with William Vredevoogd, economic-development administrator, city of Flint, 7 November 1983.

21. Ibid.

22. *Buick City Project Information.*

23. Interview with Rutherford.

24. Interview with Cameron.

25. Interview with Litzenberg.
26. Interview with Vredevoogd.
27. Interview with Genesee County's economic-development administrator, 14 November 1983.
28. Interview with Litzenberg.
29. Interview with G. Usuey, land-use coordinator, city of Flint, 7 November 1983.
30. Ibid.
31. Interview with Litzenberg.
32. Ibid.
33. Ibid.
34. Ibid.
35. Ibid.
36. Interview with Cameron.

CHAPTER 13
AUTOMOBILE POLITICS:
A VIEW FROM THE 1990s

1. Clarence Stone, *Regime Politics: Governing Atlanta* (Lawrence: University Press of Kansas, 1989), p. 6.
2. Stephen Elkin, *City and Regime in the American Republic* (Chicago: University of Chicago Press, 1987), p. 85.
3. Stone, *Regime Politics,* p. 6.
4. Clarence Stone, "Efficiency vs. Social Learning: A Reconsideration of the Implementation Process," *Policy Studies Review* 4 (1985): 484–96; Elkin, *City and Regime,* pp. 95–97.
5. Elkin, *City and Regime,* p. 95.
6. "A Decade of Auto Profits (and Losses)," *Detroit Free Press,* 16 February 1985; Motor Vehicle Manufacturers' Association, *Facts and Figures, 1990* (Detroit: MVMA, 1990), pp. 6, 7, 15.
7. Richard Bingham, "Motor Vehicle Manufacturing in the Midwest: Winners and Losers in a Recession." *Commentary* (March 1991).
8. "U.S. Car Industry Hit Hard in 1991," *Detroit Free Press,* 7 January 1992.
9. Bingham, "Motor Vehicle Manufacturing."
10. Richard Bingham and Kolawole Sunmonu, "The Restructuring of the Automobile Industry in the United States" (Paper presented at the Association of Collegiate Schools of Planning, Austin, Texas, 2–4 November 1990).
11. *Ward's Automotive Yearbook* (Detroit: Ward's Communications, 1990), p. 16.
12. Ibid.
13. Motor Vehicle Manufacturers' Association, *Facts and Figures, 1990,* p. 65.
14. John Lippert, "Jefferson Plant Hits End of Line," *Detroit Free Press,* 2 February 1990.
15. John Lippert, "G.M. Plans to Switch Production at Plants," *Detroit Free Press,* 9 October 1991; Greg Gardner, "G.M. to Wield the Ax," *Detroit Free Press,* 19 December 1991.
16. The Flint Assessor's Office reports that as of 31 December 1990, the state equalized value of the Buick City complex was as follows: ad valorem (non-abated): real, $119,535,900, and personal (equipment), $100,336,800; industrial facilities tax (abated, and thus subject to one-half the regular millage rate): real, $8,387,608, and personal, $107,236,000.

17. Interview with Bill Glowny, Assessor's Office, City of Flint, 25 July 1991.

18. Interview with Kim Vincent, Orion Township Assessor, 29 July 1991.

19. *Ward's Automotive Yearbook* (1987), p. 99; *Ward's Automotive Yearbook* (1988), p. 129; *Ward's Automotive Yearbook* (1990), p. 181.

20. Constance Prather, "A Blacker Detroit Is Source of Pride, Problems," *Detroit Free Press,* 2 March 1991, and "Figures Chart Racial Turnover in Detroit," *Detroit Free Press,* 5 March 1991.

21. Joe Darden, et al., *Detroit: Race and Uneven Development* (Philadelphia: Temple University Press, 1987).

22. Constance Prather, "$50 Million City Deficit Has No Easy Solutions," *Detroit Free Press,* 6 April 1991.

23. Bryan Jones, "Speculative City Budgeting and Federal Grants," *Research in Urban Policy* 2 (1986): 3–22; Barbara Presley Noble, "A Downgraded Detroit Cries Foul," *New York Times,* 3 November 1992.

24. City of Detroit Tax Increment Finance Authority (Central Industrial Park Project), "Official Statement in Connection with Sale of $46,100,000 Variable Rate Demand Tax Increment Bonds, Series A, and $8,100,000 Variable Rate Demand Tax Increment Reserve Fund Bonds, Series A," 29 August 1984; see also "Central Industrial Park Project Financial Statement, Year Ended June 30, 1983." Overruns would have been higher had expenditures for site preparation not been below anticipated levels.

25. Mel Ravitz, "Costs Associated with the Central Industrial Condemnation Action" (Unpublished memorandum, 11 April 1984).

26. Jack Seamonds, "Poletown Hasn't Matched Promise," *Detroit Free Press,* 31 May 1989.

27. Bill McGraw, "Church Takes on GM over Poletown Land," *Detroit Free Press,* 14 March 1990.

28. Interview with Councilman Mel Ravitz, 24 July 1991.

29. Interview with Marcus Loper, City Planning Commission, 23 July 1991.

30. John Marco, "Memorandum: Poletown," 21 September 1988.

31. Ibid.

32. Chauncey Bailey, "Chrysler Asks for Big Tax Break," *Detroit News,* 10 September 1988; Chauncey Bailey, "Council Rejects G.M. Tax Break," *Detroit News,* 24 March 1988.

33. Wilbur Rich, *Coleman Young and Detroit Politics* (Detroit: Wayne State University Press, 1989), pp. 33–34.

CHAPTER 14
THE CHRYSLER JEFFERSON PROJECT:
POLETOWN REVISITED?

1. Marjorie Sorge and Bruce Alpert, "Chrysler Jefferson Updating Proposed," *Detroit News,* 7 January 1986.

2. Bruce Alpert and James Higgins, "City Plan Would Aid Chrysler," *Detroit News,* 11 January 1986.

3. David Markiewicz, "City Offers Jefferson Plant Lures," *Detroit News,* 27 January 1986.

4. Ibid.

5. James Higgins and Marjorie Sorge, "Chrysler Maps Total Overhaul of Jefferson Plant," *Detroit News,* 19 June 1986.

6. David Markiewicz, "Chrysler Asks Aid at Jefferson," *Detroit News*, 27 July 1986.

7. Lynn W. Bachelor, "Flat Rock, Michigan Trades a Ford for a Mazda: State Policy and the Evaluation of Plant Location Incentives," *The Politics of Industrial Recruitment*, ed. Ernest J. Yanarella and William C. Green (New York: Greenwood Press, 1990).

8. Edward Miller, "State OK's Funds to Aid Chrysler on Two Big Projects," *Detroit News*, 10 September 1986.

9. Earle Eldridge, "Chrysler Project's $1 Billion Cost Is Firm, City Told," *Detroit News*, 11 September 1986.

10. David Markiewicz, "U.S. Tags $50 Million for Jefferson Project," *Detroit News*, 24 September 1986.

11. Bruce Alpert and Earle Eldridge, "Chrysler Plant Wins Financing, Land Approval," *Detroit News*, 13 September 1986.

12. Marjorie Sorge and Earle Eldridge, "Jefferson Plant Plan in Gear," *Detroit News*, 18 October 1986.

13. Marjorie Sorge and Denise Stinson, "Newest Plant over Oldest Plant," *Detroit News*, 21 October 1986.

14. N. Scott Vance, "Council OK's $1.2 Billion Chrysler Plan," *Detroit News*, 19 February 1987.

15. Marjorie Sorge, "Jefferson Plant Faces Year Delay," *Detroit News*, 15 December 1987; Marjorie Sorge, "Jefferson Ave. Plant to Operate Until 1991," *Detroit News*, 16 January 1988.

16. N. Scott Vance, "Chrysler Plant Sites Prove Costly," *Detroit News*, 26 January 1988.

17. Chauncey Bailey, "Detroit Asked to Increase Jefferson Plant Financing," *Detroit News*, 4 February 1988; Chauncey Bailey and N. Scott Vance, "$40 Million Chrysler Project Loan Approved," *Detroit News*, 4 February 1988.

18. Norman Sinclair and Brenda Ingersoll, "Court Orders Records Opened, City Lost $34 Million on Deal," *Detroit News*, 29 October 1988.

19. Brenda Ingersoll and Norman Sinclair, "City's $40 Million Land Deal Probed," *Detroit News*, 14 September 1988; Bill McGraw, "$40 Million City Land Deal Probed by the FBI," *Detroit Free Press*, 15 September 1988.

20. "Where Was City Government?" *Detroit News*, 16 September 1988.

21. Norman Sinclair, "Possible Inventory Padding Investigated in Land Deal," *Detroit News*, 18 December 1988.

22. Sinclair and Ingersoll, "Court Orders Records Opened."

23. Brenda Ingersoll and Norman Sinclair, "Companies Bought Back Machinery from City," *Detroit News*, 15 September 1988.

24. Bill McGraw, "Young Accepts Blame in Chrysler Overruns," *Detroit Free Press*, 15 July 1989.

25. Chauncey Bailey, "Chrysler Asks for Big Tax Break," *Detroit News*, 10 September 1988.

26. Chauncey Bailey, Marjorie Sorge, and Brenda Ingersoll, "Chrysler Tax Break Denied," *Detroit News*, 20 September 1988.

27. N. Scott Vance, "No New Tax Break, No Jefferson Plant, Chrysler Warns City," *Detroit News*, 18 October 1988.

28. Ibid.

29. Monroe Walker and N. Scott Vance, "Chrysler Wins City Tax Break," *Detroit News*, 20 October 1988.

30. Louis Mleczko and Dennis Pfaff, "Chrysler Plant Faces Massive Cleanup," *Detroit News*, 17 December 1988.

31. Dennis Pfaff and Louis Mleczko, "Chrysler Cleanup: $50 Million," *Detroit News,* 26 January 1989.

32. Louis Mleczko, "Site Cleanup May Delay New Jefferson Ave. Plant," *Detroit News,* 24 February 1989.

33. Dennis Pfaff, "Chrysler Gets Approval for Jefferson Site," *Detroit News,* 27 April 1989.

34. Janet Braunstein and Constance Prather, "Controversy Encircles Jefferson Avenue Plant," *Detroit Free Press,* 31 May 1989.

35. United Press International, "Jefferson Plant L-Car Production Begins," *Detroit News,* 18 March 1989.

36. Helen Fogel, "Jefferson Ave. Layoffs Extended for 1600," *Detroit News,* 23 May 1989.

37. "Chrysler Stuns Detroit, 1,700 Jefferson Workers to Lose Jobs in February," *Detroit News,* 4 November 1989.

38. David Sedgwick, "Analysts: Smart Hedge against Slump in Sales," *Detroit News,* 4 November 1989.

39. John Lippert, "Jefferson Plant Hits End of the Line," *Detroit Free Press,* 2 February 1990.

40. Ibid.

41. Chauncey Bailey, "Chrysler Cleanup Costs Climbing," *Detroit News,* 12 July 1989; McGraw, "Young Accepts Blame in Chrysler Overruns."

42. Pat McCaughan, "Chrysler Job Cost to City: $48,825 Each," *Detroit News,* 15 July 1989.

43. Vivian Toy, "Costs Per Job Soar at Project," *Detroit News,* 4 October 1989.

44. John Marco, "Memo to Detroit City Council Members: City of Detroit Obligation for the Chrysler-Jefferson Project," 29 September 1989.

45. Rob Zeigler, "Fiscal Experts for Young, Council Spar over Chrysler Costs," *Detroit News,* 13 October 1989.

46. Bella Marshall, "Memorandum to City Council: Chrysler Jefferson Project Costs and City of Detroit Obligation," 5 October 1989.

47. John Marco, "Memorandum to City Council: Chrysler Jefferson Project Costs and City of Detroit Obligations," 5 October 1989. Marco notes that the 19 June 1989 issue of *City and State* included $167.6 million in interest as part of Kentucky's costs for a new Toyota plant. However, H. B. Milward and H. H. Newman, "State Incentive Packages and the Industrial Location Decision," *Economic Development Quarterly* 3 (1989): 203–22, include neither tax abatements, tax-increment revenues, nor interest payments among project costs for the Toyota facility.

48. Bella Marshall, Letter to City Council, 31 July 1989; Economic Development Corporation of the City of Detroit, Memorandum: Jefferson/Conner Industrial Revitalization Project, Project Plan.

49. Bella Marshall, Letter to City Council, 14 June 1991: Issuance of Not to Exceed $53,500,000 City of Detroit Local Development Finance Authority Tax Increment Bonds," and attachment, "Resolution of the City Council of the City of Detroit Authorizing the Limited Tax Pledge of the City to Support the City of Detroit Local Development Finance Authority Tax Increment Bonds."

50. At least Chrysler Chairman Lee Iacocca stressed the Detroit location of his state-of-the-art plant in his "Lead, Follow, or Get Out of the Way" 1992 advertising campaign.

51. John Lippert, "Chrysler Puts Itself on Line in Detroit," *Detroit News/Free Press,* 4 January 1992.

52. John Logan and Harvey Molotch, *Urban Fortunes* (Berkeley: University of California Press, 1987).

53. Elkin, *City and Regime,* pp. 40–41.

CHAPTER 15
URBAN POWER, POLITICAL DECISION MAKING,
AND THE AUTOMOBILE INDUSTRY

1. Roger Friedland, *Power and Crisis in the City: Corporations, Unions, and Urban Policy* (London: Macmillan, 1982), p. 202.

2. Clarence Stone, in "Systemic Power in Community Decision-Making: A Restatement of Stratificationist Theory," *American Political Science Review* 74 (December 1980), has viewed urban politicians as being cross-pressured by their constituencies and by community elites. Hence, the pursuit of constituency demands is by no means guaranteed.

3. See David Vogel, "The Power of Business in America: A Reappraisal," *British Journal of Political Science* (January 1983): 34, on the tendency of business organizations to evaluate public policy in terms of effects on their own organizations, neglecting the impact that it will have on their industries or on the business community as a whole.

4. Interview with Edward Cushman, 31 January 1985.

5. Interview with Kenneth Cameron, 14 November 1983.

6. Clarence Stone, "Paradigms, Power, and Urban Leadership," in *Leadership and Politics,* ed. Bryan Jones (Lawrence: University Press of Kansas, 1989), p. 148.

7. Robert Dahl, *Who Governs?* (New Haven, Conn.: Yale University Press, 1960).

8. See Michael D. Kennedy, "The Fiscal Crisis of the City," in *Cities in Transformation,* ed. Michael Peter Smith (Beverly Hills, Calif.: Sage, 1984), pp. 91–110.

9. Bryan D. Jones and Lynn W. Bachelor, "Local Policy Discretion and the Corporate Surplus," in *Urban Economic Development,* ed. Richard Bingham and John Blair (Beverly Hills, Calif.: Sage, 1984).

10. Paul Schumaker et al., "Economic Development Policy and Community Conflict: A Comparative Issues Approach," in *Research in Urban Policy,* ed. Terry Clark, 2:A (Greenwich, Conn.: JAI Press, 1986), pp. 25–46.

11. On the proper size of local government see Vincent Ostrom, Charles M. Tiebout, and Robert Warren, "The Organization of Government in Metropolitan Areas: A Theoretical Inquiry," *American Political Science Review* 55 (December 1961): 831–42; Elinor Ostrom, "Metropolitan Reform: Propositions Derived from Two Traditions," *Social Science Quarterly* 53 (December 1972): 474–93; Robert Dahl, "The City in the Future of Democracy," *American Political Science Review* 61 (December 1967): 953–70. Matthew Holden treats metropolitan government as a problem of managing external relations but focuses mainly on intergovernmental affairs (see "The Governance of the Metropolis as a Problem in Diplomacy," *Journal of Politics* 26 [August 1964]: 627–47).

12. John Mollenkopf, *The Contested City* (Princeton, N.J.: Princeton University Press, 1983).

13. On this point, see Hal Wolman, "Local Economic Development Policy: What Explains the Divergence between Policy Analysis and Political Behavior?" *Journal of Urban Affairs* 10 (1988): 19–28.

14. Richard Child Hill, "Crisis in the Motor City," in *Restructuring the City,* ed. Susan Fainstein et al. (New York: Longman, 1983), p. 118.

15. This interpretation bears a resemblance to Robert Dahl's description of Mayor Lee's Citizens' Action Committee in New Haven (see Dahl's *Who Governs?* chap. 10).

See, however, G. William Domhoff's reevaluation in *Who Really Rules?* (New Brunswick, N.J.: Transaction, 1978).

16. See R. Allen Hays and Christopher Silver, "Can You Compensate for a Lost Home? An Assessment of the 1970 Uniform Relocation Act," *Urban Affairs Papers* 2 (Winter 1980): 33–49.

17. Oliver Zunz, *The Changing Face of Inequality* (Chicago: University of Chicago Press, 1982).

18. Douglas Yates, *The Ungovernable City* (Cambridge, Mass.: MIT Press, 1977).

19. Paul E. Peterson, *City Limits* (Chicago: University of Chicago Press, 1981).

20. C. G. Pickvance, "The Structuralist Critique in Urban Studies," in *Cities in Transformation,* ed. Michael Peter Smith (Beverly Hills, Calif.: Sage, 1984), p. 32.

21. Ibid., p. 46.

22. See Anthony Downs, *An Economic Theory of Democracy* (New York: Harper & Row, 1957).

23. See Richard A. Musgrave and Peggy B. Musgrave, *Public Finance in Theory and Practice,* 2d ed. (New York: McGraw-Hill, 1976), pp. 104–8.

24. W. A. Niskanen, *Bureaucracy and Representative Government* (Chicago: Aldine-Atherton, 1971); Albert Bretton, *The Economic Theory of Representative Government* (Chicago: Aldine, 1974).

25. Aaron Wildavsky, *The Politics of the Budgetary Process* (Boston: Little, Brown, 1964).

26. Thomas Anton, *The Politics of State Expenditures in Illinois* (Urbana: University of Illinois Press, 1966).

27. John P. Crecine, *Government Problem-Solving* (Chicago: Rand-McNally, 1969).

28. Bryan D. Jones, *Service Delivery in the City* (New York: Longman, 1980); Kenneth Mladenka, "Rules, Service Equity, and Distributional Decisions," *Social Science Quarterly* 59 (1978): 991–98.

29. John W. Kingdon, *Agendas, Alternatives, and Public Policies* (Boston: Little, Brown, 1984); see also Michael Cohen, James March, and Johan Olsen, "A Garbage Can Model of Organizational Choice," *Administrative Science Quarterly* 17 (March 1972): 1–25.

30. Kingdon, *Agendas,* p. 20.

31. Charles H. Levine, Irene Rubin, and George C. Wolohojian, *Politics of Retrenchment* (Beverly Hills, Calif.: Sage, 1981).

32. Pietro Nivola, "Apocalypse Now? Whither the Urban Fiscal Crisis," *Polity* 14 (Spring 1982): 371–95.

33. Terry Nichols Clark and Lorna Crowley Ferguson, *City Money* (New York: Columbia University Press, 1983).

34. Herbert A. Simon, "Rational Decision Making in Business Organizations," *American Economic Review* 69 (September 1979): 510.

35. Aaron Wildavsky has termed such complex feedback "policy as its own cause" (see *Speaking Truth to Power* [Boston: Little, Brown, 1979]).

36. René Thom, *Structural Stability and Morphogenesis* (Reading, Mass.: W. A. Benjamin, 1975), p. 2.

37. See Michael Peter Smith, "Urban Structure, Social Theory, and Political Power," in *Cities in Transformation,* ed. Smith, pp. 9–30.

38. Stone, "Paradigms, Power, and Urban Leadership," pp. 135–59.

39. Ibid., p. 148.

40. Marion Orr and Gerry Stoker, "Urban Leadership and Regimes in Detroit" (Unpublished manuscript, Wayne State University, 1991).

41. Charles Lindblom, "The Market as Prison," *Journal of Politics* 44 (May 1982): 324–36.

Index

American Motors, 64, 236
Anton, Thomas, 5, 34, 46–47, 246
Area Citizens for a Rural Environment
  (ACRE), 176–77, 179
Argonaut Realty, 74, 78, 191–93
Association of Community Organizations
  for Reform Now (ACORN), 155
Automobile industry:
  assembly plants, 3, 20
  black community and, 44–45
  capital spending in, 67–70, 233–34
  cities and, 3–8, 195, 206–8, 233
  decision making in, 8–14, 49, 66, 70
  decline of, 57–62, 66, 69, 165–66, 212
  growth in, 57, 63, 66–67, 205–6, 209
  mature market, 65
  Michigan economy, 4–14, 21–28, 30, 33
    38, 41, 133, 208–16
  oil shortages and, 57, 59, 66
  plant replacement in, 70
  public policy and, 4–14, 21–22, 39,
    76–77, 86, 234–37
  quotas and, 208
  regulations and, 66, 223–24
  site selection in, 75, 77, 209
  small cars in, 57–58, 67, 165, 236
  unionism in, 45, 211
  See also under Detroit; Flint; Pontiac

Barbeau, Paul, 177
Bauer, Raymond, 190
Baum, Victor, 151
Baumgartner, Frank, 18
Bay City, Mich., 3
Beckham, Charles, 182

Bielby, William, 14
Bingham, Richard, 209
Black communities:
  Coleman Young and, 45–46, 115, 118–19,
    161, 216, 244
  in Detroit, 36, 44–46, 50
  in Flint, 187–88
  mobilization of, 244
  New Detroit and, 53, 212, 216
  in Orion Township, 177
  in Poletown, 144–46, 158, 160–62
  unions and, 45
Blanchard, James, 220
Boudon, Raymond, 4
Bowen, Bruce, 46
Browne, Ernie, 118–19
Budget Planning and Stabilization Com-
  mittee, 36–37
Buick Assembly Plant, 186, 190, 194–96,
  199
Buick City, 3, 194–202
Bureau of Economic Analysis, 26–27

Carter, Jimmy, 46, 52, 99, 101, 108, 119
Cavanaugh, Jerome, 36, 45
Central Industrial Park Citizens' District
  Council (CDC), 104–5, 111–22, 132,
  150–51, 161
Central Industrial Part Joint Venture,
  137–41
Central Industrial Park project:
  CDC and, 111–17
  Detroit and, 216
  financial plans in, 95–108, 213
  GM and, 56, 76–162, 215

Central Industrial Park project, *continued*
and historic place, 92
legal suits in, 122–33, 213
neighborhood, 144–46
opposition to, 143–62
political leadership in, 216
project plan in, 93–94
public purpose in, 127–28, 132–34
"quick take" law and, 83, 123, 127,
132, 213
relocation of, 103–8, 130
site selection in, 76–89, 213
tax arrangements in, 134–42, 214–16
See also Poletown Neighborhood Council;
Young, Coleman
Charter Township Act, 193
Chene Area Business Development
Corporation, 147
Chrysler Corporation:
cutbacks at, 60–61
decision making at, 49, 56
and Detroit, 7, 29–30
Dodge Main and, 42, 55–56, 81–83, 92, 103
market structure and, 63–64
Orion Township and, 168
profits at, 62, 67, 224
subcompacts and, 58, 67
Churches, 47–48, 143, 145, 155–60
Citizens' District Council, 132, 150, 161
Clark, Terry, 28, 218, 247
Clay, Eric, 128
Clean Air Regulations, 69, 76–77, 151
Cleveland, Clyde, 136–37
Coalition making:
Coleman Young and, 46, 52, 118–22, 206,
227, 249
Detroit, 50–54, 183–84
elites and, 50
and Orion Township, 183–84
progrowth, 242–45
Cockrell, Kenneth, 116, 119
Cohen, Michael, 247
Community and Economic Development
Department (CEDD):
CDC establishment and, 111–14, 150
cost projections and, 95–96, 103, 106,
118
EDC and, 215, 243
financing, 121, 221
loans and, 99–102, 118, 221
plan approval of, 116
relocation and, 104–6, 121, 130
site provider, 92–93, 123–24
tax increments and, 117, 138–39
See also Moten, Emmett S.
Community Development Block Grants
(CDBG):

Coleman Young and, 36
Detroit City Council and, 115, 215
EDC and, 110
financing for CIPP, 95–103, 114, 213
Flint and, 200
PNC and, 147
Crandall, Robert, 66
Crecine, John, 247
Crow, Carl, 21
Cunningham, Thomas, 112–13

Dahl, Robert, 9, 48, 51, 237, 239
Davidson, C. Don, 172–75, 182–83
Dearden, Cardinal, 156, 158
Decision making:
community values in, 9–11, 183
corporate, 66, 76–77
determinism in, 246, 248
jurisdictional justice, 139, 142
nonrational, 247
peak bargaining and, 51–53
pluralism in, 9
polity/economy, 6, 22, 46, 54, 183,
190, 200–202
public-choice theorists and, 19, 247
public economy and, 202
public officials and, 6–7
public policy and, 38–39, 46, 77, 193
rationality in, 9, 19, 235, 246–47
site selection, 76–77, 183
social trends in, 6–7
See also under Automobile industry;
Detroit; Flint; General Motors Corp.
Decision rules, 51
Democratic party, 43–46
Detroit:
auto industry in, 21–23, 28–32, 36,
41–46, 70, 76, 215, 217
black community in, 36, 44–45, 50, 212
business community and, 242
city interest in, 215
coalition making in, 49, 220, 228
Coleman Young and, 4, 35–37, 50, 223
concentric sector in, 32
decision making in, 7–8, 19, 50–51,
90, 139, 141
decline in, 30–37, 39, 44, 77, 125,
129, 136
development of, 40–43, 46, 141–43
economic elite in, 46–48
economic development in, 8, 18, 36,
39, 89, 141, 227
ethnic communities in, 42–44, 235
federal aid in, 35, 37
GM and, 23, 73–162, 211–12, 228, 243,
248
police of Poletown sit-in, 156–57

policy making in, 46–48, 50–51
political leaders in, 228–29
relocation threats in, 87, 91, 124, 136–37,
  142, 224
revenue in, 33–37, 213
sectarchy and, 51, 239–40
tax arrangements in, 135–41, 213, 215
urban migration in, 32, 44
See also Central Industrial Park project;
  Detroit City Council; Young, Coleman
Detroit Association for Radical Economics
  (DARE), 119
Detroit City Council:
block grants and, 101, 117, 138–40
CDC establishment and, 111–13, 150
citizen concerns and, 114–17, 121
City Planning Commission, 111, 116,
  123–24, 126, 136
economic development and, 116, 228
HUD loan and, 92, 117
plan approval, 95, 99, 102, 108–9,
  116–18, 123, 128, 135, 151
politics in, 115, 215
reduction of power in, 45, 115, 121
tax abatement and, 117–18, 135–37,
  142, 201, 215
Detroit Economic Development Corporation
  (EDC):
CIPP and, 92–94, 109, 121, 128
Coleman Young and, 121
and Hamtramck, 109, 137–38
legal suits and, 123, 125, 128, 130
membership of, 110
powers of, 110–12, 121
site criteria and, 94, 130
TIFA and, 86, 138–41
Detroit Free Press, 119
Detroit News, 47, 221–22
Detroit Renaissance, 53
Dexter, Anthony, 190
Dodge Main:
Chrysler and, 7, 42, 56, 60–61
and GM Poletown project, 81–82, 103,
  125, 244
Hamtramck Assembly and, 42, 55–56
UAW and, 42, 45
work force of, 55–56
Dungy, Richard, 156
Durant, William Crapo, 3–4
Durant-Dort Carriage Co., 3
Dye, Thomas, 52

Economic Alliance of Michigan, 53
Economic Development Administration
  (EDA), 93, 101–2, 199
Economic Development Corporation Act,
  83–84

Economic elitism:
coalition building, 14–15, 50
Coleman Young and, 118–19
Detroit, 46–48, 51, 242
Flint, 197–98
institutional, 9–10, 52
interests of, 8–9, 11–12, 235
peak bargaining and, 53
polity/economy of, 46–48, 133
public policy, 9–15
Elections:
Detroit, 43–46, 118–19
Flint, 186–89
political leaders and, 13, 51, 235
Elkin, Stephen, 11, 15, 206, 231
Embry, Robert, 93
Environmental Impact Statement, 91–95,
  130–31, 171
Environmental Protection Act (Mich.),
  127–29
Environmental Protection Agency (EPA),
  101–2, 170
Estes, Elliott, 74, 149
Ewen, Lynda, 46

Federal Advisory Council on Historic Sites
  (FACHS), 153
Federal Council on Environmental Quality,
  91–92
Federal Trade Commission, 208
Feikens, John, 130–32, 151
Ferguson, Lorna, 28, 247
Flint:
annexation, 191–93
auto industry in, 21–23, 37, 41, 70, 76
black community in, 187–88, 238, 244
Buick City and, 196–99, 217, 235, 244
Buick Motor Co. and, 3–4
business interests in, 188
community concerns in, 188, 201–2
decision making in, 202
economic decline in, 31, 33, 37, 189
economic-development policies in, 18,
  33–39, 191, 193, 196–200, 202, 237
GM and, 7–8, 29–30, 59, 185–202,
  210–11, 240
government in, 186–89, 197–98
Mott foundation and, 189–90, 202, 242,
  252
political leadership in, 193, 202, 206–7,
  234, 248
polity/economy of, 233
public policy in, 190, 201, 238
revenue in, 33–37
site selection in, 78, 191–93
taxes in, 192–93, 200–201, 210
unionism in, 186–88, 196

Flint, *continued*
  urban renewal in, 199–200, 210
  See also Rutherford, James
Flint Area Conference, Inc. (FACI), 190
Flint Downtown Development Authority
    (DDA), 191–93
Flint Fisher, 196, 198
Flint Journal, 188
Ford, Henry, 32, 44, 63
Ford, Henry, II, 47, 49, 53, 236
Ford Motor Co.:
  capital spending at, 69
  community involvement of, 47, 53
  cutbacks at, 59–62
  decision making at, 49
  fuel economy and, 236
  lower-price market and, 57–59, 67
  market structure and, 41, 62–64
  Michigan economy and, 23, 44
  profit loss, 62–67
Fox, George, 192
Friedland, Roger, 14, 19, 234

General Motors Corp.:
  Billy Durant and, 4, 23
  black employment, 44
  Buick City and, 196–200
  capital spending at, 67–71, 73, 75, 79–80,
    88–89, 107, 165, 190, 194, 209, 213
  CIPP and, 56, 73–162
  community involvement of, 47–48,
    188–90
  cutbacks at, 59–60
  decentralization at, 49, 74, 194–95
  decision making at, 7, 49, 63, 68–70,
    73–77, 89–90, 183, 194–95, 198, 248
  Detroit and, 7, 28–29, 41, 56, 73–162,
    210, 215, 218, 228, 239, 248
  Flint and, 7, 29–30, 59, 185–202, 211, 245
  front-wheel-drive cars, 67–70, 76, 79–80,
    165, 190
  imports and, 57–58, 208
  internal competition at, 195
  market structure and, 62–64
  Nader and, 66
  plant closings at, 70, 198
  policy at, 49, 74, 188, 190, 200
  Pontiac/Orion Township and, 7, 29–30,
    56, 59, 85, 165–84, 243
  profits at, 62
  regulations and, 49, 66, 69, 73, 76, 90,
    106, 132
  small-car market, 58, 60, 67, 165, 236
  suppliers and, 196–97, 211
  tax abatements and, 85, 135–37, 141,
    166, 174–75, 200–201, 215, 222–23
  See also Site selection

Genesee County Economic Development
    Department, 198
Genesee Township, 188, 191–93
Geschwender, James, 45
Glinnan, Thomas, 43
Glusac, Michael M., 223
Good Citizens' League, 43
Gould, Stephen J., 5
Grand Trunk Railroad, 176
Greenwald, Gerald, 219, 221

Hacker, Andrew, 52
Hamtramck, Mich.:
  CIPP and, 81–83, 91, 93, 99
  EDC and, 109
  Hamtramck Assembly and, 4, 55–56
  tax arrangements, 134–41
  UDAG and, 100
Henderson, Erma, 114, 149
Henig, Jeffrey, 148
Hill, Richard Child, 21, 243
Historic Preservation, 151–52
Hodas, Richard, 147, 150, 152–53, 157,
    159
Holland, Wallace, 173, 182
Honigman, Jason, 125, 128
Hostetter, Leonard, 130–31
Housing and Community Development Act,
    95–96, 100
Housing and Urban Development,
    Department of:
  CIPP funding and, 92, 95, 130, 154, 193,
    213
  homes, 104–5
  loans and, 96–98, 101–2, 213, 219–20
  property acquisition and, 106
  relocation plan and, 93, 113
  repayment contract with, 96
  section, 114

Iacocca, Lee, 62, 220
Immaculate Conception Church, 131,
    143–47, 150, 152, 155–57, 159
Imports, 57–59, 64, 66, 70, 76, 210

Jackson, Mich., 3, 7
Japanese automobile manufacturers, 7, 58,
    66, 70, 75, 194, 208–9
Jeffries, Edward, 44
Jones, Bryan, 18
Jurisdictional justice, 139, 142

Kadushin, Charles, 47
Kahn, Albert, 42
Kan-ban inventory system, 194, 196–97
Karasiewicz, Father Joseph, 156, 159
Kelley, Jack, 136

Kelly, John, 139
Kennedy, Michael, 238
Kingdon, John, 18, 247

Lake Orion (Mich.) *Review*, 179
Landrieu, Moon, 99, 108, 126
League of Revolutionary Black Workers, 45
Leland, Henry, 43, 47
Levine, Charles, 247
Lindblom, Charles, 51–53, 243, 254
Litzenberg, Jack, 193–94, 201
Local Development Finance Authority, 227–28
Logan, John, 11
Lukens, William, 154

Marco, John, 215, 226–28
Marshall, Bella, 220–21, 226–28
Martin, George, 123, 125, 128, 131, 151–52
Martin, Patrick, 192
Michigan:
    auto industry in, 7–14, 20–33, 39, 41, 60, 133, 171, 206
    CIPP financing, 102
    decline in, 33, 36, 38, 77, 133, 210
    economic-development policies in, 7–14, 79, 83, 85, 89, 93, 104, 111, 133
    local government in, 6–11, 206, 244
    public expenditures in, 23–24, 28–29, 33, 38–39, 218
    tax arrangements in, 85, 135, 138–40, 167, 213, 227
Michigan Constitution:
    eminent domain, 85, 89, 127–30
    referendum petitions in, 178–79
Michigan Economic Security Commission, 30
Michigan Supreme Court, 125, 128–32, 151–54, 157
Miller, Gerald, 133
Milliken, William:
    CIPP and, 79, 155
    Coleman Young and, 37, 46
    Orion Township and, 170
    UDAG and, 101
Mills, C. Wright, 10, 52
Milwaukee Junction, 41–42
Miriani, Louis, 45
Mollenkopf, John, 13–14
Molotch, Harvey, 11
Moten, Emmett S., Jr.:
    EDC and, 121
    entrepreneurial skills of, 90, 108, 120, 122, 175, 222
    federal financing and, 93, 99, 126, 220–21

GM site selection and, 82, 94, 124–25, 137
GM suppliers and, 228–30
PNC and, 154
Poletown task force and, 93
project plan and, 111, 124–25, 135
tax arrangements and, 136, 138, 140
Motor Vehicle Manufacturers' Association (MVMA), 236
Mott, Charles S., 189, 242, 252
Mott Foundation, 189–91, 202
Mowitz, Robert, 50
Mundy Township, 191–92
Murphy, Daniel, 180–81
Murphy, Thomas A.:
    financing, 74
    peak bargaining, 239
    PNC and, 149
    site requirements, 94
    site selection, 4, 79–80, 124, 191
    tax abatements, 135

Nader, Ralph:
    CIPP and his organization, 114, 144, 153–56, 159
    Coleman Young and, 4, 119
    Unsafe at Any Speed, 66
National Environmental Protection Act, 130
Neighborhood Services Organization (NSO), 104–5
New Detroit, 53
Nichols, John, 45
Nivola, Pietro, 247

Oakland County, Mich., 180–81
Oakland Press, 179
O'Connor, James, 238, 253
Oil crisis, 30, 33, 57–59, 165
Olechowski, Thomas, 147, 149–50, 154, 158–60
Orion Township, Mich.:
    character of, 168
    community opposition in, 169, 171, 176–83
    GM and, 166–84, 210–11, 240
    policy making in, 166
    politics in, 168–69
    relocation threats in, 167, 171, 177–79, 183
    rezoning in, 176–79
    sewer politics in, 180–82, 184, 245
    site requirements in, 170–71, 176, 179–80, 183
    site selection in, 56, 78, 166–76
    tax abatements in, 85–87, 166–67, 174–75
    taxes in, 166–69, 211

Orion Township Planning Commission, 174, 176, 178, 180, 182
Orr, Marion, 251

Padilla, Tom, 174–75
Pailen, Donald, 221
Parenti, Michael, 10
Pastalan, Leon, 104–5
Peak bargaining, 51, 53, 239
Peterson, Paul, 8–10, 12, 53, 245
Pickvance, C. G., 246
Pierce, Samuel, 99
Pingree, Hazen, 43
Pluralism, 48, 50–51, 53
Poletown. *See* Central Industrial Park project
Poletown Area Revitalization Force (PARTF), 147, 149
Poletown Neighborhood Council:
  Coleman Young and, 120
  demands of, 107, 114, 143–44, 149–50, 160
  errors of, 157–58
  financing questions of, 114, 136–37
  inception of, 147
  internal politics in, 150
  leadership in, 158–60
  legal suits and, 84, 123–30, 132, 151–52
  lobbying efforts of, 153–54
  media exposure of, 152–53
  mobilization of, 147–49
  outside support for, 154–55
  weaknesses of, 161–62, 184
Polish Interparish Council, 147
Political leaders:
  communities and, 6, 14, 238, 248–49
  constituency and, 51, 237
  decision making and, 5–6, 241, 248
  economic development and, 234–38
  economic elites and, 10, 12, 15, 236, 242
  elections and, 9
  interests of, 8, 235, 253–54
  peak bargaining and, 245
  policy entrepreneurs, 21, 19, 51
  polity/economy and, 17
  public policy and, 244
Political power:
  Coleman Young and, 119–20
  Detroit, 48–51, 120
  economic elites and, 9–14, 63
  institutional, 10, 52
  organizational structure of, 52
  polity/economy of, 241–45
  progrowth, 14, 242–44
  sectarchy, 51, 239
Political systems, 22
Polyarchy, 51–52

Pontiac:
  auto industry in, 21–23, 37, 206
  community concerns and, 183, 240
  decline in, 30–31, 34–35, 167, 172
  economic development in, 35–39, 167, 172, 175, 242
  GM and, 7, 29–30, 59, 69, 166–76, 189–90
  plant reuse in, 173–74
  political leaders in, 173–75, 183, 233, 243, 248
  revenue in, 33–39
  sewer connections and, 180–81
  Silverdome and, 35, 37
  site selection in, 79, 167–68, 172–75, 183
  tax abatement in, 166, 174–75
Pontiac City Commission, 166, 173, 175, 182
Pontiac Downtown Development Authority, 172–73
Pontiac Plan, 172, 182–83
Pontiac-Waterford Times, 172
Pool, Ithiel, 190
Postma, Donald, 174
Potter, David, 135–36, 142, 171
Pound, Arthur, 28–29
Pryor, Jack, 138
Public economy:
  auto industry and, 23, 39
  decision making and, 6
  Flint, 186–89
  policy action and, 4–6
Public interest in Poletown project, 126–33, 138, 142
Punctuated equilibrium model, 18

"Quick-take" law, 82–83, 89, 123, 127, 132, 176, 213, 230

Reagan, Ronald:
  federal aid and, 37, 85, 101–3
  import quotas and, 70, 208
Reosti, Ronald, 124–28, 151
Relocation threats:
  Buick Motor Co., 3–4
  GM in Detroit, 87, 91, 124, 136–37, 142
  GM in Orion Township, 167, 171, 176–79, 183
Resident relocation:
  industrial renewal and, 252
  Poletown, 93, 103–8, 112–13, 121, 130, 155
Reuss, Lloyd, 194, 197
Rhode Island:
  auto assembly plant in, 7
Rich, Richard, 148
Rich, Wilbur, 216

Ridley, Richard, 131
Rutherford, James:
  Buick City and, 197
  economic development and, 206, 234
  fiscal policy of, 37
  GM site in Flint and, 190–93
  as political leader, 193, 202, 248, 254
  UAW and, 187
Ryan, James, 129–30, 132–33, 254

St. John, Anthony, 225
St. John's Catholic Church, 145, 147
St. John's Industrial Park, 199
Santiago, Jose, 174
Schumaker, Paul, 240
Secrest, Fred, 36–37
Sectarchy, 51–53
Sharp, James, 187–88
Simon, Herbert, 8, 247
Sinclair, Robert, 169
Site selection:
  Buick Motor Co. and, 3–4
  factors in, 77–78
  GM in Detroit, 4, 7, 73, 76–89, 108,
    129–31
  GM in Flint, 191–93
  GM in Pontiac/Orion Township, 166–74
Sloan, Alfred, 65, 74
Small Business Administration, 105
Smith, Roger, 74, 122, 157, 194
Solidarity House, 49–50
Spreitzer, Barbara, 165
Stempel, Robert, 170
Stepp, Marc, 219
Stilp, Gene, 153–56
Stoker, Gerry, 251
Stone, Clarence, 10, 15, 53, 206–7, 237,
    250
Stone, Herbert, 194
Stroh, Peter, 236

Tax abatements:
  GM, 215
  GM/Detroit, 89, 117–18, 134–42
  GM/Flint, 192, 200–201
  GM/Orion Township, 85–87, 166–67,
    174–75
  local government and, 197
  Poletown residents and, 112
Tax-increment financing:
  Buick City and, 200–201
  CIPP, 117, 134–42, 213–15
  Detroit, EDC, and, 86, 110, 215–16,
    226–28, 249
  Michigan, 85, 138–40, 212–13
Tax Increment Financing Authority
    (TIFA), 85–86, 135, 139, 214–15

Thom, René, 248
Thompson, Bryan, 169
Tomboulian, Alice, 173

Unionism:
  collective bargaining and, 49–50
  Detroit City Council and, 115
  local politics and, 211
  mobilization of, 218–19
  policy initiatives and, 52
Unitary interest, 84
United Automobile Workers:
  black Detroit and, 44–45
  breakthrough of, 44
  collective bargaining and, 49–50, 219
  Detroit City Council and, 115
  Dodge Main, 42
  Flint, 186–88, 196, 202, 211
  GM and, 78, 208, 231
  Orion Township, 177, 183
  policy making and, 49, 208, 218
United Way of Pontiac/North Oakland
    County, 179
Unsafe at Any Speed (Nader), 66, 243
Urban Development Action Grants
    (UDAG):
  applications for, 100, 114, 117, 220
  EDC and, 110
  establishment of, 100
  Flint, 193–94, 199
  Reagan and, 101
Urban Mass Transportation Administration,
    102

Van Tassel, Joann, 177, 181
Verway, David I., 22
Vienna Township, Mich., 191–93
Volkes, David, 152

Ward's Automotive Yearbook, 59, 61
Wayne County Circuit Court, 123, 151–52
White, William S., 189
Whitney, William, 193
Wildavsky, Aaron, 246
Wright, Deil, 50

Yates, Douglas, 245
Young, Coleman:
  black community and, 45–46, 115,
    118–19, 161–62, 216, 244
  Carter administration and, 92, 108, 119,
    175
  CIPP and, 94, 99, 108, 111, 119–25,
    130–34, 137, 149, 154, 157, 161–62
  coalition making and, 52, 118, 121, 206,
    227, 249
  Detroit fiscal problems and, 36–37, 223

Young, Coleman, *continued*
  election of, 45, 118–19, 240
  GM and, 4, 79, 124
  peak bargaining and, 206, 239
  PNC and, 149, 160–61, 244
  policies of, 45–46, 216, 218, 230, 234, 250

as political leader, 35–36, 52, 90, 108, 115,
    118–22, 132, 182, 220, 222, 228–29
  suburbs and, 50–51
  tax abatements and, 137, 141, 216

Zunz, Oliver, 42–43, 46, 244